other titles in the

irreverent guide

series

Irreverent Amsterdam
Irreverent Boston
Irreverent Chicago
Irreverent Los Angeles
Irreverent London
Irreverent Manhattan
Irreverent New Orleans
Irreverent Paris
Irreverent Rome
Irreverent San Francisco
Irreverent Seattle/Portland
Irreverent Vancouver
Irreverent Walt Disney World
Irreverent Washington, D.C.

**Frommer's**

# irreverent guide to Las Vegas

## 2nd Edition

By
Jordan Simon

HUNGRY MINDS, INC.

## a disclaimer

Please note that prices fluctuate in the course of time, and travel information changes under the impact of the many factors that influence the travel industry. We therefore suggest that you write or call ahead for confirmation when making your travel plans. Every effort has been made to ensure the accuracy of information throughout this book and the contents of this publication are believed correct at the time of printing. Nevertheless, the publishers cannot accept responsibility for errors or omissions or for changes in details given in this guide or for the consequences of any reliance on the information provided by the same. Assessments of attractions and so forth are based upon the author's own experience and therefore, descriptions given in this guide necessarily contain an element of subjective opinion, which may not reflect the publisher's opinion or dictate a reader's own experience on another occasion. Readers are invited to write to the publisher with ideas, comments, and suggestions for future editions.

Your safety is important to us, however, so we encourage you to stay alert and be aware of your surroundings. Keep a close eye on cameras, purses, and wallets, all favorite targets of thieves and pickpockets.

## Published by HUNGRY MINDS, INC.

909 Third Avenue
New York, NY 10022

Copyright © 2002 by Hungry Minds, Inc.

ISBN 0-7645-6550-8
ISSN 1524-4326

Interior design contributed to by Tsang Seymour Design Studio

## special sales

For general information on Hungry Minds' products and services please contact our Customer Care Department within the U.S. at 800-762-2974, outside the U.S. at 317-572-3993 or fax 317-572-4002.

For sales inquiries and reseller information, including discounts, premium and bulk quantity sales, and foreign-language translations, please contact our Customer Care Department at 800-434-3422 or fax 317-572-4002.

Manufactured in the United States of America

# what's so irreverent?

It's up to you.

You can buy a traditional guidebook with its fluff, its promotional hype, its let's-find-something-nice-to-say-about-everything point of view. Or you can buy an Irreverent guide.

What the Irreverents give you is the lowdown, the inside story. They have nothing to sell but the truth, which includes a balance of good and bad. They praise, they trash, they weigh, and leave the final decisions up to you. No tourist board, no chamber of commerce will ever recommend them.

Our writers are insiders, who feel passionate about the cities they live in, and have strong opinions they want to share with you. They take a special pleasure leading you where other guides fear to tread.

How irreverent are they? One of our authors insisted on writing under a pseudonym. "I couldn't show my face in town again if I used my own name," she told me. "My friends would never speak to me." Such is the price of honesty. She, like you, should know she'll always have a friend at Frommer's.

Warm regards,

*Michael Spring*

Michael Spring
Publisher

# contents

**INTRODUCTION**                                          1

**NEIGHBORHOOD MAP**                                      6

**YOU PROBABLY DIDN'T KNOW**                              7

**ACCOMMODATIONS**                                        12
   **Winning the Reservations Game  (16)**
   **Is There a Right Address?  (17)**
   **THE LOWDOWN**                                        18

   New-style glitz  (18)
   Not to be outdone  (19)
   Older money  (20)
   Don't know much about history  (21)
   Overrated  (22)
   Globe-trotting themes  (23)
   Globetrotting themes gone haywire  (25)
   Campiest themes  (26)
   When your chips are down  (27)
   Gen-X  (28)
   Family-friendly on the Strip  (29)
   Family-friendly off the Strip  (30)
   Quick getaways  (31)
   Taking care of business  (31)
   Service with a smile  (33)

Old Vegas  (33)
Better than you'd expect  (34)
Where to escape the madness  (35)
Where to tie the knot  (36)
Cool pools  (37)
For the body beautiful  (38)
Heavy lobbying  (40)
Handsomest guest room decor  (41)
Art-ful hotels  (43)
Obsessively detailed  (44)
Suite deals  (44)

**THE INDEX**                                                    **46**
*An A to Z list of places to stay, with vital statistics*
**MAPS**                                                        **53**
Las Vegas Accommodations  (53)


**DINING**                                                     **54**

**Only in Las Vegas  (56)**
**What it Will Cost  (57)**
**When to Eat  (57)**
**How to Dress  (57)**
**Getting the Right Table  (57)**
**THE LOWDOWN**                                                **58**
Where to go when you hit the jackpot  (58)
Most beautiful clientele  (59)
Overrated  (59)
Most creative menus  (60)
Where the Rat Pack might hang out  (61)
Close encounters of the romantic kind  (62)
Where to impress clients  (63)
Frozen in the '50s  (64)
Buffet all the way  (65)
Bargain buffets  (66)
The brunch bunch  (67)
Incredible edible deals  (68)
We never close  (68)
Delish deli  (69)
Chow, bella  (69)
Mambo Italiano  (70)
Service that sparkles  (71)
Decor to the max  (72)
Winning wine lists  (73)
Kidz are us  (74)
Designer Asians  (74)
Authentic Asians  (76)
Fishing around  (77)

Prime beef  (78)

Theme dining: the A list  (80)

Theme dining: the B list  (80)

For Gen-XYZ  (81)

Voulez-vous manger avec moi?  (82)

High-falutin' French  (83)

South of the Border  (84)

Southwest sizzle  (84)

Arabian nights and Turkish delights  (86)

**THE INDEX**                                     **87**

*An A to Z list of restaurants, with vital statistics*

**MAPS**                                          **97**

Dining Downtown  (97)

Dining East of the Strip  (98)

Las Vegas Strip Dining  (99)


**DIVERSIONS**                                    **100**

**Getting Your Bearings  (102)**

**THE LOWDOWN**                                   **104**

Where the hell am I?  (104)

Freebie spectacles  (104)

Best shows for kids  (105)

Thrill rides  (106)

Overrated  (107)

Au naturel  (108)

Lions and tigers and bears, oh my  (109)

Under the sea  (110)

Kids' favorite theme parks  (110)

Theme parks for grownups  (111)

Honeymoon in Vegas  (112)

Neon dreams  (114)

Kidding around  (114)

For high-tech kids  (115)

Kitsch collections  (116)

Show me the cheese: gift shops  (118)

History lessons (why not?)  (118)

Thumbs up from the galleries  (119)

Rev your motors  (120)

For your viewing pleasure  (121)

Away from the Strip  (121)

Head for the lake  (122)

Par for the course  (123)

Rockin' it  (125)

Parking it  (125)

**THE INDEX**                                     **126**

*An A to Z list of diversions, with vital statistics*

## MAPS     133
    Las Vegas Diversions (133)

## CASINOS     134
**The Rules, and the Odds (137)**
**Getting Comped (139)**
**THE LOWDOWN     140**
    Friendliest pit staff (140)
    Cheekiest waitress costumes (140)
    For nickel-and-dimers (141)
    Casinos Royale (142)
    Most witty theme (142)
    Old-style flavor (143)
    Over the top (even by Vegas standards) (143)
    Don't live up to their billing (144)
    Worth leaving the Strip to see (144)
    High-roller havens (145)
    Best bets (146)

**THE INDEX     147**
*An A to Z list of casinos, with vital statistics*

## SHOPPING     152
**Target Zones (154)**
**Bargain Hunting (157)**
**Hours of Business (158)**
**THE LOWDOWN     158**
    Best for kids (158)
    Tackiest *tchotchkes* (158)
    Souvenirs with panache (159)
    Campier than thou (159)
    For collectors (160)
    Books and record deals (161)
    Retro-fitting (161)
    Haute couture (162)
    Clubbier wear (162)
    To beautify your home (163)
    Forbidden delights (162)

**THE INDEX     164**
*An A to Z list of shops, with vital statistics*

## NIGHTLIFE     168
**Sources (171)**
**What it Will Cost (171)**
**Liquor laws and drinking hours (172)**
**Drugs (172)**

## THE LOWDOWN     172

Big throbbing dance clubs (172)
Dancing cheek to chic (174)
Boogie nights (175)
Best people-watching (175)
Drinks with a theme (176)
Class lounge acts (177)
Tit-illations (177)
Where the Rat Pack might hang out (178)
See-and-be-scenes (179)
Vintage Vegas (179)
Love shacks (180)
Where to get intimate (181)
Rainbow nights (181)
Wildest decor (182)
Rooms with a view (182)
True brew (183)
Martini madness (184)
Cocktail culture (184)
Country roots (185)
Sports bars (185)
For slackers, Goths, and nihilists (186)
Frat parties (186)
For twentysomethings (187)
For thirtysomethings (187)
For fortysomethings (188)
Where locals hang out (188)
Cigars, cigarettes (189)
The piano man (190)
Jazzin' it up (190)
Singing a blues streak (191)
Where to hear local bands (191)

## THE INDEX     192

*An A to Z list of nightspots, with vital statistics*


# ENTERTAINMENT     200

## Sources (203)
## Getting Tickets (203)
## THE LOWDOWN     204

What money does for the imagination (204)
And the Liberace award goes to (206)
The bare necessities (207)
Presto! (208)
The impressionists (209)
The crooners (210)
Off-Broadway babies (211)

Headlining showrooms  (212)
Music rooms for the hip  (212)
Yukking it up  (213)
Top-priced tickets  (214)
Best values  (214)
Family outings  (215)
Best movers and shakers  (215)
Stadium seating  (216)
Classical moments  (217)
The theatah  (218)
A sporting chance  (218)
Overrated  (219)

**THE INDEX**                                    **220**

*An A to Z list of venues, with vital statistics*


**HOTLINES & OTHER BASICS**              **229**

Airports  (229)
Airport transportation to the city  (230)
All-night pharmacies  (230)
Buses  (230)
Car rentals  (230)
Child care  (231)
Climate  (231)
Convention center  (231)
Coupons  (232)
Dentists  (232)
Doctors  (232)
Driving around  (232)
Emergencies  (232)
Events hotline  (232)
Festivals and special events  (232)
Gay and lesbian resources  (233)
Limos  (233)
Newspapers and magazines  (234)
Parking  (235)
Post offices  (235)
Radio and TV stations  (235)
Restrooms  (235)
Taxis  (235)
Ticketing  (235)
Tours  (235)
Travelers with disabilities  (235)
Visitor information  (236)

**INDEX**                                        **237**

# introduction

I was driving down the Strip, dazed, amazed, and disoriented. There was the erupting volcano, the Eiffel Tower sprouting from the Paris casino, the roller coaster zooming around the Statue of Liberty and the Chrysler Building, a giant pyramid beaming lasers as if sending a beacon to lost E.T.s. And I recalled Hunter S. Thompson's line in *Fear and Loathing in Las Vegas*: "No, this is not a good town for psychedelic drugs. Reality itself is too twisted." It holds even truer today than it did then.

A little later, I sat jawing with an off-duty dealer, one of the rare born-and-bred locals in this transient town. I trotted out my observation that Las Vegas is a town without a history, continually demolishing and imploding its landmarks (the Sands becomes the Venetian; the Hacienda, Mandalay Bay; the Dunes, Bellagio; the Aladdin...the Aladdin). With no culture of its own, it parasitically appropriates architecture, gourmet chefs, artworks, loot from around the world. Las Vegas continually reinvents itself, I opined. The dealer laughed. "Oh EVERYone says that. But really Las Vegas is just a mirror, reflecting our country's values. It's whatever you think the American Dream ought to be." And she was right on the money. Las Vegas has uncannily taken America's pulse for the last 70 years, more "dream factory" than Hollywood itself.

The supreme irony is that this Sin City was founded by Mormons in 1855, though they soon decamped for Utah (call it a premonition). By 1931, Nevada was on the verge of becoming a ghost state when, at the depth of the Depression, government officials hit upon the brilliant idea of legalizing gambling and prostitution, while easing marriage and divorce laws. It suited an era when people needed to feel alive, to indulge greedily in immediate gratification. Hoover Dam was built at the same time, boosting the country's morale with proof that America was still technologically superior and raising hopes for a better future. This provided Las Vegas with the first of many tourist attractions it could hype. The first real casinos—and neon signage—appeared shortly after, with the El Rancho Hotel inaugurating the Strip in 1941. The first theme hotel materialized in 1943: The Last Frontier filled its rooms with antique pioneer furnishings, hired Zuni artisans to create baskets and rugs, and picked up guests from the airport in a horse-drawn stagecoach.

But it was Benjamin "Bugsy" Siegel who jump-started the good times with the Flamingo in 1946. Tall, suave, and handsome, Bugsy solidified the Hollywood connection (George Raft supposedly modeled his screen persona after him). Headliners streamed in: Jimmy Durante, Martin and Lewis, Sammy Davis Jr. And where movie stars went to be licentious, so did the public. Reflecting postwar prosperity, Vegas became the ultimate "cool" frontier town: no rules, no limits, no covers, no sales (or income) tax, where anything could happen—and usually did. For a while, Mob ties glamorized Las Vegas, culminating in the Rat Pack days when martinis, cigarettes, and sex were the order of the day and night. Bugsy created a Vegas in his image: a little garish and gaudy, but smooth, with evening dress mandatory in the casinos and restaurants. His vision for Las Vegas may have been his downfall; he was gunned to death ostensibly for skimming off the cash flow, but really because, like many a movie director, he ran over budget.

Vegas has always been about cash and flash. By the 1950s, when atomic-bomb tests were held in the nearby deserts, Las Vegans were already tourism-savvy enough to put chaise longues on hotel roofs and sell tickets. Bars served atomic cocktails, casinos featured Miss Atom Bomb beauty pageants, and salons advertised atomic hairdos; when shock waves broke glass, entrepreneurs offered the shards as free souvenirs. Even today, the Department of Energy conducts free monthly tours of nonclassified areas of the Nevada Test

Site, where you can see the moon-like craters formed by deto-
nations, one of them used as a training spot for the Apollo
astronauts' lunar landings. But the thrill soon palled with Cold
War fears, and during the Kennedy Camelot era, America
became disenchanted with organized crime.

The town's unlikely redeemer was reclusive, germ-phobic
Howard Hughes, who in the mid-1960s moved into the
Desert Inn and bought hotels as if the Strip were his own private Monopoly game. Though he didn't build any monuments,
Hughes made Vegas "legitimate" for big business. By the
1970s, corporate interests had sufficient clout to urge the government to establish the Nevada Gaming Commission to control the goodfellas and the good times. By the mid-1980s, Las
Vegas was in the doldrums. Enter Steve Wynn, who changed
the face of the Strip forever by erecting the glamorous, tropically themed Mirage, with its white tiger habitat, jungle interior, and belching volcano. A string of resorts followed,
culminating in Wynn's own opulent re-creation of a Lake
Como villa, Bellagio (now owned by MGM Grand-Mirage
Resorts). Nowadays on the Las Vegas skyline, minarets give
way to turrets, domes, arches, Deco skyscrapers, Italian campaniles, even a hundred-foot-tall Coke bottle (a relic of the
defunct World of Coca-Cola attraction). It all gives rise, of
course, to some unintentionally funny juxtapositions. The
Luxor's Nile Deli serves kosher sandwiches; the NASCAR
Café brings a whiff of the grease pits to the Moroccan-themed
Sahara hotel; a headless Lenin statue looms outside Red Square
in the otherwise tropically themed Mandalay Bay. And developers, as if suffering from an edifice complex, are already fret-
ting about where to turn now that they've exhausted the
truly recognizable cityscapes like Venice, Paris, New York, and
ancient Rome.

In the early 1990s came the single stupidest marketing
ploy in Las Vegas history. The town fathers determined to clean
up Sin City's image by promoting it as a family-friendly destination—again reflecting the middle-American zeitgeist,
cashing in on the "family values" debate. When that misfired,
Wynn and other big-business dreamers like Sheldon Adelson
(the maestro who re-created Venice as the Venetian) antici-
pated the next trend, of dot-commoner kings and mutual-fund
tycoons. Las Vegas decided to go upscale with a vengeance,
aiming to appeal to that coveted 18- to 49-year-old demographic of stockbrokers, bankers, and professionals who
Internet-work even on vacation. Enter Bellagio, the Venetian,

Paris, and Mandalay Bay. All are sumptuous and dazzling, but then you see the Jumbotron sign flashing "Hermès and Prada." It's a bit like someone thrusting a 10-carat diamond ring in your face, then adding, "It's Tiffany, you know." The truth is, any schmoe with dough is still welcome. Remember the scene in *Pretty Woman* where Julia Roberts tramps down Rodeo Drive in her hooker garb and is shunned at every chic boutique? It wouldn't happen at the chichi shops of Las Vegas. Take the couple in pastel polyester (and Flintstones™ fannypacks) who stagger into the Tiffany outpost in the ultra-exclusive Via Bellagio shopping arcade, schlepping bags from Gucci and Chanel. A frosty blonde saleswoman, immaculately turned out in hauteur couture, scarcely misses a beat before unctuously asking, "What can I do for you, sir?" The man peels off several $100 bills from a thick wad and replies, "We need some souvenirs for the folks back home." It's consumerism in its purest, most naked form.

So how does the city dumb down to the lowest common denominator that has always been its bread and butter while smartening itself up for the new younger, upscale crowd? It's a delicate high-wire act, but Vegas manages to offer something for everyone: high, low, and arched brow—a *New Yorker* meets *Hustler* cartoon. Nowhere else will you see dreadlocked gangsta rappers and long-bearded Hasidic rebbes sit side by side at shows, expense-account fat cats next to fanny packers in restaurants, blue-haired grannies passing white-collar CEOs in the casinos. Tour buses circle like buzzards; neon winks like a hooker in the night; bimbos, bingo junkies, and pencil-neck geeks alike stare into the maw of the one-armed bandits.

As proud as many locals are of the town's spiffy resurgence, they're also dismayed by the increased hordes, the traffic, the condescending jokes from outsiders about Vegas being a good-time gal trying to get class. Some even wax nostalgic about the Mob days, when casinos were more generous with their comps than the corporate bean-counters: "Once, if you gambled $100, you got a big steak dinner; now you're treated like meat." I overheard a grizzled bartender at a seedy downtown casino wistfully reminisce about the days when he served Sinatra at the Sands. "You know what he told me he loved about Las Vegas: 'Loose slots and loose slits'."

Okay, so some things don't change. I saw a working girl in black leather miniskirt, 5-inch stilettos, and Gucci bag (holding who knows what) walk into an elevator on a room floor at one of the tony new resorts and casually ask "Going up?". A 6-foot-tall transvestite in fishnet stockings, blonde wig, and gray mustache bellies up to a table and no one blinks. Titillating magazines are dispensed on the streets; T&A jiggle and burlesque shows remain among the ABCs of tourism. Outside town, in Nye County, where prostitution is legal, the (in)famous Chicken Ranch has its own airstrip. The Stardust and Riviera are legendary for presenting private XXX revues, especially during Comdex (nicknamed by locals Comsex) and the Consumer Electronics Show. The Riv, in fact, brings in porn actresses; they strip and autograph their panties for panting software designers.

Any town that can pack the Seven Wonders of the Ancient and Modern Worlds into a 3-mile main drag is surely capable of being simultaneously crass and sublime, of being all things for all people. Under its neon-lit influence, even culture snobs begin to unbend, to enjoy the camp and the kitsch, to let themselves go and just have a good time. Above all else, Las Vegas feeds into the American Dream of get-rich-quick, hitting the jackpot, beating the odds. After all, Las Vegas itself, in the middle of the damned desert, defied the odds to become the entertainment capital of the world.

I recall one of Liberace's last shows. He entered in a blizzard of white sequins and announced, "I've only done a couple of numbers and I'm warm already. Why don't I slip out of this and into something more spectacular?" That could be the Las Vegas motto as it sheds its skin, reborn yet again.

# Las Vegas Area Orientation

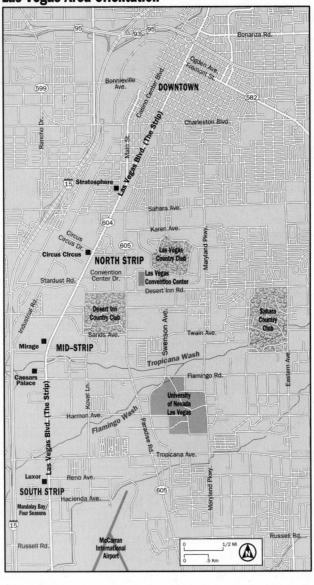

# you
# probably
# didn't know

**The Strip is in Las Vegas...right?...** Few visitors realize that they're leaving Las Vegas as they drive past **Las Vegas Boulevard South**, aka **the Strip**, just past Sahara Avenue. Yes, the airport, the **MGM Grand, Luxor, Excalibur, Bellagio, Mandalay Bay, Mirage, Venetian, Caesars Palace**—indeed, most of the famed names, aren't part of incorporated Las Vegas, but rather **Clark County**.

**Just how big are those big hotels?...** Just listen to these statistics. At the **MGM Grand**, which is the world's second-largest hotel, you'd have to sleep in a different bedroom every night for 13 years and 8 months to work your way through its 5,005 guest rooms; there are 18,000 doors (a staffer cracks that it's like Monty Hall's nightmare). The MGM Grand puts roughly 771,700 gambling chips into play annually, which if stacked up would climb 1.5 miles. In 1999, the **Las Vegas Hilton** had 5,290 phones, 603 computers, 224,936 square feet of windows, and 4,552 parking spaces; it used 153,000 decks of cards, 8,357 dice, 101,562 light bulbs, and cleaned 29.8 million pieces of laundry during the year. **Bally's** handled 3,800 pieces of luggage daily, and one million rolls of toilet paper (1,300,000,000 feet; no data available as to single- or double-ply) were flushed in one year. The **Rio**, known for its 15 sumptuous eateries, prepared 1,825,000 pastries, 73,000 cakes, and 91,000 pies utilizing 81,250 pounds of chocolate, 73,000 pounds of sugar, and 730,000 pounds of flour. **Excalibur** eats up 44,100 Cornish game hens, 15,000 pounds of hamburger meat, and 4,200 pounds of prime rib monthly. **Caesars Palace** goes through 2,080,000 maraschino cherries, 114,800 cucumbers, 11,200 ounces of caviar, and 156,000 pounds of coffee, not to mention 2,152,800 ounces of tomato juice and 584,000 ounces of vodka yearly (that's a hell of a lot of Bloody Marys). **Mandalay Bay** has 5,300 palm trees of various species; its wave pool holds 1,640,270 gallons of water and is surrounded by 1,700 tons of sand. Lucky the Clown, the 123-foot neon marquee mascot of **Circus Circus**, has 1,232 fluorescent lamps, 14,498 incandescent bulbs, and three quarters of a mile of neon tubing. The **Luxor**'s 29-million-cubic-foot lobby could shelter nine Boeing 747s stacked atop one another; the laser-lit Luxor pyramid is one of only two man-made objects (the Great Wall of China is the other) visible from outer space.

**Where can I find a legal hooker?...** Nowhere. The world's oldest profession is legal in Nevada, *except* in Las Vegas, Reno, and their counties. The nearest lawful cathouses are 70 miles distant in adjacent **Nye County** (but never fear, many even offer free limo service). Rest assured, condom use is mandatory and the gals undergo weekly blood tests. In town, mind you, hookers are plentiful; a whole strip of little motels caters to the hourly trade. Despite security efforts, there's plenty of play in the big hotels, too. "Escort services" are abundantly advertised in the Yellow Pages, and XXX-rated local rags like *Fever* and *Gentleman's Choice* are filled with "personals" from gals named Amber, Angel, and Ginger ("I may not be *Penthouse* material but I am full-service and I need the work"). Alternative encounters are also available, circumventing the prostitute prohibition by dubbing it live entertainment in your room. But any exchange of money for sexual favors is against the law, and the police aggressively pursue solicitation arrests.

**Is Vegas still married to the Mob?...** The old

romance of tommy guns, concrete boots, and pinky rings is gone forever—bookmakers have given way to book-keepers in this increasingly corporate town. Not only the Gaming Control Board but also hotel company stock-holders keep a sharp eye out, and today's pit bosses likely boast degrees from high-toned MBA programs like Wharton's and gaming degrees from Cornell and UNLV. Operations such as RICO (Racketeer-Influenced Corrupt Organizations), the Justice Department's Orga-nized Crime Strike Force, and the FBI's ongoing Thin-crust Investigation into reputed mobsters have taken the bite out of organized crime's gambling proceeds. Still, it's a messier divorce than people realize. Las Vegas Mayor Oscar Goodman himself acted for 35 years as attorney and *consigliere* to such notorious legends as oddsmaker extraordinaire Frank Rosenthal (depicted by Robert DeNiro in *Casino*—Goodman even played himself in the flick). As he was quoted saying prior to the election: "I'm running for mayor, I need your financial support. And if you don't give it to me, I'll have you whacked!" The action has simply moved from racketeering to other rackets, and ancillary businesses are often Mob-controlled. The sex industry, for one.

**Where can I stash the car?...** Despite frequent waits for drop-off and pickup, locals know it's much easier to valet than to find a parking spot and walk through acres of asphalt terraces. (Valet parking may be the only sane way to negotiate **Caesars Palace** and **Bally's**, especially since the latter surrendered its front parking lot to create its bizarre neon walkway and its back parking lot for the **Paris** casino—the remaining lot is a long schlep away, on Paradise Road.) All major hotels offer free valet service but, during holidays and big conventions, many hotels limit their valet service to their hotel guests. Bypass long waits by using valet services at the entrances of hotel shopping promenades (notably the one at **Bellagio**) or side entrances (like **Mandalay Bay**'s west side, inside the parking terrace, which is close to the casino's hippest bars and restaurants, including **rumjungle**, **Aureole**, and **Red Square**). Valet tickets are purposely not identified with the names of hotels and casinos, so hang on to your valet ticket and *remember where you parked*. Without a ticket, no amount of pleading (or moolah; acceptable minimal tips begin at $2 per car and gaming chips are okay) will prompt a Vegas valet to hand over the keys to a red Jag. Don't be like the poor soul—too many freebie drinks—who had absolutely no idea where he left his Mercedes and had to hire a private detective to find it. (It was found at a totally nude strip joint, by the way.)

**Can I walk the Strip?...** Yes, carefully. There are sidewalks along 10-lane-wide **Las Vegas Boulevard South**, and yes, you'll see masses of people walking on them. But it's deceptively far from one casino to the next, pavements are often ripped up for construction, and pickpockets and smut peddlers line the way. The worst aspect, however, is the kamikaze drivers along certain intersections, particularly the dangerous **Tropicana/Strip intersection**, where walkways were finally built between **MGM Grand**, **Tropicana**, **Excalibur**, and **New York-New York**. **Rio All-Suite Casino Resort** is linked to the Strip via a pedestrian bridge along **Flamingo Road**, since 70,000 cars use that turnoff daily. Pedestrian flyovers also connect the **Venetian** with **Treasure Island**, and **Bellagio** with **Barbary Coast** and **Bally's** (itself linked via a hall to its sister property, **Paris**). Several hotel groups operate private trams between their affiliated properties, but be forewarned: Tram stations are difficult to find, tucked in the far back corners of hotels and casinos.

**How can I avoid traffic?...** You can't, at least not along **Las Vegas Boulevard South**, which residents have nicknamed the "world's longest parking lot." Sitting in their unmoving cars, people get hotter than the desert in summer, with hardhats and soccer moms giving each other the finger. It's so slow, many motorists actually take out their laptops or write letters. Cabbies say that traffic is the number-one reason visitors refuse to return. Avoid the following treacherous intersections if at all possible: where **Sahara Avenue** crosses **Rainbow Boulevard, Decatur Boulevard, Spring Mountain Road,** or **Rancho Drive,** and where the **Strip** crosses **Flamingo Road**. Consider taking parallel north-south routes such as **Industrial Road, Rancho Drive,** and **Paradise Road**; the **Desert Inn** superarterial makes east-west traversing much easier, as it swoops over I-15 and down under the Strip. If you're traveling the western side of town, bypass **U.S. 95** in favor of **Lake Mead and Charleston boulevards.** The Interchange between **I-95** and **U.S. 95** is nicknamed the **Spaghetti Bowl** for the tangle of ramps connecting the two highways, used by 350,000 vehicles daily. Though still unfinished, it has eased congestion somewhat, as has the even newer **Beltway, I-215,** ringing town. But road engineers can't keep up with the sheer influx of both new residents (5,000 monthly) and tourists (200,000 on the worst weekends).

**Where can I pray for divine intervention at the casino?...** Perhaps it's no surprise that Las Vegas has more churches per capita than any comparably sized U. S. city. But one place of worship right off the south Strip ministers to gamblers: **The Shrine of the Most Holy Redeemer** (tel 702/891-8600, 55 E. Reno Ave.). You stagger in, only to find a most unusual "relic" on display: the lavender-and-orange Jesus Poker Chip. The novelty item, in its third edition, is an innovative idea to help pay for the parish's upkeep. The chip can't be redeemed at any casino, but the house odds are in your favor—collectible first editions have zoomed in value from $5 to $30 in just seven years. Hallelujah!

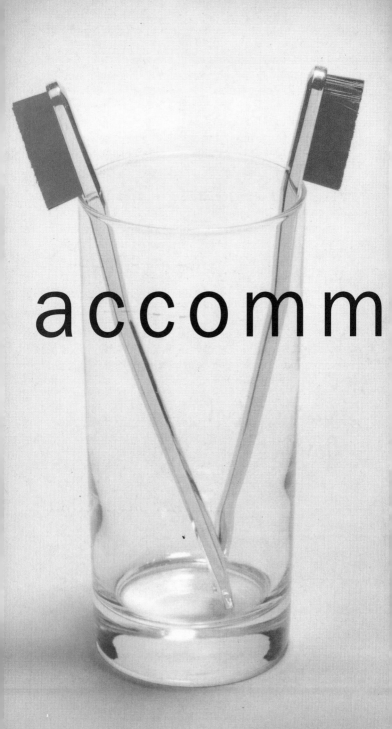

accomm

# 1

# odations

Nowhere else on
earth will you find
another skyline like
that of Las Vegas
Boulevard South—
otherwise known as
the Strip.

A Disney-esque Arthurian castle abuts an Egyptian pyramid and the Statue of Liberty. A Caribbean pirate lair stares down Venice's Saint Mark's Square. Truly, Las Vegas has shouldered aside Hollywood as America's Dream Factory. Historian Michael Ventura calls Las Vegas "the last great mythic city that Western civilization will ever create"; art critic Robert Hughes calls Las Vegas "a work of art: bad art, but art nonetheless." The extravagant pleasure palaces lining the Strip make a bold, brash architectural statement, with developers increasingly crowing about architectural integrity and authenticity. Replica landmarks are meticulously built to scale, whether half-size (the Eiffel Tower at the Paris hotel), full (the Venetian's Doge's Palace), or oversized (Luxor's Sphinx). To paraphrase Shakespeare's words about another immortal temptress: "Age does not wither nor custom stale her infinite variety."

In Las Vegas, the hotel business is a staggering success story. The city has a total room inventory of 125,000, nearly twice that of New York. The five properties at the intersection of Tropicana and the Strip alone contain more rooms than all of San Francisco. Yet the Strip has an amazing hotel occupancy level of 89.1 to 90.3 percent. Development, expansion, and large-scale renovation continue unabated. The 1,022-room Italian-themed Tuscany Suites opened east of the Strip in fall 2001, and in December 2001, The Palms resort was set to open west of the Strip on Flamingo Road, boasting a spa, cineplex, casino, 470 oversized rooms, and a gourmet rooftop restaurant run by André Rochat of André's French Restaurant (see Dining). Steve Wynn, the gaming guru who sold Mirage Resorts in 2000 to MGM Grand, Inc., purchased the ritzy Desert Inn for $275 million and in September 2001 began building the new "D.I.", erecting a 52-floor tower that will more than triple the original D.I.'s room count with 2,300 suites. On Lake Las Vegas in Henderson, the Canada-based resort developer Intrawest (Mont Tremblant, Copper Mountain, Whistler, etc.), is creating MonteLago Village, an upscale Mediterranean-style resort that will include a 350-room Ritz-Carlton set to open in 2004. Where the El Rancho Hotel once stood, a 2,000-plus-room London-themed resort/casino is on the drawing board, to feature replicas of such icons as Big Ben, the Tower of London, and Buckingham Palace (yes, there will be a changing of the guard). A Chinese-themed property, tentatively called Dynasty-Forbidden City, is also on the agenda; its parking structure will resemble the Great Wall of China.

Existing properties are expanding, too: Orleans will open a 620-room tower in mid-2002 with a 9,000-seat arena and a second casino; and the Venetian, which has remained at near-capacity since its spring 1999 opening, started building a 1,100-room tower atop its parking garage for a 2002 opening, while its "Phase Two" expansion (a new 3,000-room hotel with additional restaurants, shops, casino, attractions, and meeting space) will break ground in spring 2002.

The sheer magnitude of these properties impresses, too. Las Vegas possesses 11 of the world's 12 largest hotels and 18 of the 19 largest in the United States. It even boasts the world's largest Super 8 and Motel 6 properties. A 2,000-room property is considered average size here. No wonder they're cities unto themselves, with everything from ATM machines to fast-food courts, giving guests no reason to leave the hotel—and, more important, the casino, since gaming is still the name of the game (note that main-floor elevator buttons are marked "C" for casino, instead of "L" for lobby).

In that respect, however, things have been changing here. Non-casino revenues are increasing at nearly quadruple the rate of casino revenues, accounting now for almost half the income. Promoters these days talk of Las Vegas as a true resort, not merely a gambling destination. Every new hotel that's built includes a massive spa, glorified pool area, and fitness facilities—not to mention gourmet eateries, name-brand shops, in-house attractions, and razzle-dazzle shows. Guest rooms themselves have been improving; they're no longer dark, dingy, cramped chambers calculated to make guests flee to the casino. The typical directory of services looks like a small town's phone book—and it's printed in at least five languages (English, French, Spanish, Japanese, and German).

Developers up the ante in a high-stakes gamble for the tourist dollar. Older hotels constantly receive face-lifts (befitting a city renowned for its plastic surgeons). In the newly upscale Vegas, kitschier properties like Circus Circus and Excalibur have "classed up" their cheap-motel fantasy-suite decor. In a tornado of remodeling, MGM Grand slew the 80-foot roaring lion at its main entrance (which had spooked Asian gamblers to no end), as well as demolished the tacky Emerald City just inside (including the animatronic Dorothys, Totos, and Munchkins). Unfortunately, in the rush to play "Can you top this?" many hotels are constructed little better than mud huts in New Guinea (you may be able to hear your neighbors shower, celebrate their winnings, or consummate their quickie marriages). Typically, Strip resorts settle about 2 to 8 inches just after construction because they're built on rock-like caliche; some sections of Mandalay Bay settled as much as 16 inches, requiring 500 steel pipes to be bored into its foundation to stabilize the tower. Even the Venetian, in its quest to replicate Venice, didn't sink to that level.

The new yupscale models, however, will never be the true pampering resorts they claim to be as long as hotels cling to the old casino-centric Vegas standards of guest treatment. Service can be soulless and impersonal, including lengthy check-in periods and waits for your bags or car, even at the ultra-ritzy Bellagio. Conventioneers often arrive early and grab the available rooms; though check-in is normally 3pm, you may have to cool your jets before your room is clean. Hardly luxury coddling. You'd be amazed how difficult staffers find it to switch you from a double/double to the king you'd requested, even with 3,000-plus rooms to choose from. If necessary, make a fuss (politely); blather about being late for meetings. If you wait forever at restaurants or for room service, complain to the MOD (manager on duty) about your hypoglycemia. It might net a few coupons, or a free meal. And be prepared to flash your room key/card as often as a teenager with fake ID at a bar—security is stringent, with the elevator banks staked out by the kinds of goons one usually associates with nightclubs.

### Winning the Reservations Game

Given the 90 percent average room occupancy rate, you may not be able to book on your preferred dates, so reserve way ahead or be flexible. Also be aware that there is no rhyme or reason to pricing—any given week, certain hotels will be in greater demand than others (presumably if they host a convention or special event), and rates oscillate wildly. Major holidays, needless to say, are near-impossible. Even more important, avoid the big conventions and special events (see Hotlines & Other Basics), like Comdex, the NAB (National Association of Broadcasters), or National Finals Rodeo week. During these events, rooms are booked a year in advance; people may have to stay as far as 90 miles away in Mesquite. Even an event like the latest Mike Tyson fight can triple room rates—and not just in the host hotel. There are some rules of thumb. Most properties roughly double their prices over the weekend— except in the dog days of summer. The periods surrounding major holidays are usually slower, as are the first two weeks of January, April, June, and September (when estimated taxes are due). Keep checking the Internet or your travel agent for special deals: They come and go like airline promotions. Consider hooking onto something like a drag-racing promotion so you get the room at 25 percent off (and a free sun visor, too!). You can inquire whether or not a hotel offers casino deals, such as playing three hours straight at the $5 table to gain a free night's stay, but remember that there is a risk here—you might end up losing quadruple the room price. If you win big, on the other hand, most casinos and hotels will "comp" you with breakfast, lunch, and dinner, treat you to a suite, or upgrade you to high-roller digs, all in the interest of keeping you in the casino. High-roller suites are usually obtained via a guaranteed line of credit and a minimum amount (of both time and money) spent gambling, which varies according to property. On rare occasions, usually during slow periods, hotels release higher-end suites (expect to pay anywhere from $1,000 to $25,000 per night). Among the most luxe, with haute bachelor pad decor, are those at the Rio, Caesars Palace, Las Vegas Hilton, MGM Grand, and Mirage. You can always resort to calling the **Las Vegas Convention and Visitors Authority** reservations line (tel 800/332-5333), which can also inform you about convention schedules, or the discounter **Reservations Plus** (tel 800/805-9528). Both services are free. Among the websites you can try are *www.lasvegashotel.com*, *www.lasvegasreservations.com*, *www.ilovevegas.com*, and *www.lvholidays.com*. Each offers numerous properties at varying rates; just remember you won't get your choice of room (a higher floor for maximum views, for example).

### Is There a Right Address?

Naturally, most people want to stay on **the Strip**. Since this fabled stretch is a mere 3.5 miles long (technically walkable) and the iconic properties are lined up along it—from Circus Circus at one end to the MGM Grand, New York-New York, Luxor, Excalibur, and Mandalay Bay at the other—there is no preferred Strip address. It all depends on the ambience, theme, and facilities you seek. The old Vegas wisdom that a room is just a room no longer applies; posher digs are now available at the likes of Bellagio, Four Seasons, and the Venetian, as well as old standbys like Caesars Palace, Mirage, and the MGM Grand. Of course, you pay more for the premium toiletries, turn-down service, and spacious rooms. Prices have risen across the board with the "upscaling" of Las Vegas, but they're still rock-bottom compared to most cities.

While there are still bargains on the Strip itself, many people on a budget prefer to stay **Downtown**, where you can hit 15 casinos in a four-block radius. (Strip hotels are farther apart, though there are clusters at the southern and lower-central sections.) Another increasingly popular way to go is to choose one of the moderately priced **Paradise Road** and **Boulder Highway** properties. Three "locals' casino" chains generally offer superior value, whatever the individual hotel's location: Boyd Gaming (California, Main Street Station, Fremont, Stardust, Sam's Town), the Station lineup (Santa Fe, Reserve, Fiesta, Palace, Boulder, Texas, and Sunset Station Hotels), and the Coast chain (Gold Coast, Orleans, Barbary Coast, and the new Suncoast in tony Summerlin). Also check out Arizona Charlie's (West and East) and Terrible's. Though various properties in a chain may have different themes, they offer comparable facilities. Another benefit is that they offer free shuttles between their properties. In fact, most off-Strip properties, such as the Hard Rock, offer complimentary transport to the "action." Wherever you stay, especially if you bring the kids or don't gamble, make sure there are plenty of activities and facilities. All the properties listed below, unless stated otherwise, will include at least a pool, a restaurant, a bar, and a casino.

# The Lowdown

**New-style glitz...** In the late '90s, Las Vegas hoteliers were suddenly struck with a desire for "class," like a retired madam who madly redecorates in an effort to win over her former clients' wives. The prime class-monger is Steve Wynn, whose swan song as CEO of Mirage Resorts was the exquisite Lake Como–style palazzo **Bellagio.** Highly refined (at least by Las Vegas standards), it strives to offer the best of the best, or at least the best that money can buy: world-renowned chefs/restaurateurs, haute couture shops, a spa offering no less than eight facials, the Cirque du Soleil extravaganza "O" (see Entertainment), the Bellagio Gallery of Fine Art, and the Bellagio Conservatory (see Diversions for both). Caviar bars, afternoon teas, graceful fountains, exemplary lounge entertainment—the array begins to feel parvenu and ostentatious. Its hipster equivalent is the **Hard Rock Hotel & Casino**, where Fendi meets Fender guitars. Its witty rock music theme includes song lyrics posted in the elevators and the usual complement of gold records, guitars (formerly owned by REM's Michael Stipe, Axl Rose, and The Boss), and memorabilia (Elvis's gold lamé jacket, Ginger Spice's Union Jack bathing suit, Beach Boys' surfboards, '60s and '70s dolls of Sonny and Cher and Donny and Marie, even Andy Gibb and Bobby Sherman lunch boxes and Boy George makeup kits). The decor, with leather, gold, purple, and black accents, is kitten-with-a- whip. There are even four all-music TV channels. As if painstaking re-creations of Venetian landmarks and Renaissance artworks, vaulted ceilings, miles of marble and gilt, scintillating gourmet restaurants, upscale shops, and the largest "standard" rooms in town weren't enough, the **Venetian Resort-Hotel-Casino** has upped the Vegas status quotient with two Rem Koolhaas-designed branches of the Guggenheim Museum, one devoted to modern art and the other to masterpieces from the Hermitage in St. Petersburg (see Diversions). The **Mandalay Bay Resort & Casino** (aka M-Bay) juxtaposes old-fashioned glitz (a lushly landscaped exterior with sweeping waterfalls and fire pots shooting flames 15 to 20 feet) with newfangled pizzazz (computer and data-port capabilities in the rooms and futuristic gourmet restaurants). Raffles it ain't, but it's impressively high-tech for a fairly high-maintenance crowd.

**Not to be outdone...** These newer properties exerted pressure on Strip institutions like **Caesars Palace**, which responded by building its Palace Tower, with enormous rooms (550 to 750 square feet) that manage to be models of restraint and good taste. Decorated in gold and bronze-tan tones with cherry-wood two-poster beds, sponge-painted walls, and subdued classical prints, the rooms' only concessions to razzmatazz are huge gilt mirrors. Bathrooms feature marble vanities, double showers, and whirlpool baths. Add a clutch of truly superb restaurants, high-end shops, and world-class high-roller areas; Caesars Palace attracts clients so posh, they carelessly leave unopened champagne bottles on their finished breakfast trays. The **Mirage**'s lobby lagoon is spectacular (more so than the pool) and the recently expanded business center and spa, while not the town's finest, are superior and luxe, with lots of antique chinoiserie and polished hardwood. The restaurants (including Onda and Renoir, by celeb chefs Todd English and Alex Stratta) are superlative, the shops upscale, the look simply ravishing. Wynn's first Vegas property, the downtown **Golden Nugget**, still shows off his famed "touch of class" in an understated way. The lustrous gold-and-white building is accented with umbrella canopies and stately palm trees; even the sidewalk is emblazoned with brass-inlaid white granite squares. Public areas display miles of obsessively swept marble floors, etched-glass windows, potted plants, gleaming brass, red carpets, and stained-glass ceilings in the elevators. The cultivated room decor features burnished golden fabrics, gilt mirrors, and a vaguely turn-of-the-century (that last one) feel. Excellent restaurants include Lillie Langtry (Chinese, but resembling Marie Antoinette's drawing room) and Stefano's (trellises and lovely murals of the Tuscan countryside). The casino is refreshingly human-scale, with a certain Bond-like savoir faire; even the cabaret is intimate and tasteful. With these amenities, it would cost at least twice as much were it not located in budget-conscious Downtown.

**Older money...** Discerning moneyed guests quickly discovered the newcomer **Regent Las Vegas**, with its 11-acre complex of gardens and pools, quietly elegant casino (almost an afterthought), and Aquae Sulis spa. The Regent's Spanish Revival–style architecture blends harmoniously with the surrounding mountains, with graceful domes, campaniles, cupolas, and barrel tile roofs. Inside, the lobbies of the Spa and Palm Towers define quiet elegance, with tapestries, hand-carved and painted woodwork, terra-cotta or parquet floors, and gigantic gilt or filigreed pewter mirrors; guest rooms are huge, awash in marble and rich dark woods. The pool area, perfumed by desert blooms, takes full advantage of the breathtaking natural setting. The Regent is an oasis where good old boys convene to raise profit margins and lower golf handicaps—it's affiliated with three nearby top-flight courses: Badlands, Angel Fire, and the nationally ranked

TPC at the Canyons (see Diversions). Restaurants include an authentic Irish pub (see Nightlife) and two fancifully designed eateries run by master chef Gustav Mauler (see Dining). Though it's the largest property in its chain, **Four Seasons Las Vegas** is an oasis of serenity, perched on the 35th through 39th floors of Mandalay Bay. To enhance its guests' privacy, it has its own express elevators, its own restaurants (two) and lounges, business center, meeting space, an 8,000-square-foot pool area, and spa/fitness club. Many areas are inaccessible to Mandalay Bay guests, though Four Seasons guests have access to the larger resort's facilities. Rooms are enormous, including junior suites with separate parlor, furnished in the usual refined Four Seasons style, with hardwood furnishings (including armoires and canopy beds), down comforters, marble bathrooms, and botanical prints on the walls.

**Don't know much about history...** A handful of Strip hotels plumb the past for theme concepts, with mixed success. The awesome grandeur of ancient Egypt is actually captured in some parts of **Luxor**, erected in the shape of a Rayban-dark glass pyramid (the inclined 39-degree elevators are an engineering feat in themselves). Cracked ruins, the Cleopatra's Needle obelisk, and a mysterious 10-story-high Sphinx greet you at the entrance. The lobby re-creates an archeological dig, with exact replicas of Egyptian artifacts and statues, including a 35-foot Ramses; hieroglyphics are stenciled on the walls. Scarabs, cobras, and sacred cats stare you almost menacingly in the eye in the casino. Even the gourmet restaurants include vases, pharaoh images, hieroglyphics—thankfully without being cheesy. Over-the-top as it is, the Roman Empire theme of **Caesars Palace** works (after all, the ancient Romans themselves were given to vulgar excess). The public areas feature a miniature re-creation of Imperial Rome at its height, enhanced by holograms and fiber optics; the Garden of the Gods pools, inlaid with Carrara marble, were inspired by the Baths of Caracalla. The north edge of the property features the Quadriga statue: four gold-leaf horses and a charioteer that point the way through five triumphal arches into the Olympic casino. Everywhere you look are neoclassical statues, including reproductions of Michelangelo's *David*, the *Winged*

*Victory of Samothrace*, *Venus de Milo*, and *Rape of the Sabines*. The **Aladdin Resort & Casino** mixes and matches mythic and authentic Muslim influences, from Arabian Nights touches (the casino's giant golden Aladdin's lamp, Sinbad's Roc egg embedded in a bar's wall) to bona fide artifacts including antique Arabic royal outfits, ceramic bowls, and old wooden shutters hanging in the hallways. The connected Desert Passage mall (see Dining and Shopping) features decorative parapets, onion domes, minarets, and keyhole arches galore. Rooms are large if rather spare, with hardwood furnishings, rich Moorish colors (bronze, peacock blue), vaguely arabesque mirrors, prints of Moroccan scenes, and magnificent bathrooms where the faucets are shaped like, well, Aladdin's lamp. Sheik chic is not as important, though, as the hotel's intelligent layout, which is unlike most Vegas properties' labyrinthine designs; you're never more than seven doors from the elevator to your room. Less successful is medieval-themed **Excalibur**, where no one acts particularly chivalrous—people shove for a look at the animatronic dragon and cut ahead in the buffet lines. Many of the heraldic banners and halberds, even the actors' costumes, are faintly authentic, but the decor is cartoonish, like a Dr. Seuss rewrite of *La Morte d'Arthur*.

**Overrated...** In an ill-advised ploy to attract families, **Treasure Island** was conceived as the Mirage's kid sister—they're even connected by a tram. Though the rooms are pleasant enough, with handcrafted hardwood furnishings, old globe maps, and prints of sailing ships, you can hear the plumbing next door, and the kitschy property offers nothing memorable save for the Pirate Battle. It's certainly not worth paying the comparative pirate's ransom to stay here. In its no-man's-land at the extreme north end of the Strip, the high-rise **Stratosphere Casino Hotel & Tower** sits as if in solitary confinement. The Strat compensates with a full menu of activities and facilities; everything from the shows to the rooms is high-quality but low-cost, and its new 1,002-room tower adds hip new watering holes and a leviathan pool area overlooking the Strip. Still, its unsavory surroundings (creatively termed the "Stratosphere District") attract a high percentage of petty theft—if you stay or play there, drive or cab it. Despite diligent refurbishment, the 30-year-old

**Las Vegas Hilton** is showing its age. The mid-sized rooms are sterile in ordinary blond woods, burgundy carpets, and washed-out floral and coral fabrics. Though the hotel remains a top choice for business folk thanks to its proximity to the Las Vegas Convention Center, the disco has lost luster and its otherwise solid restaurants are hardly cutting-edge (even though the Benihana Village throws in some streams and gardens). Beautiful—if nouveau riche—as it is, the fantasy Italian villa **Bellagio** can't keep the gawkers out, which diminishes its otherwise haute ambience. Same story at the **Venetian**, which should only get worse as it more than doubles in size as planned by 2004. Can they maintain its high standards and authentic feel?

**Globe-trotting themes...** If you can peel your eyes from the half-scale Eiffel Tower at **Paris**, you'll note replicas of other famed landmarks: the Opéra, the Louvre, and the Arc de Triomphe, along with bas-reliefs of famous French figures and an entrance skillfully evoking a *belle époque* metro station. The 34-story hotel itself is modeled on the 800-year-old Hôtel de Ville, the Paris City Hall. Cobblestone paths wind everywhere and the shopping areas (wine, cheese, lingerie, mini-Eiffel Towers stamped Paris Las Vegas!) re-create Parisian street scenes circa the 1920s, striving for that *The Sun Also Rises* feel. There are nine Gallic-themed eateries, and on every hand you'll see Parisian street performers (mimes, musicians, magicians, sword-swallowers), or at least American imitators. Elegantly appointed guest rooms feature crown molding, gilt mirrors, rich French fabrics in cool blues and mauves, and custom-designed inlaid-wood furnishings (including armoires as closets)—so why no bidets? Unlike the other Vegas "cities," the **Venetian** presents full-size replicas of its landmarks: the Doge's Palace, the 315-foot Campanile Tower, the Rialto Bridge, the Bridge of Sighs, and the Ca d'Oro Villa. Interiors were meticulously duplicated from actual paintings, frescoes, and statues. The Gallery area features copies of artworks by Titian, Bellini, and Canaletto. Okay, so the Grand Canal is only a quarter-mile long and 3 feet deep, not to mention oddly clean, with motorized gondolas; okay, so the cobblestone "neighborhoods" lining the canal are full of glass-blowers, jugglers, opera singers, and living statues. Still, the St. Mark's Plaza looks very convincing—at least, until you spy the neon

Jimmy Choo sign and hear La Streisand playing on the sound system. **New York-New York**'s charm starts with the scaled-down version of the skyline: Statue of Liberty in a miniature New York Harbor (complete with a tugboat to hose her down), Brooklyn Bridge, Chrysler and Empire State Buildings, storefronts, even gargoyles. Inside, on the walkway into Little Italy, manholes emit steam and mailboxes are covered with graffiti. Cobblestone street scenes are re-created down to the parking meters and fire escapes. Stroll through a Central Park with tall, spreading, lifelike trees surrounding a pond and foot bridge—and banks of slot machines (well, it IS a gamble walking through the park at night). Just like its namesake, **Monte Carlo** is opulent indeed—its exterior features three grand arches, the center topped by a Renaissance-style marble grouping of angels, not to mention cascading fountains; the lobby has crystal chandeliers, marble columns, artfully aged French landscape paintings, and Aubusson-style rugs. It manages to seem refined without going for Ba-roque. **The Orleans** sports the requisite French Quarter look—trompe l'oeil green shutters and wrought-iron balconies outside, French doors and intricate latticework, and a festive mauve/key lime/coral color scheme inside. Rooms are enormous, many with separate sitting areas and period touches such as brass bedsteads and patterned wallpapers. Just don't expect proper mint juleps or Sazeracs (or much Dixieland) in the lounges. In a town that generally neglects its Wild West roots, **Sam's Town** sticks to its six-guns, setting the tone with its enormous bronze "Spirit of Rodeo" sculpture, with three proud cowpokes on horseback carrying banners. A "log cabin" facade surrounds Mystic Falls, a glassed-in re-creation of a Rocky Mountain aerie, complete with animatronic beavers and wolves (request a room with this interior view). Dance halls and saloons (see Nightlife) attract genuine boot-scooters. Bona fide antique barn doors, covered wagons, and saddles are strewn throughout; rooms have rustic pine furnishings, Native American rugs, and rough-hewn ceramic lamps with cowhide shades. **Sunset Station** duplicates sunny Spain, but it's all over the map, from Barcelona—the free-form, hallucinogenic Gaudi Bar (see Nightlife)—to the Andalusian-village public spaces, with arcades, barrel tile "roofs," and flower-filled shuttered "balconies." Pleasant restaurants like Sonoma Cellar and

Costa del Sol carry the theme through with beamed ceilings, flamenco guitars, and bullfight posters; the
cookie-cutter guest rooms have cast-iron lamps, polished cherry wood, and pretty wallpaper stenciling. The
Moroccan/Moorish motif of the **Hyatt Regency Lake Las
Vegas Resort**, 20 minutes east of the Strip, is carried out
with great flair, from the facade's arched windows, deep
loggias, and concrete grilles to its palm-studded desert
oasis landscaping. Genuine Moroccan hammered-iron
lamps and majolica urns decorate the public areas;
arabesque tracery, handpainted armoires, and pewter mirrors accent the guest rooms, most of which have sweeping
lake views. Its marvelous Café Tajine—named for a savory
Moroccan casserole)—delights with Spanish tiled tables,
copper salt and pepper shakers, and an array of traditional
teapots, ewers, and mortar and pestles.

**Globetrotting themes gone haywire...** **Mandalay
Bay** wants to offer the "colonial" experience suggested by
Kipling, or at least the steamy tropical ambience of a
Somerset Maugham novel. (Just for the record, the city of
Mandalay in Burma is fictional anyway.) Thematically, it
really spans the entire Asian continent, with a dash of
South Pacific for good measure. And the theme is happily
junked to accommodate Brazilian, Russian, Italian,
Cajun, and nouvelle American restaurants that lure trendoids. Still, there are exotic notes aplenty. Weathered
stone idols stand sentry throughout. Lily ponds, fountains, faux grottoes, waterfalls, hibiscus prints, and porcelain chinoiserie dot the public areas. Buddhas and
Confucius bless various dining spots. Tropical plants,
birds, and fish are seemingly everywhere. **Bellagio** is an
overgrown Lake Como villa (with even the lake), with a
*porte cochère* modeled after Milan's Galleria and trees
imported from Piedmont and Tuscany—but any specifi-
cally Italian influence ends there. The upmarket Via Bellagio shopping/dining area, for all its marble and
gold-plated fountains, is more Rodeo Drive; the casino
area is almost gaudy with orange and red accents.
Winking signs advertise Armani and Tiffany from the
soigné "lakeside" restaurants and lounges—hardly old-
world class. The oversized guest rooms are surprisingly
undistinguished, if handsomely appointed with marble
floors and surfaces, imported striped and plaid fabrics,

and the expected top amenities. Downtown's **Main Street Station** sports a wildly divergent collection of antiques, artifacts, and collectibles, including Buffalo Bill's private rail car, a fireplace from Scotland's Preswick castle, 19th-century Brussels street lamps, a piece of the Berlin Wall for guys to pee on outside the brew pub, and woodwork, crystal chandeliers, and stained glass pilfered from various American mansions. The large guest rooms feature "period" touches, including plantation-style window shutters and massive gold-framed mirrors. The **Stratosphere** features a clutter of unenthusiastic, seemingly unfinished themes winding up through the property's shopping/food court levels: Paris (with fin de siècle street lamps, mini Eiffel Tower, and replicas of Art Deco Metro entrances), Chinatown (with pagodas and dragons—and a Victoria's Secret outlet), and New York City (old Coney Island photos adorning the Nathan's).

**Campiest themes...** Aside from a surprisingly elegant lobby and spa, the public spaces of **Treasure Island** are as Yo Ho Hokey as can be. The exterior supposedly represents a Caribbean shanty town (complete with lagoon for the Pirate Battle—see Diversions), though it's a weird conflation of Mediterranean (barrel tile roofs, arcades), Pacific (tiki thatching), Caribbean (Creamsicle colors, fretwork balconies), and Hollywood (mermaid figureheads) elements—crowned by a huge skull and crossbones. As you cross the hemp-and-wood "bridge" into the hotel, goats bleat and roosters crow on the sound system. Inside, buccaneers with cutlasses, parrots, and treasure chests jut from the walls. Luckily, the guest rooms don't overdo the theme. **Excalibur** evokes *Monty Python and the Holy Grail*: A purplish dragon languishes in a moat that resembles a mildewed bathtub with clogged drain (well, that might be historically accurate), wildly colored turrets and towers bristle from the roof, and hand-applied stars spangle mock-stone wallpaper. The hell with Camelot, it's as if Mad King Ludwig had dropped acid before designing Neuschwanstein. Fake concrete arabesques, hideous keyhole arches, half-hearted minarets, onion domes—the **Sahara**'s remodeled decor actually makes you long for the tacky old neon camel. The onion-domed *porte cochère* is attractive, but the entrance with psychedelic stained glass looks like it was designed by a sultan on peyote, and the casino is a headache waiting to happen (with gold-painted ceilings and fake jewel–encrusted columns).

**When your chips are down...** There are plenty of motels on the north side of the Strip, with deceptively quaint names like the Pollyanna and the Laughing Jackalope. I wouldn't recommend most of these *Leaving Las Vegas* spots, dubbed by locals "tramp-oline hotels." But there are several relatively safe, clean, even appealing budget properties around town, especially Downtown. The **Gold Spike**'s $22 standard room ($33 suite) rate is valid 365 days a year. Rooms are surprisingly clean, though linens and curtains have the grayish tinge of too much laundering (could be worse). Suites are large if spare, with wood-canopied beds and black naugahyde furnishings. For every night you stay, you get a free breakfast or two-fer meal offer in the 24-hour restaurant (which serves $2.50 complete roast beef and ham dinners); the lounges serve 50¢ well drinks. The older rooms at the vintage **El Cortez Hotel & Casino** are dead plain, but rates start at $18 and some still sport the original wooden floors and tiled baths. The mini-suites in the newer tower are also cheap and quite spacious, many with separate sitting and dressing areas. Popular with compulsive-gambler seniors, El Cortez is a couple of blocks removed from the safety of the Fremont Street Experience and lacks a pool. **Jackie Gaughan's Plaza Hotel & Casino**, which sits next to the Downtown bus terminal and includes the unused Amtrak station (low-rent tour groupies stagger drunkenly through the lobby), is a good budget bet for those who want the feel and services of a large convention hotel. Rooms are serviceable, if strangely shaped, with standard blue carpet and floral spreads. The North Tower rooms arguably feature the best views of the pyrotechnic sound-and-light Fremont Street Experience (see Diversions). The lobby is incredibly garish, with strobing lights bouncing off brass railings; the casino specializes in $1 tables and nickel slots. Other facilities include a theater (usually with artfully nude X-travaganzas) and a year-round sun deck with a quarter-mile jogging track, pool, and tennis court.

Moving on to the Strip, the **Glass Pool Inn** achieved renown for its elevated pool with portholes, where photographers shot spreads for *Playboy* back in the '60s. The motel rooms probably haven't changed since. Fluorescent lighting, fake pine paneling, madras spreads, and—if you're lucky—an honest-to-God avocado-hued bathtub and toilet make this one a collector's item of sorts.

**Gen-X...** The cyber-yuppie crowd loves **Mandalay Bay** for its post-millennial cool, a futuristic fusion of pan-Asian, Russian, and European elements; it's *Blade Runner* meets the Forbidden City. Music folks like Mandalay Bay for its on-site House of Blues, but actual rockers more often head over to the **Hard Rock** to join an effortlessly sexy and cool clientele. Even the staff rocks: The April 2001 *Playboy* featured a "Girls of the Hard Rock Casino" spread. There's a remarkable collection of rock-music memorabilia, even in the rooms—about the only thing you have to provide are your own groupies. Though **Bellagio** is often thought of as a "mature" resort, stroll around the pool and you'll see not an ounce of cellulite in sight—the younger men all look fashionably pec-toned, the women as if they're awaiting their second callback for a Victoria's Secret ad. Bent on entering the new millennium, **Caesars Palace** has scrapped its old-fashioned venues in favor of high-tech restaurants and bars, while rooms have been completely redone. The **Rio All-Suite Casino Resort** still has its party-hearty neon-confetti Carnival decor, but the amenities are thoroughly up-to-date: Peerless restaurants; hip bars and shows; enormous, sexily appointed rooms; a cutting-edge convention facility; art collection; spa; tropical lagoon pool area; and one of the country's finest golf courses, Rio Secco. The **Aladdin** courts Young Turks by throwing all the latest technological bells and whistles into its huge but comparatively undistinguished guest rooms—stuff like cordless phones and your very own computer. And while both the hotel and connected Desert Passage retail complex boast serious eateries, nothing in town compares to the suavely sophisticated London Club, a European-style private gaming and dining area with stunning art-filled decor and exemplary food. The tables and slots are high stakes indeed, but anyone can savor the cosmopolitan ambience.

**Family-friendly on the Strip...** Admittedly, the great experiment to make Las Vegas a family destination failed abysmally, but it still serves the market surprisingly well, if only because Vegas manages to bring out the big kid in every visitor anyway. Always ask if the hotel is offering a special deal, or if kids under 12, 15, or even 18 can stay free with their parents (yeah, just what that restless hormonal teen craves). Boy, do they pour it on at **Circus Circus**: Clown costumes dangle from ceilings and antique Barnum & Bailey and Ringling Brothers posters adorn public dining areas. Ringmasters walk about in bright purple jackets, clowns offer free face painting; the Midway (see Diversions) features great old-style arcade games, free three-ring acts, even popcorn in huge dispensers; the Adventuredome (see Diversions) is the world's largest indoor theme park. Older kids will appreciate **Luxor**'s 18,000-square-foot Sega VirtuaLand, a kids' Arcade-ia where Sega test-markets its latest interactive video games, simulations, and shoot-outs. The hotel's occasional animatronic camels, Indy Jonesian motion-simulator rides, and IMAX theater will also enchant kids. Baby-sitting services allow parents to wallow in the luxurious spa, dine at the romantic gourmet eateries, or play in the lively casino. Like a parody of Disney World on an episode of *The Simpsons,* **Excalibur** features 265-foot-tall bell towers, turrets, machicolated battlements, and draw-bridges in colors Crayola hasn't yet invented. Inside you'll find moats, Arthurian knights and fair damsels, suits of armor, wandering minstrels, jesters, jousters, even free puppet and magic shows; kids happily spend their parents' farthings on the Fantasy Faire level's motion-simulator rides and arcade games. Alas, the formerly blood-red guest rooms with faux-stone wallpaper have been stripped of nearly all medieval embellishments save for ye olde carved headboards, cast-iron lamps, and valances patterned with coats-of-arms. **Treasure Island** is always jammed with families who enjoy the nutty nautical decor. It's marginally cheaper than its sibling, the **Mirage**, yet only a tram ride away from the Mirage's kid-appealing attractions like the Secret Garden, Dolphin Habitat, and White Tiger Habitat (see Diversions). The **MGM Grand** has jetti-soned its kitschy animatronic *Oz* characters and Grand Adventures Theme Park, but it offers instead the delightful Lion Habitat (see Diversions) and an excellent

Activities Center for 3- to 12-year-olds. Disney movies are pushed, bathrooms are "Munchkin-sized," and cartoon characters make occasional appearances, but tweeners can play air hockey, foosball, Nintendo, and pool; there's a video arcade including virtual-reality games right across the hall. Dauntingly elegant as it may seem, the **Four Seasons** is surprisingly attuned to children's needs. The Kids' Club will note kids' names and ages when you make reservations, then present them with personalized T-shirts, a stuffed animal, and milk and cookies upon arrival. All furnishings are child-proofed; kids receive their own menu along with coloring book and crayons at the Verandah restaurant.

**Family-friendly off the Strip...** Technically on the Strip but far north of the activity, the **Stratosphere** enchants kids with its thrill rides, cool Strat-o-Fair Midway (see Diversions), and its sheer dizzying height; parents appreciate room rates made even more attractive by numerous promotions. It also attracts a fair share of Spring Break types in baggy pants and bad buzz cuts. Among the many entertainment offerings at **The Orleans**, which is also off-Strip, kids enjoy the 70-lane bowling alley, 18-screen multiplex, enormous Time Out arcade, and the Kids Tyme child center with a gigantic 3-D Jungle Jim and fun activities like puppet shows, finger painting, even day trips. The festive New Orleans decor includes Mardi Gras costumes, masks, and plaques from various crewes hanging and dangling everywhere, and the good-sized rooms give families space to spread out. Social centers for locals, the Station hotels are very family-oriented, especially **Sunset Station**—aside from the 13-screen cineplex, it boasts a Sega station (Tuesdays from 5 to 11pm you can play all the video games you want for a mere $10). All the Station properties offer a Kids Quest daycare center, with karaoke shows, video games, a play gym, high-tech Jungle Gym, and vivid playful colors like turquoise and mauve. As if its Wild West theme wasn't already a kid-pleaser, **Sam's Town**, out on the Boulder Highway, is bidding for even more family business by adding a video arcade, kids club, and 18-screen cineplex by the end of 2000. The **Hyatt Regency** offers the company's award-winning Camp Hyatt program and a fully licensed childcare center. Kids

3–12 can go hiking with naturalists, or sailing or fishing on Lake Las Vegas, and learn how to make dream-catchers, sand paintings, and petroglyphs like the local Native Americans. Kids stay half-price in a second room, based on availability, and can choose from their own menus. It's that rare resort that understands that children are guests, too.

**Quick getaways...** **Best Western Mardi Gras Inn** is just one block from the Strip and the Convention Center. The casino is rudimentary—just slots, video poker, and keno—but the pool/spa area is pleasant and the tiny restaurant showcases some worthy jazz and golden oldies acts. Rooms are sleek, with arches, torchère lamps, and a muted gray-and-green color scheme, as well as wet bar, fridge, and coffeemaker (several have full kitchenettes). The tariff is low, and they rarely light the "No Vacancy" neon. **Hotel San Remo** has an unbeatable location a block from the Strip's Tropicana intersection. It offers all the expected facilities—casino, cabaret (where "Showgirls of Magic" flash a fair amount of skin), restaurants (Italian, Japanese, steakhouse)—at bargain prices, right down to a $5.95 prime-rib special in the 24-hour coffee shop and a great slot club. The standard rooms are cramped, with turquoise upholstery and carpets clashing with fussy French Provincial furnishings; suites, however, are more subdued, even monochromatic, with two-poster beds. **La Concha Motel** has a marvelous Strip location, but neither a casino nor a restaurant. It's done in standard motor-court style, but set back enough from the Strip to keep noise levels down, and you've gotta love the funky office, a 1961 design by L.A. architect Paul Williams, looking like a pale pink conch shell backed by sharks' fins (or billowing sails). The rooms are good-sized, decorated in frilly floral fabrics. It's quite popular among convention-eers with cheapskate bosses.

**Taking care of business...** The **Las Vegas Hilton** enjoys location location location: right next to the Convention Center. Savvy management provides something for the older business traveler (golf course, elegant restaurants) and the new whiz kids, like Star Trek: The Experience (see Diversions) and a dance club (see Nightlife). Standard rooms are plain, though the marbleized desks are long enough to be real working desks. Suites are classier in decor, individually decorated (including four fantasy-theme versions) with hand-carved four-poster beds, modern artworks, crystal chandeliers, and tall wrought-iron lamps. In addition to its own extensive meeting facilities (500,000 square feet, which in Phase Two will nearly double), the **Venetian** is connected to the Sands Convention Center, making it a whopping 1,700,000-square-foot corporate playground. The 85,000-square-foot main ballroom is the world's largest without columns. In keeping with the rest of the resort, the meeting space has fastidiously duplicated frescoes, murals, and statues, as well as Venetian-glass chandeliers and textured wallpaper. **Paris** offers 140,000 square feet of pillarless function space, including the largest ballroom in Las Vegas, prosaically named the Paris. The convention area is patterned after the Hall of Mirrors at the Palace in Versailles: It's lined with towering mirrored arches, while crystal chandeliers hang from recessed ceilings with gold-leaf cornice moldings, ideal for the CEO who fancies himself Louis XIV. Moreover, Paris is connected via "Le Boulevard" to its sister property, **Bally's**, which offers another 175,000 square feet. Meeting planners can one-stop-shop at the combined sales office for their functions. **Riviera**'s lively "adult" rep (right down to the vulgar gold tassels on guest-room furniture in the newer towers) already appeals to certain conventioneers; an added inducement is its 158,000-square-foot convention center expansion, which is already booked into 2003. The Palace Tower meeting space in **Caesars Palace** is fit for any corporate emperor: marble pediments atop etched bronze elevators, replicas of Roman frescoes and murals, and barrel-vaulted ceilings. Fruitwood-paneled boardrooms, many with views of the stunning pool areas, offer plush leather executive chairs, and private mini-offices with phones are available. The business center even has a notary on staff. **MGM Grand**'s separate 300,000-square-foot Conference Center is perhaps the most sophisticated part of this sprawling, amenity-packed hotel. The smart postmodern decor features striking abstract wood "torches," fake palms, and stained-glass panels; boardrooms, many with outdoor views, feature plush leather armchairs, marble tables, curved glass pendant lamps, and decorative porcelain in cabinets.

**Service with a smile...** The **Four Seasons** boasts 10 staff concierges, including six out of the 13 Nevada members of Les Clefs d'Or, the profession's highest award. Their "I Need It Now" program redresses packing lapses: The Concierge Kit includes everything from batteries to birthday candles, cuff links, sleeping masks, thermometers, and reading lights—all delivered within 15 minutes. Guests who go for a run are handed bottled water and a cold towel upon their return, while poolside loungers are offered complimentary Evian spritzing, fresh fruit, even cucumber slices for their eyes. Even The Verandah restaurant anticipates every conceivable need: a kosher kitchen was installed and black napkins are provided for those wearing standard N.Y./L.A. black, lest the white linen shed. With such an attentive staff, there's actually more of a "Raj" ambience here than at its downstairs neighbor, Mandalay Bay. **Bally's** has long been lauded for its smooth, friendly service, including some of the most helpful dealers in town and most gorgeous pool attendants. Despite its size, Downtown's **Golden Nugget** has remarkably attentive service: Doormen promptly open doors and the front desk staff or concierge apologize sincerely if they keep you waiting more than 30 seconds—virtually unheard-of elsewhere. The **Bellagio** staff is unfailingly cordial, which is amazing considering some of the prima donnas checking in; they never raise a voice (though you suspect major dishing goes on behind the scenes). **MGM Grand's** staffers act like former cheerleaders; in an effort to counteract the place's massiveness, they're instructed like Stepford folk to chirp "Have a Grand Day"—even in the wee hours when you request your wake-up call.

**Old Vegas...** The Rat Pack landmarks are gone, but a few hotels, while keeping up with the latest trends, still retain that '60s time-warp feel. **Stardust** has been featured in numerous flicks, including *Showgirls, Mars Attacks!,* and *Casino,* with its vintage cigarette girls, cartoonish neon, multihued carpets, mirrored columns, and crystal disco balls in the casino/reception area. Its sign is a blast from the past: a huge spangled fireworks display of stars going supernova. Built well after the Rat Pack heyday, **Bally's** has since been surpassed in many ways, but it upholds old-style professionalism—the restaurants are uniformly excellent, the unthemed casino elegant without pretension, the rooms fairly large (450 square feet) with tasteful gold-toned fabrics and blond or inlaid-wood furnishings. Its quiet style appeals to a loyal, discriminating clientele that doesn't want glitz. And dig the reception desk's great mural of Las Vegas characters in action. Downtown, **El Cortez** may be ugly, but it's genuinely historic—it was Bugsy Siegel's first Vegas property, with the town's oldest casino, built in 1941. Crusty Runyonesque codgers mill around in the smoky haze of its resolutely old-time gaming floor, where there are an astounding 2,100 slot machines, 11 single-deck blackjack tables, and a classic round-the-clock game of $1–$3 Texas Hold 'Em. Several "updatings" have mercifully left the **Tropicana**'s fun, funky ambience unspoiled. It's a hoot, with a neon "thatched" exterior, jungle animals painted on elevator walls, and tiger-skin rugs in the gourmet Savannah restaurant. The Tropics Lounge offers free afternoon shows, in which Joe Krathwohl ("The Birdman of Las Vegas") cajoles his pyrotechnically hued parrots, macaws, and cockatoos into acrobatics, disco dancing, daredevil stunts, and slightly off-color repartee. The original (Island) tower carries out the theme with rattan furnishings, pastels, and even the occasional mirror above the bed for those wild nights, though guests can opt for more subdued room decor in the Paradise Tower, which has French Provincial style with gold high-back chairs and armoires. The **Riviera** motto could well be "Anything Goes": Transvestites are sometimes sighted at gaming tables, and special collectible chips with porn star portraits are printed for convention groups. Though the hotel specializes in top-notch topless shows, The Top of the Riv is a classy, classic showroom that still opens for the occasional name act. Despite its aggressive modernization, **Caesars Palace** still purveys that inimitable Vegas crass/class combo. Several remodeled rooms, while handsome in muted earth tones, include features like mirrored ceilings, frosted-glass swinging bathroom doors, and whirlpool tubs rimmed with Roman frescoes. And those over-the-top high-roller suites are still the town's coolest: You expect a crooning Frank to swagger by, martini shaker in hand, trying to make up with Ava or Mia.

**Better than you'd expect...** Despite a raft of nostalgi-cally honky-tonk attractions, **Circus Circus** displays sur-prising restraint in other areas. The redecorated rooms are now actually quite nice and subdued; the sizable junior suites have muted tones of gold, silver, gray, and cream, with armoires and wet bars. The busy "back to the future" casino decor of the **Stardust** thankfully isn't carried through into the rooms. In fact, lodgings are mostly in soft dun and gray tones, with distinctly Deco-ish touches—modernist curved cabinets and black torchère lamps. Rooms in both towers have received major face-lifts; the reconfigured 765-square-foot suites, now with hot tubs, are amazing bargains. A major overhaul in 1998 softened the sultan-on-a-budget decor (except for public spaces) at the **Sahara**; refurbished rooms favor sand colors contrasted with effusively hued spreads, with pictures of mosques and casbahs on the walls. The Sahara delivers good value, with such on-site attractions as the NASCAR Café, Speed Coaster, and Speedworld (see Diversions) and a showroom featuring the terrific magician Steve Wyrick (see Entertainment). Ignore the neon-splashed prison-like exterior of the **Barbary Coast**—inside are opulent public rooms gleaming with oak wainscoting, brass accents, crystal chandeliers, and stained glass. Guest rooms follow suit with oak wainscoting, etched mirrors, original paintings, and textured wallpaper; only the suites go for a glaring '70s-era contemporary look. Pyramid-shaped **Luxor** has plenty of campy attractions in its public spaces, yet its new rooms and lobby are surprisingly restrained, and the spa and gourmet restaurants are ultra-luxurious—good amenities for this price. Avoid the drab tombs in the original pyramid—the novelty of the sloped windows wears off quickly, and many of the Strip views are now obscured by the second tower.

**Where to escape the madness...** The **Four Seasons** is like a Bali "High" overseeing the South Seas nuttiness below in Mandalay Bay; you can descend from your aerie and enjoy the mega-resort's facilities, but M-Bay guests can't impinge upon your tranquil experience (though the food-and-beverage outlets are, naturally, open to the public). Villas and suites offer even more seclusion for those who want it. **Alexis Park** is just minutes from the Strip, yet light years away in look and ambience. Its tastefully decorated suites sport soft desert hues, and lush landscaping cocoons it from the Vegas frenzy; most telling of all, it doesn't even have a casino. It's a fave of celebrities who want to keep a low profile, like Tom Cruise, Julia Roberts, Garth Brooks, and Robert DeNiro. **Regent Las Vegas** is set miles from the action in the soigné 'burb Summerlin. Though it offers an exquisite domed "European" casino (read: no theme elements), its emphasis is on restful golf and spa packages. The setting is glorious, taking full advantage of the views of Red Rock Canyon's spires and Toiyabe National Forest. The 21-acre **Hyatt Regency Lake Las Vegas** also provides a true resort experience, on the shores of the largest private artificial lake in the United States (3 miles long and 135 feet deep). The resort controls tee times at the Jack Nicklaus-designed Reflection Bay golf course (see Diversions), and a Tom Weiskopf–designed par-72, 18-hole course will be completed in 2002. There are two pools, a water slide, and private sandy beaches, as well as bass fishing, windsurfing, boating, and other water sports on the lake. The hotel's persimmon- and terra-cotta-hued exterior blends with the stark ruddy desert surroundings yet contrasts with the lake, which ripples from turquoise to tourmaline. Natural light floods the public spaces, from the Spa Moulay to the small but tasteful Casino Baraka, where two-story windows drink in that mesmerizing lake-and-mountains view.

**Where to tie the knot...** Nearly every major hotel offers at least one chapel and full wedding-planning services, often including in-house florists, photographers, videographers, and bands (for non-hotel chapels and marriage info, see Diversions). Most also provide themed nuptials of varying levels of campy tastelessness. **Excalibur**'s Canterbury Chapels, gussied up with barrel-vault ceilings, stained-glass windows, and chandeliers with dangling crowns, offer a fairy-tale affair where you're actually dubbed "faire maiden and noble knight." As one couple, married in full medieval garb as King Arthur and Guinevere, exited the chapel, the groom grinned, "Get ready for a lotta lancing, babe." **MGM Grand** offers spectacularly theatrical weddings on its *EFX* set (see Entertainment), with nymphs conjuring Merlin in a haze of fog to perform the ceremony; the bride and groom can even literally take the plunge on the SkyScreamer (see Diversions). Its cinema-themed Forever Wedding Chapels are decorated with sepia-toned celebrity wedding stills (from real and reel life). The dressing rooms are to die for, with marble vanities, frosted-glass lamps, and BIODROGA products from the spa. True to its exotic jungle theme, **Tropicana** offers an Island Wedding Chapel set on an actual island with palm trees, waterfalls, fountain, and swans. The chapel is a thatched hut with a bamboo altar, palm-frond fans, and polished hardwood floors. No themed spectacles at **Bally's** tasteful Celebration Wedding Chapel, but it's notable for its renewal-of-vows ceremony and gay-friendly attitude (drag queens often serve as maids of honor). Sumptuous fringed draperies frame windows of hand-blown amethyst Venetian glass in **Bellagio's** two chapels (never fear, ceremonies are carefully scheduled not to overlap). Most packages include complimentary limousine to the courthouse where you get your license. Beware: The floral fragrance can choke you upon entering. **Paris** also offers glitz and glamour in its Chapelle du Jardin (murals of garden scenes adorn the curved walls and the ceiling) or Chapelle du Paradis (gold leaf and paint, with a ceiling mural of painted cherubs). The **Riviera's** Royale Wedding Chapel & Floral Shoppe is as flamboyant as the rest of this property. It features trompe l'oeil murals of mountains through a window, flowers galore against an all-white backdrop, a mini-grand piano, lavender lighting, and a theater curtain painted on the exit door.

**Cool pools...** **Mandalay Bay** doesn't just have a pool—it has a bamboo-gated 11-acre aquatic environment with a replica beach that has sand, undertow, the whole bit. There's also a jogging track, lazy river ride, and four pools, including one where you can actually hang ten, surfing 6-foot waves. **Hard Rock's** new pool is so hedonistic you could imagine you're at Hef's Playboy mansion. Exhibition is rampant: "Full moons" are common from the rooms overlooking the pool, and the hotel website features a live pool cam. It's lushly landscaped with palms, a lagoon, grotto, mini-beaches, hidden Jacuzzis, and connecting lazy rivers. Wild purple lounge chairs give it pizzazz, there's swim-up gaming, and the likes of Dennis Rodman, Ben Affleck, and Arab sheiks retire with willowy models to private cabanas. Caligula would have approved of the 4.5-acre Palace Pool Complex and Garden of the Gods at **Caesars Palace**, its fountains playing around three column-lined pools inlaid with marble and granite surrounded by fragrant Mediterranean gardens. The main Temple Pool is crowned by a giant rotunda shading a central island cooled by mist from giant fountains. Statuary includes centurions in full gallop and mythical griffins (half-eagle, half-lion); even the lifeguard stands are decked out like thrones. Amid the **Tropicana**'s vintage Vegas tropical setting—palm trees, several waterfalls, swim-up cocktail bar and blackjack, guests in tacky Hawaiian print shirts and muumuus—you'll find an Olympic-sized pool (one of three) and three hot tubs scattered throughout 5 acres of lush foliage. The **Flamingo Hilton** also provides acres of greenery, a series of linked pools, waterfalls, water slides (popular with the kiddies), and—you got it—pink flamingoes, both live (in wading ponds) and immortalized in plaster or bronze. **Bellagio** places its six swimming pools in a formal, 5-acre garden setting complete with imported Italian cypress trees, arbors, urns, and pattering fountains. Almost 300 pine trees sway in the desert breeze nearby, remnants of the old Dunes golf course. The most classic "traditional" pool on the Strip is at the **Glass Pool Inn**, which got its name from the portholes in the tiny above-ground pool with mermaids painted on its sides. Back in the '60s, the Glass Pool became famous for cheesecake poses from starlets and model wannabes. Sundays at 4pm the tradition continues, with photo shoots accompanied by live music at the pool. While you're waiting to see what sleazebag shutterbugs and would-be *Sports Illustrated* swimsuit-issue centerfolds show up, you can hoist a long-neck in the adjacent (what else?) Bikini Cafe.

**For the body beautiful...** Be prepared to pay exorbitant fees to use the splendiferous fitness centers at several of the major casino-hotels. The **Regent Las Vegas**'s Aquae Sulis (Latin for "waters of the sun") offers a United Nations of healing treatments: Asian shiatsu and reflexology, Swedish massage, and Native American hot stone therapy. If all you want to do is work out, there's top-notch cardiovascular and weight-training equipment, as well as personal trainers and stress-management consultations. The ravishing locker rooms feature domed skylights and intricate glazed tile panels decorated with aquatic motifs. **Bally's** spa/fitness center provides state-of-the-art equipment, saunas, steam rooms, hot tubs, et cetera, but those in the know swear by the Belavi face-lift massage—you're slathered with various creams and oils, then toned with herbal mists, finished with a honey-lift masque while you enjoy reflexology treatments. The tennis pros here are said to be the best in town. The **Hard Rock**'s RockSpa skews more toward the vain than the varicose-vein crowd with a state-of-the-art fitness center that includes a cross-training climbing wall, stair machines, treadmills, stationary bikes, and Cybex weight training. The spa's Kerstin Florian skin-care products are utilized in thermal mineral water therapy, aromatherapy, and herbal therapy. Besides massages, facials, and body wraps, guests can get chamomile scrubs, Hungarian Moor mud baths, mineral crystal baths, cellular repair facials, acupressure lifting massages, or Vitamin C antioxidant treatments. The Garden of the Gods at **Caesars Palace** has a fitness center offering all the usual treatments, as well as a rock-climbing wall, virtual-reality stationary bikes (you're in the Tour de France!), and Zen meditation chamber. Don't miss the 110-minute Passage to India, a package that includes a dry-brush massage, warm-oil full-body massage, and scalp massage that drips warm oil lightly onto the "third eye." The 30,000-square-foot Spa at **Mandalay Bay** has 12 treatment rooms, steam rooms, saunas, and whirlpools; treatments include massages, reflexology, aromatherapy, facials, and body wraps. M-Bay's exotic theme is carried out in the decor (stone fish fountains, wicker furnishings, porcelain vases) and an array of tropical ingredients (Pacific Island salt crystals, kiwi-seed exfoliants, mango-butter hydrators). The fitness center, overlooking the lagoon, is a prime place to see people huffing into cell phones, watching the stock ticker on *Moneyline* as they pedal stationary bikes and stride on treadmills. Ironically, the most "Eastern" facility is the Spa by Mandara at **Paris**, its 24 treatment rooms fitted out with Balinese teak tables, embroidered Thai silk hangings, and Oriental rugs. You can exfoliate, detoxify, and hydrate any number of ways, but the most intriguing options are the antioxidant green-tea body wrap and, *naturellement*, a caviar facial. You get a workout

ACCOMMODATIONS | THE LOWDOWN

just traipsing the whopping 112 acres of **MGM Grand**, which, though clearly laid out, is also seemingly endless. But traditionalists applaud the fitness center's high-tech virtual-reality climbers and bikes and computerized circuit-training equipment. The spa (beautifully designed with lacquered stripped bamboo, Buddhas, Japanese sketches, Tibetan rugs, water walls, abstract art, and ceramics) offers such signature treatments as Chi Yang energy facials (involving Chinese acupressure and herbal treatments) and various forms of exfoliation, such as milk-and-honey and Parafango (a mix of paraffin and Austrian moor mud). When all is said and done, though, the king of Vegas spas is the **Venetian**'s 65,000-square-foot outpost of the ultra-chic Canyon Ranch SpaClub. Nutritionists and therapists poke, pinch, and prod clients to determine their fitness level or ergonomic profile, then prescribe a personalized regimen of diet and exercise. Guests put that regimen into action at the vast fitness center on the lower level (complete with 40-foot climbing wall) and the Canyon Ranch Café, with its organic, additive-free fitness cuisine (dishes like crab mushroom quesadillas, sesame ginger chicken satays, and luscious fresh-fruit smoothies). The spa's 48 treatment rooms host massages, facials, wraps, scrubs, balneotherapy, and body treatments from around the globe. Between an exfoliating scrub and an aromatherapy massage, luxuriate by candlelight in the hammered-bronze Royal King's Bath, filled with rose petals and essential oils. Or experience a heated body cocoon: You're slathered with peat, clay, seaweed, or goat butter, then mummified and immersed in a virtual water bed. The Rasul Chamber, with its ornately tiled heated chairs and floor, is the spot for an ancient Middle Eastern ritual: Five muds of varying properties are applied by a therapist or better yet, your significant other, after which a sudden downpour from the fiber-optic "night sky" ceiling rinses you off. Alas, the entrance/waiting area for the entire sanctuary is bustling and impersonal (the pool complex and staircase to the health club are located on the same level).

**Heavy lobbying...** Step into the **Mirage** and you've entered a rain forest with real orchids, elephant ears, and banana trees, not to mention a lagoon with waterfalls and rushing rapids, a couple of somnolent white tigers, bronze mermaids, and a coral reef (actually a 20,000-gallon aquarium stocked with more than 1,000 brilliant-hued fish, as well as several menacing sharks and gliding rays). It even smells tropical, with a faint perfume of vanilla and ginger. The lobby of **Mandalay Bay** seems tame by comparison, featuring only a 14-foot shark-filled pagoda/aquarium along with towering bamboo cages filled with parrots and cockatoos (desk clerks sometimes have to scream to make themselves heard above the birds' screeching). The **Caesars Palace** entrance is a riot of gilt bas-relief, carved and mirrored ceilings, friezes, and reclining marble nudes alongside black marble floors and crystal chandeliers. After more than 30 years, it's still Vegas glitz at its best. But for sheer camp, nothing exceeds the excess of **Excalibur,** with its mock medieval stained-glass ceiling, glowing dragons, brightly colored heraldic flags, suits of armor on wooden horses, and amazing turreted chandeliers.

The majestic 70-foot rotunda dome in the **Venetian**'s lobby glistens with 24K gold leaf and a montage of 21 Renaissance paintings. The tile floors are the real thing, scavenged from condemned palazzi. Marble and Murano glass gleam everywhere, and a photo of Venice canals provides a trompe l'oeil effect behind the reception desk. Less awesome, but handsome all the same, is **New York-New York**'s registration area, with its Art Deco bronze touches, '40s Times Square photos, and a marvelous mural of the New York skyline at dawn.

**Handsomest guest room decor...** Hard Rock's rooms are wonderful contrasts of hip and classic. The decor is mostly gold (as in record, babe) or silver tones: French windows, leather headboards, parchment-and-iron lamps, cushy contoured velour chairs, and stainless-steel sinks in the marble bathrooms. The music theme is smartly carried out with subtle instrument motifs in curtain fabrics, and walls hung with black and white photos of legends like Jimi Hendrix, Janis Joplin, and James Brown. Despite the tropical rain forest theme downstairs, the **Mirage**'s large rooms favor more subdued, shimmering taupes, beiges, and bronzes with black accents, crown moldings, hardwood and rattan furnishings, magnolia prints, marble entryways, and separate vanities. Rise above the Egyptian kitsch of **Luxor**: Its new wing's guest rooms are quite stylish, with blond wood furnishings, sponge-painted golden walls, and subtle stencils of sunbursts and ancient jewelry. Door handles replicate the Ra sign of life or Isis snake amulet. Well, okay, the faux columns are a mite much. Some of **New York–New York**'s rooms are cramped (just like Manhattan apartments, come to think of it), but they're deliciously Deco-ish: vivid colors, cubistic paintings, curved headboards, and inlaid burled wood furnishings, with ziggurat and chevron patterns subtly incorporated throughout. The surprisingly inexpensive suites let loose, with zebra-, tiger-, or leopard-print lounges and antimacassars, streamlined torchère lamps, chessboard-patterned furniture, marble vanities, and black tubs and sinks. **MGM Grand**'s rooms replicate MGM Studio's bungalows with Art Deco flair: burled and inlaid wood furnishings, platinum accents, curvilinear chaise longues, all in tones ranging from copper to chocolate. Mini-suites feature groovy violet chairs or 1960s swingin' singles leopard-print loveseats: Martha Stewart on mescaline. Even the hallways impress, with blown-glass lamps and sepia photos of MGM stars. Illuminated at night, the emerald green buildings emit a sensuous glow into the rooms. The huge rooms at **Mandalay Bay** strike a nice balance between ultramodern comfort and an exotic motif, with glazed porcelain plates, hardwood armoires, pineapple-carved beds, leopard skin armchairs, prints of plants and butterflies, and abstract tropical fabrics. And in an ultra-cool move, rooms on M-Bay's 34th floor are decorated in fabulously funky House of Blues art naïf style. **Rio All-Suites Casino Resort** offers 600-square-foot junior suites with modified canopy beds, tables of smoked glass and cast iron, richly hued velour furnishings, and floor-to-ceiling windows (most with splendiferous Strip views). The **Venetian**'s sumptuous standard rooms are the town's largest: 700 square feet with sunken living rooms and 130-square-foot Italian marble bathrooms. Ferns drape everywhere; iron railings mark off separate areas; armoires are hand painted and armchairs trimmed in gold gilt. As for amenities, the data port, fax/printer, mini-bar, and two 27-inch TVs should satisfy any latter-day Borgia. The **Regent**'s two towers both feature stylish rooms in golden hues, with striped imported fabrics, plush armchairs, and large desks for working; best of all, most offer invigorating views of Red Rock Canyon. The **Stratosphere**'s rooms are now among the town's spiffiest, especially for the price, with Deco-ish paintings, dramatically patterned fabrics, and cherry wood furnishings with black lacquer accents. Rooms in the new tower are similar but lighter, in blond woods. The commodious rooms at **Monte Carlo** have a fin de siècle feel—gilt frames, potted plants, cherry wood furniture, rose-patterned carpets, and striped tan wallpaper with fleur-de-lys friezes.

**Art–full hotels...** Sure, Venetian and Caesars Palace reproduce famed paintings and statues, but the real thing also exists in Vegas hotels (and not just in The Bellagio Gallery of Fine Arts or the Venetian's two Guggenheim branches; see Diversions). **Four Seasons** echoes the exotic motif of its downstairs neighbor, Mandalay Bay, with antique porcelain and bronze-and-cloisonné statues from China, Bali, and India scattered throughout the museum-like marble hallways. **Main Street Station** culls antiques and artifacts from around the globe: ornate doors, transom, and stained-glass windows from actress Lillian Russell's Victorian mansion; bronze doors from London's turn-of-the-century Kuwait Royal Bank; carved oak fireplace and sideboard from Scotland's Prestwick Castle; fluted cast-iron columns from the Royal Army barracks at Windsor Castle; an Art Nouveau chandelier from the Figaro Opera House in Paris; even the Schlitz Milwaukee mansion's mahogany-and-walnut elevator serving as a phone booth. Artworks by Picasso and Rauschenberg are scattered throughout **Bellagio**'s restaurants, but the cultural coup is Dale Chihuly's immense glass ceiling installation, "Fiori di Como," which resembles, depending on your point of view, a profusion of glass jellyfish, a floral explosion, or someone's 1960s LSD nightmare. The **Rio** is known for lavishly mounted traveling exhibits ranging from Tsarist treasures to Titanic artifacts, but amid the property's jazzy razzmatazz, it's easy to overlook a splendid permanent collection of contemporary art, most on display in the entrance corridor and lobby of the Samba Theatre: works by Cy Twombly, Robert Rauschenberg, Ellsworth Kelly, and Nan Goldin. The mezzanine features a 20-foot-long sculpture of powder-coated stainless steel by Micah Lexier. Most extraordinary is the 32-foot-high, 22-foot-wide diptych mural by Charles Brown and Mark Evans, a shimmering mosaic of overlapping scenes from famous theatrical events of the 20th century.

**Obsessively detailed...** The signature landmark at **Paris** is its 50-story Eiffel Tower replica. To ensure authenticity, designers obtained Gustave Eiffel's original drawings. Although Las Vegas's Eiffel Tower is a half-scale replica, elevators can't be half-scale, so it's made of stronger welded steel, but rivets duplicate the original's wrought-iron appearance. French is used throughout (even the parking levels are named for historic figures or landmarks, such as Sacre-Coeur and Georges Pompidou) to the point of cutesy overkill, and some guests complain that the restaurants serve only, *quelle horreur*, French food. But any hotel that convinces the phenomenal Gaston Lenôtre to open his only *patisserie* outside Paris is *très authentique*. The **Venetian** design team not only took thousands of photos on site, they hired an architectural consultant from Venezia to ensure accuracy right down to the last detail. Every color exactly matches those in the landmarks; every pediment, capital, frieze, and other embellishment is precise; in an air-conditioned on-site sweatshop, laborers hand-chiseled elaborate replicas of statues, right down to the cherubs' toenails. Marble in the floors comes from the same quarry that yielded the stone for the original Doge's Palace. **Luxor** features a painstaking replica of King Tut's Tomb, with "artifacts" fashioned according to ancient Egyptian methods (see Diversions). Tasteful **Bellagio** didn't strain for authenticity as much as its glitzy rivals, but its designers did import hundreds of genuine Italian cypress trees at a cost of several million dollars.

**Suite deals...** A note of quiet elegance is struck immediately in **Alexis Park**'s lobby, with its beige terra-cotta floors, overstuffed chairs, and brass chandeliers. It offers the requisite high-end restaurant, a select spa, and three pools scattered around the property. The landscaping is lovely, with greenery and rock fountains transporting you from the desert. Suites come in 10 different layouts in classic sun-drenched Mediterranean decor. Even the standard suites feature a fridge and mini-bar, while more than half the units boast a fireplace (fake logs, natch) and hot tub. Great for seduction of clients or dates. The anonymous but clean chain member **AmeriSuites,** just across the road from the Hard Rock, has no casino or restaurant but offers plenty of gratis extras, such as a shuttle, tiny fitness room, heated outdoor pool, full buffet breakfast, laundry facilities, full business center, high-speed Internet access, and even popcorn and *USA Today.* The smallish units are attractively appointed, with stained-oak furnishings, moss-green carpets, leaf-print fabrics; microwave, fridge, coffeemaker, hair dryer, and iron are standard. Homey **Desert Paradise Resort,** a gated time-share condo complex, has no casino, bar, or restaurant, but continental breakfast, fitness center, pool with BBQ grills, and Strip shuttle are complimentary. Management throws occasional wine-and-cheese parties to introduce everyone. The one- and two-bedroom units—in attractive Mediterranean red barrel tile and faux stucco—are fully equipped with kitchen (including dishwasher and microwave), washer/dryer, irons, patios, and walk-in closets. The decor goes for the upscale Sun Belt condo look: lots of handsome cast-iron and glass knick-knacks, gold sunburst mirrors, Deco-ish sconces, hardwood furnishings, and vaguely Southwestern fabrics.

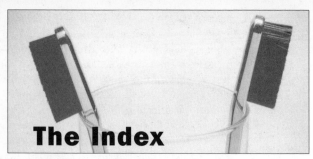

# The Index

| | |
|---|---|
| $$$$$ | over $200 |
| $$$$ | $150–$200 |
| $$$ | $100–$150 |
| $$ | $50–$100 |
| $ | under $50 |

Prices are for a standard double room (averaged between weekday and weekend tariffs), excluding nine percent hotel tax, and do not reflect special promotions, seasonal rates, or peak periods. All properties accept AE, D, DC, MC, V.

**Aladdin Resort & Casino.** Exceptional restaurants, witty decor, a marvelous Performing Arts Center, and the high-roller London Club.... *Tel 702/785-5555 or 877/333-WISH, fax 702/736-7107. 3667 Las Vegas Blvd. S. www.aladdincasino.com. 2,567 units. $$$$*
**(see pp. 22, 28)**

**Alexis Park Resort and Spa.** A 20-acre all-suite getaway just minutes from the Strip. No casino.... *Tel 702/796-3300 or 800/453-8000, fax 702/796-4334. 375 E. Harmon Ave. 496 units. $$$–$$$$$* **(see pp. 35, 44)**

**AmeriSuites.** Comfortable suite property for business travelers and families on a budget.... *Tel 702/369-3366 or 800/833-1516, fax 702/369-0009. 4520 Paradise Rd. 202 suites. $$–$$$* **(see p. 45)**

**Bally's Las Vegas.** Near the top in every category and blissfully theme-free.... *Tel 702/739-4111 or 800/634-3434, fax 702/739-4405. 3645 Las Vegas Blvd. S. 2,814 rooms (including 265 suites). $$$–$$$$*
**(see pp. 32, 33, 37, 39)**

**Barbary Coast Hotel.** A surprisingly elegant smaller Strip hotel at sensational prices.... *Tel 702/894-9954 or 800/634-6755, fax 702/894-9954. 3595 Las Vegas Blvd. S. 196 rooms. $$* **(see p. 35)**

**Bellagio.** Luxe, lavish, and slightly nouveau, this re-creation of a villa on Lake Como is made for modern Medicis.... *Tel 702/693-7111 or 888/987-6667, fax 702/693-8546. 3600 Las Vegas Blvd. S. 2,688 rooms (including 388 suites). $$$$$*
**(see pp. 18, 23, 25, 28, 33, 37, 38, 43, 44)**

**Best Western Mardi Gras Inn.** Limited restaurant and minimal casino, but close to the Strip and a tremendous value.... *Tel 702/731-2020 or 800/634-6501, fax 702/731-4005. 3500 Paradise Rd. 314 rooms. $$*
**(see p. 31)**

**Caesars Palace.** The town's first truly luxe (and themed-to-the-max) property has maintained its standards. Trendoid restaurants, lavish showroom.... *Tel 702/731-7110 or 800/634-6661, fax 702/731-6636. 3570 Las Vegas Blvd. S. 2,471 rooms and suites. $$$–$$$$$*
**(see pp. 19, 21, 28, 32, 34, 38, 39, 41)**

**Circus Circus.** An exuberant property-as-giant-arcade that appeals to the kid in everyone.... *Tel 702/734-0410 or 800/634-3450, fax 702/734-5897. 2880 Las Vegas Blvd. S. 3,744 rooms (including 130 suites). $–$$*
**(see pp. 29, 35)**

**Desert Paradise Resort.** Former cookie-cutter condos transformed into suites—homey accommodations at a decent price.... *Tel 702/257-0010 or 877/257-0010, fax 702/257-0363. 5165 S. Decatur Blvd. 111 units. $$–$$$*
**(see p. 45)**

**El Cortez Hotel & Casino.** El cheapo no-frills, but adequate hotel that caters to a senior crowd.... *Tel 702/385-5200 or 800/634-6703, fax 702/382-1554. 600 E. Fremont St. 308 units. $* **(see pp. 27, 34)**

**Excalibur.** The campiest theme in town—medieval mediocrity, but kids dig Camelot a lot.... *Tel 702/597-7777 or*

*800/937-7777, fax 702/597-7040. 3850 Las Vegas Blvd. S. 4,008 rooms. $$–$$$*
**(see pp. 22, 26, 29, 36, 41)**

**Flamingo Hilton.** A pallid replacement for Bugsy Siegel's original, but still a good moderate Strip option, with decent-sized rooms in warm jewel tones.... *Tel 702/733-3111 or 800/732-2111, fax 702/733-3353. 3555 Las Vegas Blvd. S. $$$–$$$$* **(see p. 38)**

**Four Seasons Las Vegas.** Understated luxury, occupying Mandalay Bay's 35th to 39th floors.... *Tel 702/632-5000 or 877/632-5000, fax 702/632-5222. 3960 Las Vegas Blvd. S. 424 rooms (including 86 suites). $$$$$*
**(see pp. 21, 30, 33, 35, 43)**

**Glass Pool Inn.** A total throwback motel with peculiarly cheesy allure. No casino.... *Tel 702/739-6636 or 800/527-7118, no fax. 4613 Las Vegas Blvd. S. 100 rooms. $* **(see pp. 28, 38)**

**Gold Spike.** Basic Downtown property, but bountiful amenities for the price.... *Tel 702/384-8444 or 800/634-6703, fax 702/384-8768. 400 E. Ogden Ave. 109 rooms. $* **(see p. 27)**

**Golden Nugget.** With a light-handed Victorian theme, this Downtown gem may be the most refined of MGM Mirage's properties.... *Tel 702/385-7111 or 800/634-3454, fax 702/386-8362. 129 E. Fremont St. 1,911 rooms. $$–$$$* **(see pp. 20, 33)**

**Hard Rock Hotel & Casino.** Hedonistic hangout for a hip under-40 crowd, fabulously witty.... *Tel 702/693-5000 or 800/HRD-ROCK, fax 702/693-5010. 4455 Paradise Rd. 670 rooms (including 68 suites). $$$$*
**(see pp. 19, 28, 37, 39, 41)**

**Hotel San Remo.** This comparatively small, friendly property boasts a great location and solid low-end value.... *Tel 702/739-9000 or 800/522-7366, fax 702/736-1120. 115 E. Tropicana Ave. 711 rooms. $$* **(see p. 31)**

**Hyatt Regency Lake Las Vegas Resort.** Sublime setting

between lake and mountains, luxurious facilities and amenities (including water sports and golf), minutes from the Strip... *Tel 702/567-1234 or 800/55-HYATT, fax 702/567-6112. 101 MonteLago Blvd. 496 units, including 47 suites and 10 casitas. $$$$–$$$$$*
**(see pp. 25, 30, 36)**

**Jackie Gaughan's Plaza Hotel & Casino.** A rather impersonal, shabby, but inexpensive downtown hotel with all the expected facilities.... *Tel 702/386-2110 or 800/634-6575, fax 702/382-8281. 1 Main St. 1,037 rooms. $–$$*
**(see p. 27)**

**La Concha Motel.** Cozy rooms, friendly service, pool, and ideal location for the price..... *Tel 702/735-1255, fax 702/369-0862. 2955 Las Vegas Blvd. S. 351 rooms. $–$$*
**(see p. 31)**

**Las Vegas Hilton.** Despite its age, the Hilton does everything well, serving a discerning business clientele.... *Tel 702/732-5111 or 800/732-7117, fax 702/732-5243. 3000 Paradise Rd. 3,174 rooms. $$$–$$$$*
**(see p. 31)**

**Luxor Hotel & Casino.** With just enough Egyptian theme to be fun, arguably the best middle-priced entry in town.... *Tel 702/262-4000 or 800/288-1000, fax 702/262-4406. 3900 Las Vegas Blvd. S. 4,467 rooms (including 473 suites). $$–$$$* **(see pp. 21, 29, 35, 42, 44)**

**Main Street Station.** Handsomely outfitted Downtown yuppie hangout.... *Tel 702/387-1896 or 800/465-0711, fax 702/386-4466. 200 N. Main St. 406 rooms. $$*
**(see pp. 26, 43)**

**Mandalay Bay Resort & Casino.** A hip, corporate frat party with a South Seas theme. Cutting-edge fun, from the House of Blues theater to the top-notch eateries.... *Tel 702/632-7777 or 877/632-7000, fax 702/632-7190. 3950 Las Vegas Blvd. S. 3,276 units. $$$$–$$$$$* **(see pp. 19, 25, 28, 37, 39, 41, 42)**

**MGM Grand Hotel & Casino.** The world's second-largest hotel, it remains a king of the Vegas jungle thanks to

ACCOMMODATIONS | THE INDEX

**50**

savvy improvements and faultless facilities.... *Tel 702/891-1111 or 800/929-1111, fax 702/891-1030. Las Vegas Blvd. S. 5,034 units (including 756 suites and 29 villas). $$$–$$$$*

**(see pp. 29, 32, 33, 36, 40, 42)**

**Mirage.** Remarkable jungle lobby, elegant rooms, excellent restaurants, and generally impeccable service.... *Tel 702/791-7111 or 800/627-6667, fax 702/791-7446. 3400 Las Vegas Blvd. S. 3,044 rooms (including 279 suites). $$$–$$$$$* **(see pp. 20, 29, 40, 41)**

**Monte Carlo Resort & Casino.** This cultivated property offers a combination of old-fashioned romance and up-to-date amenities.... *Tel 702/730-7777 or 800/311-8999, fax 702/730-7250. 3770 Las Vegas Blvd. S. 3,002 rooms (including 265 suites). $$$–$$$$*

**(see pp. 24, 43)**

**New York-New York Hotel & Casino.** Merely average restaurants, pool, and spa/fitness club, but otherwise a thoroughly admirable property.... *Tel 702/740-6969 or 800/NY-FOR-ME, fax 702/740-6969. 3790 Las Vegas Blvd S. 2,033 units. $$–$$$* **(see pp. 24, 41)**

**The Orleans Hotel & Casino.** This popular Big Easy–themed resort doesn't take itself too seriously, and has great diversions for the kids.... *Tel 702/365-7111 or 800/675-3267, 4500 W. Tropicana Ave. 840 rooms. $$–$$$* **(see pp. 24, 30)**

**Paris.** Obsessive replica of the City of Light, with near-authentic Gallic élan. The food is ooh-la-la.... *Tel 702/967-4111 or 888/266-5687, fax 702/967-3836. 3655 Las Vegas Blvd. S. 2,916 units (including 295 suites). $$$–$$$$* **(see pp. 23, 32, 37, 39, 44)**

**Regent Las Vegas.** Suburban off-Strip location and luxury style makes this resort feel more like a Phoenix/Scottsdale golf resort than a Vegas property.... *Tel 702/869-7777 or 877/869-8777, fax 702/869-7771. 221 North Rampart Blvd. 540 rooms. $$$$–$$$$$*

**(see pp. 20, 36, 38, 42)**

**Rio All-Suite Casino Resort.** Exemplary property—huge

rooms, superlative restaurants, a model beach/grotto pool, fine spa, extensive gaming, and nightlife.... *Tel 702/252-7777 or 800/PLAY-RIO, fax 702/253-0090. 3700 W. Flamingo Rd. 2,563 units. $$$* **(see pp. 28, 42, 43)**

**Riviera Hotel & Casino.** This slightly tarnished golden oldie markets itself as "The Alternative for Grownups".... *Tel 702/734-5110 or 800/634-6753, fax 702/794-9451. 2901 Las Vegas Blvd. S. 2,075 rooms (including 158 suites). $$–$$$* **(see pp. 32, 34, 37)**

**Sahara Hotel & Casino.** A bargain at the edge of the Strip, popular with families and seniors.... *Tel 702/737-2111 or 888/696-2121, fax 702/791-2027. 2535 Las Vegas Blvd. S. 1,709 units. $$* **(see pp. 26, 35)**

**Sam's Town.** A virtual Western theme park, complete with dance halls, saloons, and a re-creation of the Rocky Mountains. One of the best buys in town.... *Tel 702/456-7777 or 800/634-6371, fax 702/454-8014. 5111 Boulder Hwy. 650 units. $$–$$$* **(see pp. 24, 30)**

**Stardust Resort & Casino.** Old holdover that remains one of the best values in town, catering to middle-American sales reps and tour groups.... *Tel 702/732-6111 or 800/824-6033, fax 702/732-6296. 3000 Las Vegas Blvd. S. 2,431 units. $$–$$$* **(see pp. 33, 35)**

**Stratosphere Casino Hotel & Tower.** Despite a poor location, the tallest structure west of the Mississippi offers solid value with a shot of glitz. *Tel 702/380-7777 or 800/99-TOWER, fax 702/383-4755. 2000 Las Vegas Blvd. S. 2,446 units. $–$$* **(see pp. 22, 26, 30, 43)**

**Sunset Station Hotel & Casino.** Stellar example of this chain's family values, featuring an attractive Mediterranean theme.... *Tel 702/547-7777 or 800/6-STATIONS, fax 702/547-7606. 1301 W. Sunset Rd., Henderson. 448 units. $$–$$$* **(see pp. 24, 30)**

**Treasure Island.** Popular but overly themed sibling resort to the Mirage.... *Tel 702/894-7111 or 800/944-7444, fax 702/894-7446. 3300 Las Vegas Blvd. S. 2,891 units. $$$–$$$$* **(see pp. 22, 26, 29)**

ACCOMMODATIONS | THE INDEX

**Tropicana Resort & Casino.** Strip property that offers kitsch and glitz with a wink.... *Tel 702/739-2222 or 800/634-4000, fax 702/739-2469. 3801 Las Vegas Blvd. S. 1,874 units. $$–$$$* **(see pp. 34, 37, 38)**

**Venetian Resort-Hotel-Casino.** Admirable duplication of Venice, including ceiling frescoes and a Grand Canal. Remarkable dining and shopping.... *Tel 702/733-5000 or 888/2-VENICE, fax 702/733-5404. 3355 Las Vegas Blvd. S. 3,036 units. $$$$$*

**(see pp. 19, 23, 32, 40, 41, 42, 44)**

# Las Vegas Accommodations

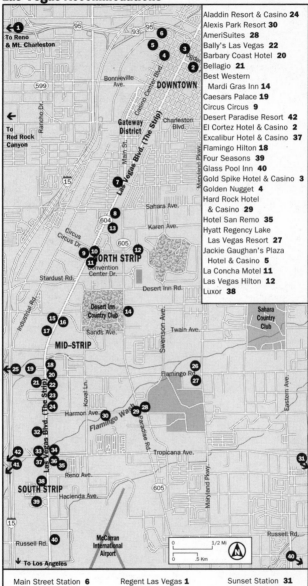

Aladdin Resort & Casino **24**
Alexis Park Resort **30**
AmeriSuites **28**
Bally's Las Vegas **22**
Barbary Coast Hotel **20**
Bellagio **21**
Best Western
 Mardi Gras Inn **14**
Caesars Palace **19**
Circus Circus **9**
Desert Paradise Resort **42**
El Cortez Hotel & Casino **2**
Excalibur Hotel & Casino **37**
Flamingo Hilton **18**
Four Seasons **39**
Glass Pool Inn **40**
Gold Spike Hotel & Casino **3**
Golden Nugget **4**
Hard Rock Hotel
 & Casino **29**
Hotel San Remo **35**
Hyatt Regency Lake
 Las Vegas Resort **27**
Jackie Gaughan's Plaza
 Hotel & Casino **5**
La Concha Motel **11**
Las Vegas Hilton **12**
Luxor **38**

Main Street Station **6**
Mandalay Bay **39**
MGM Grand **34**
Mirage **17**
Monte Carlo Hotel
 & Casino **32**
New York-New York **33**
Orleans **41**
Paris **23**

Regent Las Vegas **1**
Rio All-Suite
 Casino Resort **25**
Riviera Hotel & Casino **10**
Sahara Hotel & Casino **8**
Sam's Town **26**
Stardust Resort
 & Casino **13**
Stratosphere **7**

Sunset Station **31**
Treasure Island **15**
Tropicana **36**
Venetian **16**

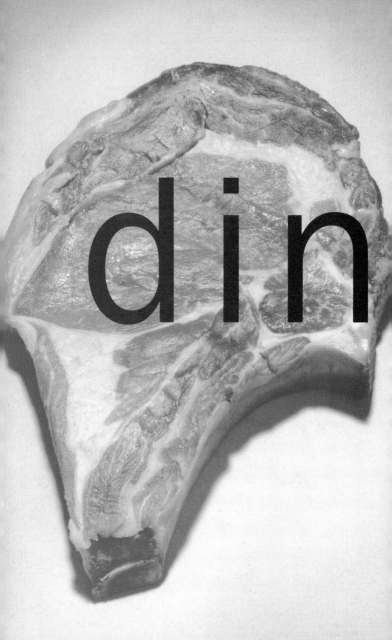

# ing 2

Used to be that Las Vegas was the city where the preferred greens were crisp laundered C-notes. You had two dining choices:

zcafeteria-style all-you-can-eat buffets or ornate gourmet rooms with strolling violinists and champagne waterfalls, serving continental cuisine frozen in the Kennedy era (the latter designed for high rollers—90 percent of the meals were comped). Today the baby radicchio/arugula crowd has arrived en masse. Credit it to Wolfgang Puck, who in 1992 opened a branch of his trendy L.A. gourmet pizzeria, **Spago**, in the Forum Shops at Caesars, of all places. It was an instant smash, still his biggest-grossing restaurant with sales in excess of $12 million annually. Once Puck raised the bar, everyone rushed in to fill the culinary void, and the dining scene has undergone a change of epic proportions. Today, most of America's hottest chefs or restaurateurs are in Las Vegas, though usually in absentia—they're too busy checking on their other outposts, promoting their cookbooks, or taping their TV shows— leaving the kitchens to be run by hand-picked acolytes (several of whom leave the nest to open their own buzzing off-Strip eateries). Las Vegas even boasts more Master Sommeliers (seven of the world's total 76) than any other city. Unfortunately, these star restaurants seem to be on steroids, conceived on an even grander scale than the originals. And past the top 40 or 50 eateries, there's a significant drop-off in quality. But those 40 or 50 can stand against almost any restaurant in America—in every respect save, perhaps, service, due to the shallow pool of trained high-end restaurant labor.

There's so much competition, even for local business, that hotel buffets have done away with the ghoulish goulash, mousy moussaka, and pallid paella. Now, live chef's stations are de rigueur, as are fresh ingredients and fresher recipes. Following the dining-as-entertainment trend, hip Vegas eateries also incorporate lavish specialty bars and/or morph into late-night dance clubs (see Nightlife for still more choices). This anecdote overheard at **Le Cirque** tells it all: As one Valentino-clad woman confided to another about her stodgy date, "He's boring and a terrible lay. I would have broken up with him long ago, but all these new restaurants keep opening."

## Only in Las Vegas

Las Vegas offers nothing truly original, unless you count the all-you-can-eat buffets that began in the 1940s with El Rancho's Midnight Chuck Wagon: a $1 late-night meal as an inducement to keep customers in the hotel after the second show. What is unique is that in one mega-hotel you can find a themed fast-food court, a 24-hour restaurant, a massive buffet, a deli, and several other eateries, ranging from theme to steakhouse to gourmet—and room service to boot. The basic idea is the same: Keep customers on the property at any cost.

## What It Will Cost

The price ranges from a $2.99 steak dinner to a $6,000 bottle of wine and $150 prix fixe menu at the gastronomic temples. Some of the most fabulous deals, advertised all over town, are offered in the wee hours in the casino/hotel 24-hour coffee shops (often far more attractive than the dingy diners and truck stops elsewhere in the country). Coupons in the free rags and the newspapers can help save on meals, and joining a slot club may snag you VIP passes to avoid long buffet lines. Tip the standard 15–20 percent at restaurants.

## When to Eat

Buffet lines at peak hours can entail a wait of an hour or more (room service is even worse, especially at 3am after a crappy night at the craps table). Consider going late for breakfast (after 9am); before 11:30am or after 1:30pm for lunch; and as early as 4:30 or after 8pm for dinner.

**Real meal deals**

*The historic (1906) Golden Gate (tel 702/385-1906, 1 Fremont St.) serves a legendary 99¢ shrimp cocktail round the clock: more than 100 shrimp swimming in a big sundae glass. San Remo's Ristorante di Fiori (tel 702/739-9000, 115 E. Tropicana Ave.) has a $5.95 prime rib special (salad, baked potato, veggie, and roll). The Gambler's Special at Arizona Charlie's Sourdough Café (tel 702/258-5200, 740 S. Decatur Blvd.; tel 702/951-5900, 4575 Boulder Highway), available midnight till 7am, rolls a lucky seven: seven different breakfasts, each 77¢—or, anytime, a top sirloin (or ham) steak plus two eggs, toast, and potatoes for $2.49.*

DINING | INTRODUCTION

## How to Dress

Usually anything goes, even at the pampering palaces of dining, which sneer only at shorts and slogan T-shirts. Still, Las Vegas is cultivating that swankier image, remember. So jacket (and sometimes tie) for guys and appropriate evening garb for dolls are recommended at the gourmet rooms in **Bellagio, Las Vegas Hilton,** the **Venetian, Caesars Palace,** and the **Rio,** as well as a smattering of other top restaurants around town. Dress codes, if any, are noted in the Index below.

## Getting the Right Table

Even in the dead of winter or summer, the trendy eateries require reservations up to two months ahead. Scope out the territory in advance: If you want a window or patio seat, request it—or else your romantic anniversary dinner will be accompanied by a symphony of clashing plates or a serenade of shouts from the kitchen. As in any other gastronomic capital, the only way to ensure prompt service and a prime table is by being a regular or a celebrity. Tipping the maître d' at see-and-be-scenes is now regarded as gauche. If you notice empty tables, request a better one; most maître d's will accommodate you. If all else fails, walk out—there are probably five or ten other restaurants in the hotel, and many more within a few minutes' walk.

# The Lowdown

**Where to go when you hit the jackpot...** Perversely located on a balcony overlooking the frenzied Rio casino, **Napa** makes you forget the revel below with shimmering abstract artworks and a centerpiece bronze sculpture of leaves whirling up to a huge oval skylight. From the banquettes, diners can watch the open kitchen turn out well-nigh perfect food. Chef Mark Demers carries on the work of Napa's founder, the late Jean-Louis Palladin, whose elaborate concoctions use fresh, often unusual American ingredients (Hudson Valley foie gras, Yukon gold potatoes, and Delaware smoked eel), caviar and truffles, and hearty game like antelope loin and partridge. Bellagio has a trio of high-ticket restaurants that really stand out. Bucking the bigger, bolder trend, **Le Cirque** is intimate (80 seats) by Vegas standards, with only three seatings, making you feel like a member of a private club. The French gourmet fare is deceptively simple, in brilliant counterpoint to the whimsical circus theme. Despite its "power" look, clientele, and feel, the innovative steak house **Prime** is surprisingly unstuffy. Jackets aren't required (though New York black always works); there are even ponytails, earrings, and tattoos in evidence. Then there's **Picasso**, which spotlights an approximately $30 million collection of the namesake artist's originals, plus carpet and furniture designed by Picasso's son, Claude. The Mediterranean-style vaulted dining room sets off chef Julian Serrano's masterworks, inspired by Pablo Picasso's stomping grounds in the South of France and Spain. Serrano is one of only two Vegas star chefs in residence; the other is Alex Stratta at Mirage's **Renoir,**

who worked under Alain Ducasse in Monaco's Hotel du Paris and won a James Beard Award at Mary Elaine's in Scottsdale. Five-course degustation menus, especially paired with wines, showcase his signature dishes—things like foie gras with pineapple pepper crisps dusted with coriander over balsamic reduction and out-of-this-world braised short ribs with caramelized shallots. Tasting menus are also a great idea at **Eiffel Tower,** nestled in the 11th floor of the half-scale replica at Paris: Terrine of foie gras with marinated figs might segue into tournedos Rossini with truffle sauce. The Venetian's **Lutèce** has an austere, monochrome modern decor that reflects the uncluttered cuisine: sautéed foie gras in blood-orange reduction with a splash of Sauternes, a whole 2.5-pound lobster poached in court bouillon with puréed English peas. Coveted window seats overlook Venetian's Grand Canal, Mirage's volcano, and Treasure Island's pirate battle.

**Most beautiful clientele...** At Emeril Lagasse's **Delmonico Steakhouse**, at the Venetian, Robin Leach wanted a dessert that wasn't on the menu: He laid a model out nude on his table and slathered her with whipped cream and chocolate sauce (merely a whipped cream fight, according to Leach). The equally well-connected Lagasse has since banned Leach, though that hasn't stopped *Lifestyles of the Rich and Famous* types from stampeding this upscale meat-ery. Chi-chi Chinese **P. F. Chang's China Bistro** is a sea of MTV types with earrings and goatees, fresh-faced collegiate jocks, manicured JAPs with nails out to here, and distinguished politicos with slicked-back gray hair (there's a special area in the kitchen for power dinners). The Hard Rock's **Mr. Lucky's** is packed with sultry trendoids, leggy models, and members of the band. The restaurant is exotically decorated, with high star sightings and nouvelle California food (frankly, the more calories, the better the dish). Owned by former dancers Kirk Offerle and Connie Chambers, the two tiny but sophisticated branches of **Jazzed Café and Vinoteca** are after-the-show gathering spots for lissome toned dancers of both sexes—open late, off the Strip, with superb Italian food, wines, and espresso.

**Overrated... Michael's** serves sublime Continental food in a prototypically "classy" wood-paneled setting. But after all these years, why is it still such a high-ticket hot ticket? The celeb clientele may be loyal, but they don't get the brush-off lesser-knowns endure here. At **Emeril's New Orleans Fish House**, everything seems harried and hurried during peak hours, and the normally superlative fish can be overcooked. At these prices, that's unforgivable. And really, Emeril, a big "BAM! WHOP! SMACK!" for the crass advertising of your merchandise on the menu. The **Rosewood Grille** is bustling and impersonal; though the kitchen still excels, it's clearly been coasting complacently on its rep—and the bill's bigger than the much-vaunted lobsters. With **Spago**'s signature items now in supermarket frozen-food sections, the menu at this trendsetter almost parodies itself. Former head chef, now partner, David Robins is helping reinvigorate the old Wolfgang Puck warhorse, however, with less complex dishes like roasted pumpkin ravioli with spinach, endive, and hazelnuts in sage brown butter, or a pear and radicchio salad with endive, candied pecans, and foie gras crostini.

**Most creative menus...** At **Napa**, the groupie waiters breathlessly describe the chef's byzantine preparations: crisp roast suckling pig in rosemary *jus* paired with marshmallows and sweet-potato mousseline, or a duck consommé embellished with black truffles and cubes of foie gras, topped with foie gras–infused whipped cream. The endlessly inventive Julian Serrano at Bellagio's **Picasso** roasts scallops in a robust veal reduction with black truffles or sautés them in an ethereal saffron-infused beurre blanc; slightly smoky medallions of fallow deer are counterpointed by caramelized green apples and Zinfandel sauce. Perhaps the single most brilliant, gutsy dish in Vegas is at Mark Lo Russo's **Aqua**: seared *ahi* tuna crowned with sautéed foie gras, with spinach and a crispy potato cake enveloped in a rich port wine reduction and meaty portobellos. An even more audacious variation substitutes sea scallops, caramelized rhubarb-lime compote, and endive. The MGM Grand also has three very creative kitchens: As sincere flattery, Caesars' **808** "borrowed" both Aqua's signature *ahi* tuna/seared foie gras combo and its fabled cart service (including one for caviar, vodka, champagne, and condiments). Chef Jean-Marie Josselin successfully walks the tightrope between fusion and confusion, creating such inspired collages as braised veal cheeks with day-boat scallops in demi-glacé, or porcini-crusted *ahi* with foie gras spring roll and dried cherry Pinot Noir glaze. **Neyla**'s haute-Moroccan fare features seductive dishes like hand-rolled crab cigars stuffed with shiitakes with tomato-coriander relish and tamarind molasses, or tilapia encrusted with pistachio and pumpkin seeds with a roasted beet, mango, and vanilla vinaigrette; Mark Miller's nouvelle Southwestern **Coyote Café and Grill** counterpoints flavors like cumin and pumpkin seed or cranberry and chipotle, as in blushing lamb chops goosed by ancho-herb crust and rosemary-pear chutney; and **Nob Hill** pays tribute to San Francisco cuisine starring Bay Area produce—as in Liberty Farm duck raviolis with creamy polenta and roasted Chino Farm vegetables in foie gras sauce. In Mandalay Bay, **Aureole** chefs John and Megan Romano follow Charlie Palmer's "progressive American cuisine" by layering fresh seasonal regional ingredients in textured skyscrapers of food. Try caramelized pheasant atop truffled potato purée accompanied by Oregon chanterelles and sweet Italian *cipollini* onions. CIA grads Michael and Wendy Jordan, the husband-and-wife chef team who own **Rosemary's** on West Sahara, turn out signature dishes like pan-seared honey-glazed salmon with Granny Smith apple cabbage slaw and candied walnuts, and veal sweetbreads with bourbon sweet potatoes and crab-pecan relish in an andouille reduction. At the Venetian, **Tsunami** serves *uni*, tuna, and salmon marinated in the likes of sake, Cuervo 1800, or Bacardi Limón and finished with combinations of avocado, daikon, wasabi, pickled ginger, Tabasco, mint, and Thai chili sauce; **Postrio** freshens up Wolfgang Puck's formulas thanks to chef John LaGrone, whose tasting menus might showcase seared sea scallops with morel *agnolotti* and white asparagus, or grilled Hawaiian swordfish with spicy shrimp jambalaya and red pepper coulis. Downtown's unlikely jewel, **Second Street Grill**, sparkles with Rachel Breen's Chinese marinated duck confit and shrimp tacos in papaya salsa, and blackened *ahi* atop stir-fry vegetables swimming in Chinese mustard and wasabi beurre blanc sauces.

**Where the Rat Pack might hang out...** The Downtown basement location, with cozy curtained booths, exposed brick-and-hardwood walls, and vaulted brick ceiling, gives **Hugo's Cellar** a speakeasy air, reinforced by a bar where the city's finest classic martinis are served in decanters buried in ice baths. The retro menu includes tableside salad service from giant carts, "Hot Rock" items grilled on stones, the occasional flambé, and decently executed standards like *escargots en croûte*, herb-crusted rack of lamb, and swordfish *en papillote* with julienne vegetables. A '50s-style marquee glows "Cocktails" above tufted oxblood leather doors leading to **A.J.'s**, the Hard Rock's faithful re-creation of the Rat Pack era's macho glam look—dark woods, sheer curtains, curved leather booths, and a serpentine elevated bar whose martinis are as mouthwatering as the slabs of meat on display. The guys would also wax nostalgic at Harrah's **The Range**, where 40-foot wraparound picture windows spectacularly front the Strip (dead-on views of the Mirage volcano) and a piano bar has live entertainment nightly, including jazz trios composed of true singin' hepcats. The retro-swank Italian **Manhattan of Las Vegas** on Flamingo Road is more smart-ass than smart, but Frankie and Dino would slip right into the plush booths like old shoes, snob-nobbing alongside such regulars as Wayne Newton, Johnny Depp, Ernest Borgnine, and the McGuire Sisters. And no place in Vegas has more limos waiting outside.

**Close encounters of the romantic kind...** The three tiny timbered rooms at Downtown's **André's French Restaurant** have that rustic look—stuccoed walls embedded with straw and hung with country crockery, arches crawling with vines—and plenty of nooks and crannies for amorous tête-à-têtes over unfussy French food. The longtime French standard **Pamplemousse** has a rosy glow—maroon and mirrored walls, pink and plum napery, wood beams, and the kindest lighting in town, in pink bulbs, for the gracefully aging clientele. Piaf, Mouskouri, Aznavour, and Brel warble on the sound system. Downtown at the Lady Luck, the **Burgundy Room**'s Deco style, with red velour banquettes, hardwood and brass accents, and posters by Dalí and La Poucette, suggests something out of *Gigi*. Dim lighting and well-spaced tables complete the romantic ambience. **Neyla** at the MGM Grand has a sensuous souk-like ambience: stained-glass chandeliers, arches, Berber rugs, billowing canopies, and a working hookah at the room's center, with a selection of fruit-infused Turkish and Iranian tobaccos that provides instant aromatherapy. The Middle Eastern fusion food awakens the senses, too, with unusual combinations of exotic ingredients. The cozy oak-panelled warren of rooms at **Mon Ami Gabi** set the stage for *l'amour*; there are atmospheric black and white photos of sidewalk cafes inside, and the real thing outside, beneath the "Eiffel Tower" with a breathtaking view of Bellagio's dancing fountains across the Strip. Water walls and fountains provide a soothing backdrop for conversation at **Café Lago**, especially on or beside the patio, which overlooks Caesars' illuminated Garden of the Gods pool complex.   Another romantic touch: top-flight pianists, including acclaimed David Osborne (a Bobby Short-in-the-making). Posh **Valentino** features dimly lit private nooks, rose or tangerine velvet curtains, and Murano glass flowers and lighting fixtures. Lovers can lock gazes here over a superlative bottle of Gaja Barbaresco and refined risotto (perhaps with dried berries and bacon-wrapped quail).

**Where to impress clients...** Bellagio's ultra-contemporary, hyperactive **Aqua** has the requisite "hot/cool" quotient for wheeling and dealing; everyone talks rapidly into cell phones as their eyes follow who's entered. As you might expect at Bellagio, it's hung with fine artwork: specially commissioned Rauschenbergs. Its neighbor **Prime** dresses for success with an Aubusson wool tapestry by Lichtenstein, paintings by Robert DeNiro, Sr., and a five-paneled water-themed canvas by Joseph Raffael. Designer Michael DeSantis gave this sizzling steak house a grand manor-house library look in a stunning royal-blue-and-chocolate color scheme; rooms can be curtained off for greater privacy. Picture windows overlook the dancing fountains. Mandalay Bay's gourmet American **Aureole** manages to be both a relaxing dining experience and a frenetic power room. Though the high-tech space seats 400, designer Adam Tihany has cleverly broken it up with half-walls and water curtains. Earth tones, paper lamps, brass-and-wood sconces, and towering floral arrangements impart the feel of a plush boardroom; for serious deal-hammering, head for the Swan Court area, just nine tables and four booths surrounded by picture windows overlooking a waterfall, swan-filled pool, and gardens. Only the prix fixe tasting menus can be ordered back

*Mandalay*

here, but all the better to sample the stellar regional American cuisine. Tihany also designed the same hotel's Italian charmer, **Trattoria del Lupo**, which strikes a nice medium between the neighboring youthful party restaurants and expense-accounter Aureole. The look is secluded Milanese piazza: wrought-iron gates, wooden ceiling beams, huge earthenware pots, elegantly tiled floors. Just down Paradise Road from the Convention Center, **McCormick and Schmick's** has the look of a Northwest lumber baron's fishing lodge: white tablecloths, cherry-wood paneling, parquet floors, tiled fireplaces, green velvet drapes, stained glass gleaming with fish motifs, and trophy fish on the walls. Seafood is flown in fresh daily, whether from Fiji or Canada's Fundy Bay. In the Forum Shops, **The Palm** is the power-broker steak house incarnate; sensationally priced lunch specials lure both local honchos and celebs such as Tiger Woods, George Lucas, and Christina Aguilera. The re-invented **Spago** has been softened with carpeting, cork panels, and decorative glass walls, but its enormous, undivided space is still a quintessential see-and-be-scene: Diners risk whiplash as regulars like Julia Roberts, Danny DeVito, Joan Rivers, and Nicolas Cage make the rounds. **The Tillerman**'s "big deal" look features a cathedral ceiling with retractable skylights, a thicket of ficus trees and carved pillars, glazed terra-cotta tile, and enough stained glass for a chapel. The oak-paneled lounge is an ideal place to sip single malts while puffing on stogies from the vast selection. The Brennan family of New Orleans opened a Desert Passage outpost of **Commander's Palace**, a handsome series of rooms whose mahogany wainscoting, etched glass, golden beaded lamps, and historic black and white photos transport diners to the French Quarter. Asian pooh-bahs do power dim sum at the Venetian's **Royal Star**, which was designed by LAX architect Jin Wa according to *feng shui* principles: A serene Buddha and large amethyst crystal at the entrance promote good fortune and harmony. The layout represents an imaginary dragon, with the kitchen as brain, the elegantly appointed VIP rooms as the stomach.

**Frozen in the '50s...** A clutch of old-time "high roller" rooms are in a gastronomic time warp. With plush red velvet flocking and mahogany wainscoting, stodgy

**Michael's** at the Barbary Coast does a fine job with fine-dining standards like rack of lamb, chateaubriand, stone crabs in season, lobster, veal chops, and cherries Jubilee. The vintage Italian restaurant **Bootlegger Ristorante** has a great retro fireside cocktail lounge with faux-stone walls, flickering table lamps, large planters, and red red red napery. The pianist plays everything ever recorded by Bennett, Martin, and Sinatra. Co-owner Lorraine Hunt, the former singer/current Lieutenant Governor, occasionally belts out a tune. **Rosewood Grille** is a real "dad" type of restaurant, where you expect a stern lecture on life in between courses. You know the look—booths, dark wood paneling, red carpets, crisp white napery. The invariably excellent lobster, stone crabs, lamb and pork chops, crab cakes, scampi, and wine list are overpriced—just the way dads usually like it. Off the Strip, **Lawry's The Prime Rib** replicates the L.A. original's Art Deco inlaid woods and brass; Benny Goodman and Glenn Miller waft through the background and the extraordinary prime rib is served tableside from elephantine brushed-steel carts. The original **Ferraro's** on Flamingo Road is an Italian throwback, from its pink-neon facade to mirrored columns and walls; piano players croon standards in the lounge as couples rise spontaneously to touch dance. Waiters at the well-aged **Burgundy Room** Downtown murmur "excellent choice" no matter which of the fine-dining clichés you opt for—flaming tableside preparations, beef Wellington, steak au poivre, veal Oscar, or fettuccine Alfredo. Nearby **Huntridge Drugstore Restaurant/Tavern** serves occasional steak specials in its tavern area, open 24/7; it's *the* classic Vegas dive, with zilch decor and ambience, just as it's been for 40 years. Domestic brewskis are a buck, and the crowd is Hunter S. Thompson meets Charles Bukowski: neo-punks, strippers, off-duty cops, all unconcernedly scratching private parts in full view.

**Buffet all the way...** Sequined ribbons loop everywhere at the Rio's **Carnival World Buffet**, with its booths upholstered in Crayola-bright colors and servers dressed in skimpy carioca outfits. Twelve distinct global dining experiences—Brazilian, Cantonese, Italian, Mexican, BBQ, Japanese sushi and teppanyaki, et cetera—showcase live-action preparations. No wonder the lines are among the longest in town. In gorgeous Tuscan marketplace surroundings, **Bellagio Buffet** offers the most upscale items:

from venison to an exceptional gathering of marine delights, such as crab legs, oysters on the half shell, sushi, and the occasional lobster tail. Each station at Paris's **Le Village Buffet** refers to a different French province, with food to match—duck braised with Riesling wine from Alsace, sautéed sea bass with artichoke crust from Provence, coq au vin from Burgundy, and fricassee of scallops with roasted forest mushrooms from Normandy. The **Golden Nugget Buffet** is the most elegant Downtown, with frosted glass, mirrored ceilings, marble-topped serving tables, and swagged curtains. The food is excellent but limited, though the salad bar entices with almost 50 items. Bally's **Big Kitchen Buffet** is a splendiferous spread in swank surroundings (crystal chandeliers, plush carpeting, upholstered armchairs) for mid-range prices. Its creative entrees include Cajun rubbed pork chops, steak in peppercorn sauce, seafood casserole in creamy dill sauce, king crab legs, and crispy duck. **Café Lago**'s six live-action lunch buffet stations range from Asian fare and creative pastas to grilled seafood, rotisserie poultry, and carved meats, with flaky home-baked breads and crisp salad items.

**Bargain buffets...** The spreads at locals' casinos offer the best price/quality ratio (gotta keep 'em coming back, given the competition). The global smorgasbord at Fiesta's **Festival Buffet** includes Italian, Mexican, and Chinese stations; a Mongolian grill; and a fire-pit barbecue turning out some of the tenderest ribs in town, not to mention shish kebab and smoked sausage. Specialty nights might add sashimi, Hawaiian poi, or fresh shellfish and clams. At Main Street Station, the pretty brick-walled **Garden Court Buffet** offers rotisserie, wood-fired brick-oven gourmet pizzas, Chinese stir-fries, BBQ, carving, Hawaiian, Mexican (delectable salsas and guacamole), even Southern cooking, at very decent prices ($9.99 for dinner most nights). At Luxor's Indiana Jones–themed **Pharaoh's Pheast,** the Mexican, Chinese, and Italian stations are the best; desserts are bland. The **Circus Circus Buffet** looks marvelous—abstract circus paintings, barrel vault ceilings—but alas, they forgot to upgrade the food (hey, dinner's a mere $7.99); the stainless steel counters and menu ranging from pancakes to prime rib shouts cafeteria. Still, come here for a taste of

Vegas at its most surreal: Baptist church groups, bewildered Japanese tourists.

**The brunch bunch...** Many buffets ladle on the eggs Benedict/Florentine/whatever like there's no tomorrow, but beware of champagne brunches, which usually serve inferior sparkling wine, and only a glass or two at that. Not so **Bally's Steakhouse**, where Sunday's $54 Sterling Brunch entitles you to an endless stream of Perrier-Jouët NV Brut. Ice sculptures are laden with piles of shrimp, sushi, lobster, caviar, and oysters on the half shell; floral arrangements frame sumptuous entrees like roast duckling with black-currant and blueberry sauce, steak Diane, ostrich, or chicken roulade with porcinis and pistachios. With local and national touring acts stirring the soul, the **House of Blues** Sunday Gospel Brunch is as much revival meeting (up to 300 people shouting "Amen!") as brunch. There are two seatings (10am and 1pm), both all-you-can-eat with unlimited champagne (a decent domestic label) and a finger-lickin'-good menu of fried chicken, jambalaya, maple-smoked ham, shrimp remoulade salad, smoked chicken and andouille hash, and fabulous banana-bread pudding and peach cobbler. **Commander's Palace** has its own Jazz Brunch ($35), which includes a kick-ass Bloody Mary, Eggs Sardou (poached eggs over artichoke hearts and creamed spinach topped with hollandaise), and Creole bread pudding soufflé with silken bourbon whisky sauce. **Bellagio Buffet**'s champagne brunch offers your typical crab legs and prime rib, but also exotic items like wonderfully smoky strip loin of elk and saddle of wild boar. **The Steak House** at Circus Circus serves a very reasonable champagne brunch ($21.95, kids half-price); the clubby dining room crawls with families gorging on crab claws, oysters on the half shell, seafood crêpes, and the requisite prime rib and filet mignon. **Golden Nugget Buffet** is revered for its renditions of former owner Steve Wynn's mother's recipes for bread pudding, blintzes, and matzoh ball soup. At Fiesta's **Garduno's Cantina**, $10.99 will bag you some turbo-charged chili-packed selections, festive mariachi music, and free-flowing margaritas. The best non-hotel brunch bet sits in a nondescript strip mall: **Wild Sage**, whose extensive menu starts with cinnamon French toast, a smoked ham and cheddar omelet, and Belgian waffles with berry compote and vanilla whipped cream.

**Incredible edible deals...** Cheap as the Strip buffets can be, there are even better bargains around if you look for them. **Huntridge Drugstore Restaurant Tavern** serves up a mean chow mein at an honest-to-god Downtown drugstore lunch counter for under $5—cheaper and more filling than a TV dinner. In a strip mall just off the Strip, **Sam Woo BBQ** has even less atmosphere, but the crispy crackling barbecued flesh, not to mention glistening noodles, are almost as cheap. At hipster hangout **Mr. Lucky's**, $5.95 buys a damn fine steak cooked to order, three barbecued shrimp, a choice of potato (heavenly garlic mashed) or broccoli and a salad. It's available 24/7, but not on the menu, so ask your waiter. After hours, **Venetian** serves delicious half-price specials; it's a great place to spot Rich Little, Marisa Tomei, and cheesecake (no, not ricotta—showgirls and strippers often stop for a late-night bite). **Mediterranean Café and Market** is a fave UNLV student hangout for inexpensive gyros, veggie-friendly dishes, and free entertainment. **El Sombrero** is jammed and jamming with Downtown denizens, from deputy mayors to dope counselors, all enjoying high-octane authentic Mexican for under $10.

**We never close...** Every major casino (except Bellagio) has a 24-hour cafe, but if you want something more stylish, try these. Mandalay Bay's **Raffles Café** serves a United Nations menu with real flair: A small sampling includes Buffalo wings, brie and avocado bruschetta, chicken piccata, halibut and chips, quesadillas (some gussied up), and gourmet items like chilled lobster gazpacho or Chilean sea bass with chanterelles. Caesars' debonair **Café Lago** is nearly as global, with standouts including ginger crab cakes with mango and black beans and chilled lemongrass poached shrimp with cucumber and tomato horseradish sauce. **Mr. Lucky's** is like walking into a Calvin Klein shoot, where buff males and waifish females strike poses on a Route 66 set with battered highway signs, brushed-aluminum tables, leather booths, rock 'n' roll memorabilia, and rescued neon signs from demolished hotels. As you'd expect at the Hard Rock, the food is not your usual coffee shop fare— herb-roasted chicken with garlic mashed potatoes, anyone? At Circus Circus's **Pink Pony Café,** everything is cotton-candy pink with Valentine-red trimmings: pink ponies in the carpet, pink pony paintings, even a bubble gum–hued carousel. Somehow it manages to be playful rather than nauseating, and the food is straightforward burgers and grills, with Chinese after 5pm.

**Delish deli...** Stage Deli at Caesars' Forum Shops tries hard to duplicate its New York namesake with "graffitied" walls and Broadway show posters; the service, too, is as brusque as the original. "Skyscraper" 5-inch sandwiches (good for two meals) are named for Vegas entertainers: Buddy Hackett, Wayne Newton, Don Rickles, Tom Jones, David Copperfield, Jay Leno (he's the triple-decker turkey, pastrami, roast beef, Swiss, cole slaw, and Russian dressing). Knishes, pierogis, and blintzes—they even whip up a fair egg cream. On Maryland Parkway, **Celebrity Deli** serves the same without the theme and fanfare. In addition to perfectly lean corned beef, pastrami, and brisket, there's decent stuffed cabbage, potato pancakes, borscht, and matzoh ball soup. It's a glorified coffee shop with the usual star portraits (Wayne Newton, Tom Jones, Frank Sinatra, Bill Cosby) and gum-cracking professional waitresses.

**Chow, bella...** Bellagio's **Osteria del Circo,** Le Cirque's Tuscan cousin, dishes up all the standards, from melon and prosciutto to tiramisù. The flavors sing lustily, whether it's a mascarpone and prosciutto pizza, ricotta-and-spinach ravioli in sage-accented brown butter, or grilled jumbo shrimp artfully arranged atop plump cannellini beans, diced tomato, and basil sprigs. Save room for pastry chef Gregory Gourreau's delectables: panna cotta with black-currant syrup and the explosive *bomba di cioccolato*. At Mandalay Bay's **Trattoria del Lupo,** former Spago chef Mark Ferguson has adapted "peasant" dishes to American tastes with smashing success: Sample the prosciutto-wrapped monkfish with artichokes, peas, and fava beans, or the seared porterhouse with caramelized fennel and lemon. Adventuresome Marco Porceddu of **Francesco's** runs the gamut from chicken and spinach ravioli with snap peas in rose sauce to an otherworldly risotto flavored with butternut squash, mint leaves, truffle oil, and mascarpone cheese. The cozy room is a tranquil oasis in Treasure Island, with wood chandeliers and columns, floral fabrics, and artworks by celebrities such as Tony Bennett and Phyllis Diller. From a seat at the bar at either off-Strip branch of **Jazzed Café and**

**Vinoteca**, you can watch owner Kirk Offerle in the kitchen cooking the velvety risotto (try *al prosecco,* made with sparkling wine) or eggplant Parmigiana. Piero Selvaggio's suave Santa Monica hit **Valentino** has been cloned at the Venetian. Pellegrini displays an assured touch in his seasonally changing menu: foie gras–studded filet mignon, duck lasagna, lamb osso buco, and scrumptious freshwater shrimp risotto. Go for the antipasto at MGM Grand's flashy **Olio**: It has the world's largest (40-foot) antipasto table, with dozens of choices, including grilled artichoke stuffed with goat cheese and *arancini* (deep-fried rice balls oozing ricotta). Gustav Mauler, the chef-owner of **Oxo/Spiedini**, two restaurants across from each other in Summerlin's Regent, turns out succulent spit-roasted meats with impeccably balanced seasonings and marinades, such as garlic- and fennel-crusted center-cut pork loin chop and spice-rubbed duck with orange caramel sauce. **Elements/Tremezzo**, a linked pair of Tuscan-themed restaurants just steps apart in the Aladdin, incorporate imported olives, Parma prosciutto, Taleggio cheese, wild mushrooms, and figs in creative dishes (witness lamb with morels, cepes, and Swiss chard or risotto with grilled portobellos, *trevisos,* porcini, and truffle oil). Don't skip the feathery tiramisù martini (yep, in a glass) for dessert.

**Mambo Italiano...** When it comes to old-fashioned Chianti-and-cannelloni joints, Las Vegas is well stocked. Well away from the Strip, **Bootlegger Ristorante** was founded in 1949 and seems not to have changed since. Old family photos hang everywhere, the main dining room features dark leatherette booths and a canopied bar, and the lounge is a riot of red. Chef Maria Perri's family recipes include toasted ravioli, fried mozzarella and calamari, lasagna, pizzas, and 10 milk-fed veal dishes, from piccata to pizzaiola. Pinky rings, big hair, and plunging décolletage are still in fashion at **Piero's**, just off the Strip. Waiters confide specials like consiglieres, and shadowy booths and alcoves foster deal-making and discreet groping. The food is inconsistent, but the osso buco melts, the cioppino is hearty, and the *linguine alla vongole* is about as good as it gets. The luxe **Manhattan of Las Vegas** on Flamingo Road is the kind of place Tony from *The Sopranos* would find romantic, with soft lighting and enormous private booths. The signature seafood *mezzaluna* (half-moon-shaped) pasta floats in a gossamer crab sauce; the veal is invariably excellent, as are the genuine Caesar salad and decadent tiramisù. Scenes of Venice cover the walls, inside and out, at the **Venetian**, where top choices include grilled veal chop, chilled roasted eggplant, and marinated pork neck bones with pepperoncini. **Ferraro's** regulars swear by the meltingly tender osso buco, a 3-inch-thick veal shank in silken demiglacé so renowned the kitchen prepares an average of 70 to 80 nightly. Go for the signature pastas (lemon linguine with fennel, garlic, and shrimp, or farfalle with lobster chunks, peas, and sun-dried tomatoes in Cognac sauce) and exquisite risotto specials.

**Service that sparkles...** At tony, tiny **Le Cirque**, the seamless service is orchestrated with balletic precision. In the Manhattan original, Sirio Maccione dictates who sits where, like a White House dinner; here things are much more relaxed. The front door staff is remarkably adept at placating moneyed bullies and overdressed trophy wives. At Caesars, the **Empress Court** black-clad wait staff glides silently as spies attending to your every whim, like minions of the last emperor in the Forbidden City. It isn't just the long-stemmed rose presented to every female customer—every aspect of service Downtown at **Hugo's Cellar** has an attentive, old-world manner. Salads are prepared with a flourish and a smile, and the alert waiters are friendly without being overly familiar. Tableside presentations are frequent at **Aqua**, with its congenial waiters tossing toast points or riffling slices of apple with all the unruffled poise of casino dealers. Specialized carts prowl the dining rooms; one may be devoted to home-made ice creams, another to caviars with choice of Perrier-Jouët champagne or vodka. The immaculately tuxedoed waiters at old-world haute-style **Eiffel Tower** never blink at outrageous outfits, apologize when *you* have to rush the meal to make a show, and even move empty chairs to let you snap bird's-eye shots of the Bellagio fountains and Paris balloon. **Renoir**'s black-clad wait staff is unobtrusive yet intuitive, genuinely trying to relax guests in the somewhat intimidating room, or swiftly but diplomatically escorting inebriated high rollers to the back to sober up.

**Decor to the max...** The Mirage's **Samba Brazilian Steakhouse** has a witty look that's more skewered than the meats sizzling on the open spits. Eggplant-colored ceilings and mango walls accentuate the free-flowing architectural lines; the plates are as colorful as Fiesta Ware, salt and pepper shakers are shaped like balloons, and a red-and-green contraption signals the wait staff (green means "bring it on," red means "wheel me out"). Adam Tihany designed **Le Cirque** at Bellagio as a subtler, more intimate version of its New York sister, with vividly colored Italian silks draping sensuously and lit, tent-like, from within. Yes, there's a circus theme, with big-top murals on cherry-wood walls and jugglers and clowns etched on Lalique frosted-glass panels. David Rockwell gave the Hard Rock's chic Mexican **Pink Taco** an updated, tequila-soaked *On the Road* look with corrugated metal, distressed wood, swinging bare-bulb fixtures, even an enormous hubcap chandelier. Leather, canvas, burlap, and denim are incorporated into upholstery and wall hangings; the tin-topped Tequila Bar features a pony-skin drink ledge. At the Forum Shops, Spago's Chinese cousin **Chinois** is fusion-designed, like the food—on the one hand, bamboo, Asian statues, a rock garden, and porcelain vases, on the other hand a riot of curved and textured surfaces and intense gem colors worthy of a Miró painting. Mandalay Bay's **House of Blues** has the world's largest folk art collection, including a life-size Elvis outside, doll-filled coffins, and funky seating areas formed by hammered license plates, bottle caps, and olive oil and coffee cans. Mist from a faux grotto cools **Kokomo's** at the Mirage, where rattan and bamboo furnishings nestle amid a tropical rainforest of banana trees, royal palms, orchids, and other exotic blooms. **Olio's** 100-foot-long tiger-wood entrance leads to a hip, retro lipstick-red lounge with beaded curtains. An 8-foot-high roaring fireplace separates the bar from the multitiered dining room, where sensuous fiber optics change the back wall from magenta to turquoise. At **Oxo/Spiedini**, Oxo is the wilder of the pair, with its psychedelic-hued cow murals by Russian neo-Impressionist Sergey Cherep and its neon tic-tac-toe boards flashing above the entrance. Spiedini is subdued by comparison: Circles and curves abound, with wild handblown glass fixtures everywhere. A sort of upscale spa look prevails at **808**: Bamboo stalks adorn tables, golden light radiates from onyx fixtures, glass walls laminated with rice paper divide sections, bronze and aluminum fish sculptures grace the Tamo ash-wood walls, and a simulated riverbed of burnished copper pebbles flows on the ceiling to the ostentatious exhibition kitchen. The original funkadelic **Jazzed Café and Vinoteca** has walls in different shades of blue covered with lurid artwork (a woman's navel in denim cut-offs, a Warhol-esque JFK portrait with a bull's-eye in forehead); the newer West Sahara branch is even more outrageous, with walls and velvet sofas in mauves, crimsons, and teals.

**Winning wine lists...** At Mandalay Bay, **Aureole** features the best range and some of the fairest prices in town, with a particularly superb selection of Burgundies, Bordeaux, and (hot trend) Austrian whites to complement the finely wrought American food. You can't miss the four-story wine tower made of stainless steel and glass, with cool chicks clad in *Avengers*-style cat suits, harnesses, and crash helmets rappelling up and down to fetch bottles for customers. Yet the tower holds only a quarter of the restaurant's 45,000 bottles (the rest are conventionally stored). Two thousand wines are available, ranging from $25 to $45,000. The wine list comes as an e-book, with a touch-sensitive flat screen presenting vintage charts and wine-maker profiles. You can even reserve your wines in advance on the site, eWinetower.com. Aureole's wine director, Andrew Vadjinia, also oversees the **Charlie Palmer's Steakhouse** list, which focuses on boutique producers, including an extraordinary selection of California cult wines as well as varietals of first-growth Bordeaux and rare California Cabs. At the Rio, **Napa** showcases Barrie Larvin's collection of 65,000 bottles, including 25 vintages of Château Lafite-Rothschild; not all are available, but the menu lists more than 600 bottles, with more than 100 by the glass. Building on the wine rep of its L.A. parent, **Valentino** has an encyclopedic list (27,000 bottles, over 1,200 labels) that's unmatched for boutique Italian producers. **Eiffel Tower** features a smartly chosen page of wines by the glass, a remarkable Alsatian list, high-ticket varietals, and older Bordeaux (back to 1949 Haut-Brion)—and a sizable selection of fine bottles under $50. **Pinot Brasserie**'s well-priced, comprehensive list travels from Margaret River in Australia to Monbazillac and offers mini-flights. The **Commander's Palace** list helpfully separates bottles not only according to region and varietal, but body (light and velvety to full and smooth, round and balanced to complex and rich). Most wines (Italy and the Southern Hemisphere are favored) fall in the $25 to $40 range, with several offered by the glass or in half-bottles. Jay James maintains an enviable master list for all Bellagio restaurants, including **Le Cirque**, **Prime**, **Picasso**, **Aqua**, and **Olive's**; if you desire something on another restaurant's list, you can request it from the big book. **Smith and Wollensky's** meaty list is admirably balanced, with an impressive number of larger magnums and double magnums (which age better). **Rosemary's** seeks out top-value, lesser-known varietals (Malbec to Mourvèdre) and regions (Argentina to Washington). The menu contains dozens by the glass (not to mention 20 by "demi-pitcher" and two pages of half-bottles) and also recommends beer pairings from Chimay Trappist Ale (Belgium) to Blanche de Chambly (a Quebec white beer brewed on lees). Downtown, **André's French Restaurant** offers impressive varietals of all the first-growth Bordeaux (15 vintages of Lafite); a long brass bar at the entrance features plentiful wines by the glass.

**Kidz are us...** At the MGM Grand, **Rainforest Café** offers a wonderland (on acid) of animatronic animals and other faux-natural touches—tropical rainstorms sweep the room every quarter hour; at night, shooting stars cross the ceiling. The food's surprisingly edible, with a kid's menu including Amazon burgers and Planet Earth Pasta. Excalibur's **Sir Galahad** is one mature restaurant where the kids may not squirm—they'll be too busy goggling at the suits of armor and heraldic banners and watching waiters in Robin Hood green tights carve up enormous prime ribs. Jugglers, harlequins, and singers keep kids distracted at **Postrio's** "outdoor" cafe on the Venetian's St. Mark's Square. Wolfgang Puck's designer pizzas don't fit the pizzeria mold, but youngsters may educate their palates with variations like the spicy lamb sausage, garlic, pepper, and sweet-onion pizza.

**Designer Asians...** M-Bay's futuristic **China Grill** mixes East and West with aplomb—broccoli rabe dumplings with roasted tomatoes and star anise and pan-seared foie gras with caramelized mango, palm sugar, and cashews. The BBQ lamb ribs fall off the bone. The look is very high-tech, with bronze mesh on the domed ceiling, and changing-color mood lighting. At the adjacent Rock Lobster, conveyer belts pass sushi and bite-sized crustacean tapas on colorful plates, and video monitors serve up financial news, fashion, and, duh, rock videos. At the Hard Rock, **Nobu** showcases owner Nobu Matsuhisa's "new-style sushi and sashimi," with stunning dishes like raw fluke with *ponzu* and heated olive oil. The striking space, designed by David Rockwell, features water walls, live trees, bamboo screens, and walls hung with laminated seaweed; the sushi bar glows ethereally within a curved plane of floor-to-ceiling river rock. Despite Chinese warrior sculptures and pagoda murals, the atmosphere at **P. F. Chang's China Bistro** is totally American, with halogen lights and a postmodern warehouse-y look. Northern-style short ribs, vegetarian dumplings, and crispy honey shrimp are old reliables. Wolfgang Puck does for Asian food at **Chinois** what he did for pizza at Spago: He tarts it up with unlikely yet savory ingredients. Grilled crab claws with mild *shishito* green chilis and plum-infused mayonnaise: Shinto Southwestern? Sweet-and-sour sesame chicken with yams and snap peas: Yangtze Delta food? **Second Street Grill** is an unexpected delight in a seedy Downtown hotel: a subdued Deco-ish room serving Hawaiian-accented food minus the Trader Vic's flambéed flamboyance. Lemon chicken potstickers are wonderful, as is the whole fresh fish (which could be mahimahi, *ahi* tuna, or *opaka paka*) steamed in tea leaves with coconut, cumin, and coriander notes. Second Street Grill's former chef Jean Marie Josselin has moved on to **808**, named after Hawaii's area code; its mix of Pacific Rim and coastal Mediterranean cuisines gives rise to intriguing combos like seared Hudson Valley foie gras with quince compote and lime-ginger glaze, or day-boat scallops and white truffle mashed potatoes floating in Japanese pear Riesling broth. On West Sahara at **Mayflower Cuisinier**, Hong Kong–raised chef-owner Ming See Woo is renowned for her Asian-French-Californian "mixed culture" fare: ginger-chicken ravioli with Szechuan peanut-scallion sauce, Mongolian grilled lamb chops in creamy cilantro mint sauce, and grilled salmon in ginger beurre blanc. The Venetian's **Tsunami** has an immense pan-Asian menu, a free-form gastronomic merger. The melting sushi is endlessly innovative, as are the specialty infusion cocktails with names like Typhoon Rita and Tsunami Surfer. The decor—*Blade Runner* meets Kabuki via David Hockney—violates every *feng shui* principle, with jutting eaves, shifting perspectives, and clashing colors, but who cares?

**Authentic Asians...** **Sam Woo BBQ** is a storefront in Chinatown Plaza (yes, Vegas has a Chinatown, virtually all in one strip mall), serving amazing BBQ and noodle dishes into the wee hours. Adventuresome eaters can sample unshelled fried salt- and chili-crusted prawns or a hot pot of intenstines, turnips, and pig's blood. Downtown, the 1960s vintage **Huntridge Drugstore Restaurant Tavern** could be where the Beav and his family ate Chinese, with classic chow mein and chop suey on the menu—chef/owner Bill Fong actually hails from China. **Empress Court** at Caesars may look futuristic, with star-spangled ceilings, rough stone floors, heavy metal curtains, and green-lit fiberglass columns (gotta fit into Caesars' ancient Rome look somehow), but the food is classic authentic Cantonese and Szechuan cooking: cashew chicken, prime sirloin with onions and green peppers, abalone with sea cucumber. At the Rio, **Fortune's** looks like it cost a fortune, with walnut wainscoting, serene murals, and more than $100,000 worth of Chinese porcelain and other artifacts. The food is just as artful: beef tenderloin with asparagus in black pepper sauce, shrimp in silky mayonnaise with honey walnuts and sesame seeds, and healthful "nouvelle" Chinese items such as egg-white fried rice. Hong Kong hotshot Kevin Wu celebrates China's regional cooking at the Chinese antique–studded **Royal Star**. Revelations include abalone with yellow morels and "six-hour" spare ribs braised with Northern Chinese seasonings and brown rock sugar. A separate kitchen turns out wondrous dim sum lunch—dumplings, buns, and cakes served tableside in traditional carts. In the bizarre, ugly strip mall Commercial Center, **Lotus of Siam** stars the cooking of Saipin Chutima from northern Thailand. Fresh, classic Thai seasonings—lemongrass, galingale, Kaffir lime leaves, Thai basil—awaken the palate in *nua dad deaw* (spicy beef jerky) and *nam kow tod* (minced sour sausage). Raw shrimp marinated in astounding hot fish sauce lingers in the memory like a first kiss. The big hotels have numerous tasteful Japanese restaurants to accommodate the Asian gambler clientele, but **Mizuno's** at the Tropicana is a standout: antique shoji screens and temple bells, a glass "stream" lit with twinkling lights, cut-glass dividers etched with irises and cherry blossoms, and chefs slicing and dicing with ginzu knives at marble teppanyaki grill tables. Near the Strip, **Hamada of Japan** goes touristy with stone temples, fans, kimono-clad staff, even an antique suit of samurai armor, and the teppan room does the usual ginzu tricks with meats and veggies. Still, real Japanese folks come here for the sushi: marvelous eel and toro (fatty tuna), not to mention the fried clam Vegas Roll. Just stay clear of karaoke nights.

**Fishing around...** **The Tillerman** is the old-fashioned "serious" seafood spot, and the seafood (usually at least 10 fresh specials daily) is truly special: planked salmon, sautéed scallops, Dungeness crab cakes, shrimp in garlic cream, Alaskan king crab legs—nothing fancy, but invariably perfectly cooked. At the spare but striking **Emeril's New Orleans Fish House**, the fish is so fresh it glistens on the plate; Lagasse uses his star power to fly in just-caught Okeechobee frogs' legs, Alabama free-range chicken, and Lake Superior pike. Look for Louisianan and Portuguese influences on the menu: Creole salmon with wild mushrooms and andouille sausage étouffée; roasted lobster stuffed with "Reverend Al's" oyster dressing with fried spinach leaves, lobster butter sauce, and tasso hollandaise. A la carte entrees at Bellagio's sleek **Aqua** include *ahi* tuna tartare in sesame oil infused with Scotch bonnet peppers, porcini-crusted wild turbot, and Maine lobster pot pie. Upscale **McCormick and Schmick's** serves 32 fresh fish selections, changed twice daily (for lunch and dinner), geographically pinpointed (as in chunky Oregon Dungeness crab cakes with red pepper aioli, Idaho rainbow trout stuffed with bay shrimp and spinach risotto, wonton-crusted Florida red snapper with black bean asparagus sauce). You can never go wrong with the chowders, steamers, and calamari. At the Venetian, **Pinot Brasserie** serves the freshest, most succulent shellfish anywhere; waiters shuck shells at the oyster bar in rubber boots just as they would in Montparnasse. In Desert Passage, **Josef's Brasserie** is another pearl, shelling out remarkable oysters, clams, and mussels (ah, that marinière), with seafood airlifted daily from both coasts. At **Elements/Tremezzo**, while the meat dishes are exemplary (steak tartare, wood-grilled filet mignon), the marine offerings excel, from caviar to clams to crab cakes. Musts include the lobster martini with crispy artichoke and chive dressing, peppered *ahi* in red wine sauce, and any sushi. Delicate seafood at **Lutèce** is counterpointed with fresh crunchy produce in refined sauces, such as applewood-smoked codfish on arugula salad with white truffle oil, or lobster medallions with port wine and roasted grapes. Lobster is king at the Strip's handsome-but-uppity **Rosewood Grille,** which needs three huge tanks to house its leviathan crustaceans, many weighing in at over 10 pounds. At **Francesco's**, the seafood really shines: *strozzapreti* with crab, shrimp, and zucchini in a light saffron sauce or prosciutto-wrapped scallops over seafood couscous in mint oil and a balsamic reduction. In addition to the inspired sushi and sashimi, the Hard Rock's **Nobu** offers simple cooked seafood that is saturated with flavor, such as miso-inflected cod and creamy, spicy cracked crab. The Mirage's **Kokomo's** has an exotic lagoon setting; no, they don't haul fish out of the faux grotto, but the seafood is fresh and consistently fine. Try the delectable coconut shrimp with sweet Maui onion and jalapeño chutney or delicate escolar with truffles and pasta. Off the Strip, **La Barca Seafood Restaurant** offers scintillating Mexican seafood, including fish tacos, a 45-ounce shrimp cocktail, *escabeche,* and a chopped clam tostada that will have you dreaming of mermaids.

**Prime beef...** Vegas may have more great steak houses than even Kansas City. **The Steak House** at Circus Circus remains the ringmaster of meateries. It's classic men's-club territory, with oil portraits, parquet floors, tapestries, gas lamps, and stuffed peacocks and deer mounted on the walls. Peek in the glass-enclosed dry-aging room, where slabs hang like abstract sculpture. Steaks are cooked over an open-hearth mesquite charcoal broiler, imparting a slight smokiness. Don't overlook the very good Caesar salad, excellent black bean soup, and marvelous oysters. Arnie Morton, founder of the Chicago Morton's, is paid tribute to at **A.J.'s** at the Hard Rock, owned by Arnie's son Peter Morton; the ineffable retro masculine look matches the macho cuts of beef that often surpass those at the Vegas branch of Morton's. **Bally's Steakhouse** seems straight out of a Polo Ralph Lauren ad: green-and-white-striped fabrics, mahogany wainscoting, enormous banquettes, carved wood railings, and fox hunt prints. It's pricey, but you can't beef about the incomparable dry-aged cuts. Bellagio's **Prime** may look like a classic steak house, but when chef Jean-Georges Vongerichten adds his Alsatian roots and Asian influences, you get items like short ribs with horseradish spaetzle or five-pepper New York steak with two-celery purée and chickpea fries. At the Venetian's restrained **Delmonico Steakhouse**, antique tables occupy a stark white glass-enclosed room with barrel-vaulted ceilings and chocolate-brown banquettes, but there's nothing monkish about the richly flavored meats. Wet-aged for two weeks then dry-aged for two more, they're served dripping with herb butter. Cajun twists include smoked shrimp cakes with Creole meunière sauce and grilled vegetable relish, and andouille sausage potato hash. At **Charlie Palmer's Steakhouse**, meat-lovers are bullish on the dry-aged Black Angus or pepper-seared hangar steaks, served with such scrumptious sides as porcini ragout or double-baked potato with truffle cream. In the great French bistro tradition, **Mon Ami Gabi** offers several variations of steak frites (try the Roquefort) and a peerless hangar steak in Bordelaise sauce with an ineffable peppery kick. **Josef's Brasserie**'s charcuterie table tempts with an array of luscious sausages, smoked meats, and cheeses; the seared foie gras paired with pears simply melts in the mouth. At **Samba Brazilian Steakhouse,** skewered rotisserie meats are roasted over coals at the open kitchen, then carved table-side with machete-like knives. Downtown's **Pullman Grille** has a classy antique Victorian look, but the tender mesquite-grilled steaks, marvelous prime rib, and classic steak au poivre in creamy bourbon sauce are far less expensive than at Strip counterparts. Ride on out to the Boulder Highway for **Billy Bob's Steakhouse**'s huge "cowboy" and "cowgirl" cuts that taste straight from someone's ranch, in peppercorn, Béarnaise, and honey Dijon sauces. The BBQ is damn fine, too; to be really macho, order Rocky Mountain oysters (bull's testicles), which are crunchy, greasy, and luscious. **The Range** at Harrah's offers some nice variations on standard steak house fare, such as filet mignon in gorgonzola onion croustade; for starters, try the creamy Five Onion soup served in a huge hollowed-out onion, and don't miss the Cabernet-sautéed mushrooms. **The Palm** (Forum Shops at Caesars) retains the caricatures of local celebs and politicos on the walls but has lost the sawdust-strewn tile floors and curmudgeonly waiters of its New York progenitor. The humongous steaks and lobsters are as delectable—and pricey. **Smith & Wollensky** has replicated the Manhattan original's green-and-white building, right down to the polished wood floors and crisp white napery. Alongside the steak "classics" (T-bone, porterhouse, filet, New York sirloin) you'll find roasted pork shank with jalapeño applesauce, jumbo crab cakes, and 24-ounce Cajun ribeye. And then there's **Lawry's The Prime Rib**: The L.A. original served only prime rib, considered by many the best anywhere. What should you order at this off-Strip offshoot? Prime rib, prime rib, and prime rib, with creamed spinach.

**Theme dining: the A list...** You enter Luxor's **Isis** along a colonnade of caryatids and through glass doors embossed in gold with the "Wings of Isis." It's Tut's tomb reconceived as a '70s bachelor pad, with stars sewn into the fabric ceiling, cheetah-skin chairs, pyramid paintings, metal cobras, pharaoh-motif plates, and three Ramses statues standing sentry. With its beheaded Lenin statue outside (complete with bronze pigeon droppings), Mandalay Bay's **Red Square** is a bizarre mix of Tsarist (red velour curtains and banquettes, fringe lamps) and populist (sickles, murals of proletariat rallies) decor. The Texas-sized **Star Canyon** at the Venetian is hotter than habañeros, thanks to festive ambience and innovative culinary accents like jalapeño-polenta croutons. The decor is a riot of copper and leather accents, earth-packed ceilings, rawhide chairs, steer's horns, barbed wire, and wood planks branded with the names of Texas cities. Naturally, country-and-western music hoots and hollers. Main Street Station's **Pullman Grille** is a treasure trove of Victoriana; intricately carved entrance doors designed by Stanford White, an ornately carved oak fireplace from Scotland's Prestwick Castle, a 19th-century mahogany-and-etched-glass bar, and the "Louisa Alcott" Pullman parlor car, transformed into a cozy cognac-and-cigar bar where Hollywood types (Jim Belushi, Chuck Norris) often gravitate.

**Theme dining: the B list...** You enter the MGM Grand's **Rainforest Café** underneath a huge aquarium, passing animatronic elephants, leopards, gorillas, and giant pythons hiding behind faux palms, cascading waterfalls, and mock rocks covered with fake flowers. The only living creatures are the fish and a few listless parrots (and the relentlessly perky waiters—or are they robots?). Dishes have cutesy names like Jamaica, Me Crazy (grilled pork chops with jerk seasoning and apple chutney) and The Wallaby's Wok (linguine wok-tossed with organic sun-dried tomatoes, toasted pine nuts, and fresh basil). **Billy Bob's Steakhouse** is a Western fetishist's dream: saddles, lariats, yokes, whips, spurs, ten-gallon hats, steer horns, elk racks, antler-and-wagon-wheel chandeliers from beamed ceilings, rock and log walls. The live guitarist has the Willie Nelson thing down pat. Excalibur's prime-rib joint **Sir Galahad** features suits of armor, royal portraits, coats-of-arms, cast-iron chandeliers and sconces, Tudor-style wood-and-stucco walls, and the usual medieval accoutrements. **Circus Circus Buffet** brings the big top look upscale, with abstract paintings of saltimbanques and harlequins, still lifes in Fauvist hues, and black and white torchères, but for a sheer riot of circus decor, **Osteria del Circo** wins hands down. It's Barnum-&-Bailey-as-brothel; bright reds and yellows, with multi-hued fabric "tubes," peering chimps, clowns, and dragons adorning the ceiling, and equally loud uniforms. Luxor's **Pharaoh's Pheast** duplicates an archeological dig with wood braces supporting the ceiling, papyrus, pottery shards, hieroglyphs, sarcophagi poking up through the floor, faux-sandstone walls, and servers in khaki dig duds. The centerpiece of Paris's **Le Village Buffet** is a charming country *maison* whose picture windows display to-die-for desserts. Dine "outside" in the courtyard with stone arches and gas lamps or in a quaint cottage filled with lace curtains, copper pots, and painted French country tiles. **Raffles Café** sports a colonial-tropical look, with an exotic color scheme (peacock blue, sage, mango, plum), Indonesian pottery, elaborately carved teak chests, a mosaic fountain, and folding shutters opening onto the patio.

**For Gen-XYZ...** **Mr. Lucky's** confers instant hipster status the minute you walk in—and you can walk in anytime, 24/7. Artfully weathered furnishings and upscale comfort food give it just the right casual buzz. The decor, wait staff, and clientele are equally sleek and lacquered at **P. F. Chang's China Bistro**. The service, unfortunately, is slacker-than-thou. With its artful Mediterranean-inspired food, **Olive's** is a "name" restaurant (Todd English) at casual prices. The look is playful, with yellow-and-white-striped columns, mosaic floors, and hand-painted ceramic walls swirled with childlike designs. The noisy patio is primo at lunch (cheaper selections). A hotshot booze-and-schmooze scene ignites the glacial **Red Square** vodka bar (it's one long sheet of ice). The 170-plus vodkas range from Russian sharpshooters like Red Army to familiar top-shelf brands (Belvedere, Peconica, Ketel One). The functional stainless steel unisex bathroom plastered with posters exhorts you to "join the party"—very comradely, *da*? Its M-Bay neighbor **China Grill** features a garden of "bathroom huts," small unisex single-seat bathrooms with translucent doors, large mirrors, and TVs. Wednesdays 10pm to 5am, the Dragon nightclub fills its circular black granite floor with trust-fund pretties in clingy couture gyrating to hip-hop, house, and acid jazz. The cigar-friendly bar at **McCormick & Schmick's** offers plentiful microbrews and single malts; Young Turks stream in for delicious $1.95 happy hour appetizers (shrimp bruschetta, spicy potato tacos). The sensational food at the Hard Rock's **Pink Taco** is almost incidental to the tequila bar (over 60 varieties) crammed with twentysomething singles proudly and loudly losing their inhibitions. Tri-level **Tsunami**'s pan-Asian fare, designer sakes, pulsating sound system, and black-and-blood-red decor give it a futuristic opium den allure. High-tech murals shift constantly: A panel seems one solid color, but ascend a few steps and suddenly pagodas, cherry blossoms, and calligraphy materialize, then dissolve into a fleeting, haunting geisha. That's *before* downing a killer infusion. **Olio** offers a groovy scene with playful decor, gorgeous hostesses, awesome antipasto bar, and tiny dance floor vibrating late to the DJ's R&B/jungle mix. Add a private screening room with remote-control gadgetry (try to score invites to "Soprano Sundays" and "West Wing Wednesdays"). And how cool is the gelato bar, where PYTs in mini-skirts and silver platform boots scoop 21 flavors (try the green-apple tiramisù) from holes in a chrome-plated wall?

**Voulez-vous manger avec moi?...** Downtown, the long-established **André's** is a charmingly cluttered cottage without a trace of Gallic hauteur. Stay away from the fusion experiments and stick with brasserie fare—duck breast confit with dried-cherry balsamic sauce, and foie gras terrine with Sauternes aspic and black-pepper brioche. Just off the Strip, **Pamplemousse** defines rustic French bistro, from the complimentary basket of crudités, olives, and hard-boiled eggs to the escargots in Burgundy sauce, roast duck, rack of lamb, and a marvelous "hobo" steak encased in salt. Tuxedoed waiters recite the convoluted menu, testing both their memory and their occasionally mangled French. **Josef's Brasserie** has the French bistro look down pat: murals of French village scenes, iron-and-glass chandeliers, corrugated ceilings, and large antique gilt mirrors. The kitchen expertly executes standards like mussels meunière, salade Niçoise, and bracingly garlicky escargots. Soups (roasted red pepper puréed with sweet potatoes and butter) and salads (haricots verts, beets, and olives in truffle and walnut oil) are *magnifique*. **Pinot Brasserie** also fits the part: gilt-trimmed ceilings, brass and copper accents, burgundy leather banquettes, walnut walls, and imported French architectural artifacts. Lunches are unbelievable bargains: grilled ribeye in foie gras red wine sauce, tender steamers in garlic wine butter sauce with frites. Lobster bisque perked with armagnac and crème fraîche is voluptuous as a courtesan. **Mon Ami Gabi**, a branch of Gabriel Sotelino's hot Chicago property, gets the Gallic classics right, from coq au vin to coquilles Saint-Jacques. You could easily feast on the superlative salads (baby mesclun with watercress coulis and citrus vinaigrette) and appetizers (baked brie, escargots drowning in basil and garlic), but the hangar steak and steak frites are near-definitive.

**Highfalutin' French...** Calling Bellagio's **Le Cirque** a French restaurant oversimplifies things. Chef Marc Poidevin extracts the purest flavors and intensifies them through canny pairings—filet mignon topped with foie gras and brilliantly undercut by tart shallot marmalade; roasted duck with honey-spice glaze and figs; or my favorite, a classic *cuisine paysanne blanquette de lapin* (rabbit in white-wine cream sauce). A five-course degustation features seasonal specialties. **Eiffel Tower** daringly juxtaposes flavors, textures, even colors. Witness flaky Arctic char with chunky flageolets and zucchini topped with potato and basil crisps (the latter an almost phosphorescent green). The porcini flan is the gustatory equivalent of a silk peignoir.

**South of the border...** The colorful, family-run **Lindo Michoacan** admirably avoids gringo-izing its food. Chicken mole is dark and bittersweet, and real Mexican dishes such as beef tongue, tacos, goat stewed in beer, *carnitas* (succulent slow-braised pork), and steak cooked in Coca Cola (*si*, it's a popular Michoacan method) grace the menu. Unlike many greasy taquerias, **Viva Mercado** stresses healthful cooking: No animal fats are used, and there are several vegetarian specialties. Dino-sized burritos and create-your-own chimichangas are joined on the menu by lobster and fish tacos. Try the intriguing Mex-Ital Marisco Vallarta (orange roughy, shrimp, and scallops swimming in coconut tomato sauce with capers and olives). Off the Strip, the weekends-only **La Barca** is like entering a fiesta, with a great mariachi band, splashy murals of Mexican history and folklore, and remarkable Mexican seafood. A relic from the 1950s, **El Sombrero** is an unprepossessing Downtown dump, with a couple of serapes and sombreros sufficing for decor. But the clientele is a vibrant mix of yuppies and ethnic laborers, all rocking to the tremendous jukebox of Latin American songs. Dirt-cheap enchiladas, tamales, tacos, and flautas are served in asbestos-proof *colorado* (red) and *verde* (green) chilis. At the Mirage's **Samba Brazilian Steakhouse,** try duck tamales and coconut prawns; the *caipirinhas* (sugar-cane liquor and limes) deliver a knockout punch. **Pink Taco's** Tacho Kneeland earned his chops with the Too Hot Tamales, Mary Sue Milliken and Susan Feiniger (and often surpasses their Border Café in Mandalay Bay). He reinvents tacos and quesadillas (his sand dab tacos and pink salsa is marvelous), but also turns out properly spicy *achiote*-rubbed chicken and chicken-and-cheese enchiladas in tomatillo sauce.

**Southwest sizzle...** Stephan and Alena Pyles' **Star Canyon** sizzles at the Venetian, with all the items that practically created new Texas cuisine: tamale tart with creamy garlic flan, molasses-grilled quail with arugula, poached pear, and Cambozola cheese, and such delicate dishes as halibut in a fennel-orange sauce. With its pumpkin-colored walls adorned with photos of New Mexican staples like chilis and etched art-glass and copper panels, the MGM Grand's **Coyote Café and Grill** has a festive yet elegant Southwestern feel, right down to the waiters' bolo ties and chili-patterned plates. Try the chipotle-marinated shrimp on blinis with avocado relish or the portobello tamales paired with sun-dried tomato corn salsa and portobello cream sauce. The cafe features an authentic exhibition *cazuela* (casserole oven) and *comal* (grill) under a ceramic hood, not to mention more than 60 tequilas by the glass. **Garduno's Cantina** serves nasty margaritas and dumps classic green chili sauce from New Mexico recipes over the tacos and enchiladas, but the seafood-stuffed jalapeños, *posole* (hominy), and *carne adovada* are superb. The tableside guacamole preparation is quite a show. **Born in the USA...Commander's Palace** weaves together Creole, Cajun, and Southern elements (though the sass has been softened). Start with definitive turtle soup au sherry or shrimp remoulade; other faves include veal chop Tchoupitoulas (topped with goat cheese in a brandied wild mushroom demi-glacé) or pan-roasted Gulf oysters with a confit of artichokes and double cream sauce bread crumbs. Don't miss the signature side, Creole smashed new potatoes with andouille sausage. **Rosemary's** lures locals and muckety-mucks (the Clintons, Liz Taylor) alike to Summerlin. Begin with a fabulous seasonal soup (perhaps truffle potato or sweet corn with melted chive butter), move on to an appetizer like prosciutto-wrapped figs with goat cheese, arugula, herb pesto, and a balsamic vinegar extraction—but the must-have is Hugo's Texas barbecued shrimp with Maytag blue-cheese slaw. The flourless chocolate cake is molten sin. Spago and Chinois expats—ebullient hostess Laurie Kendrick, brother Wes Kendrick, and husband Stan Carroll—serve seasonal haute all-American comfort food at **Wild Sage**. Come here for fresh-baked breads, sensational daily soup specials (duck and heirloom bean, potato and Swiss leek, saffron spring corn), and "Puck-ishly" extravagant entrees like sautéed monkfish with saffron rice pilaf and roasted-pepper coulis, or signature crab cakes with field greens and smoked tomato salsa. Even TV dinner staples like chicken potpie, macaroni and cheese, and killer meatloaf with mashed potatoes and onion gravy are hits here. At **Nob Hill**,

**DINING | THE LOWDOWN**

Aqua's Michael Mina pays homage to San Francisco in an airy, Zen-like space in muted beige and cream hues. Mina worked with San Francisco chefs to re-create their signature dishes, as well as his own take on the likes of cioppino, crab louie, and lobster potpie. A 100-square-foot bread oven offers a selection of just-baked sourdough or foccacia. Despite the Marxist-chic decor, **Red Square**'s menu is U.S.A. all the way: fried Bell & Evans chicken with buttermilk mash and red beans; steak tartare; crab cakes with basil mustard mayonnaise; and veal and shiitake meatloaf. **House of Blues'** roadhouse food is soul-satisfying, too—besides gumbo and grits, you'll find Memphis-style ribs with Jack Daniels sauce, cedarplank salmon with watercress-jicama salad, and Voodoo Shrimp served with rosemary cornbread. The Oxo in **Oxo/Spiedini** specializes in juicy mesquite-scented meats and such nouvelle American dishes as crab cake with remoulade sauce, blackened scallops with sweet pearl onion coulis, herb-rubbed chicken breast with mango and corn relish, and a smashing sea bass in pineapple soy ginger marinade with wasabi mashed potatoes.

**Arabian nights and Turkish delights...** The MGM Grand's **Neyla** mates Turkish, Egyptian, and Lebanese cuisine with broader Mediterranean influences—witness the duck breast lacquered with tamarind and jasmine topped with macadamia nuts, or the dry-aged strip steak smothered in seven spices and stuffed with feta cheese. You can easily make a meal of the traditional meze, tapas-style portions of stuffed grape leaves, kebabs, merguez sausage, falafel, spinach pie, etc. Near UNLV, **Mediterranean Café & Market** serves excellent homemade hummus, particularly fine grilled kebabs, thick Turkish coffee, and to-die-for baklava cheesecake. Ignore the misguided decor—weird murals (cavorting Greeks and animals), plastic vines on the ceiling, and marbleized tables. The UNLV crowds love when the vivacious owner makes like Zorba the Greek.

# The Index

| | |
|---|---|
| $$$$ | over $50 |
| $$$ | $35–$50 |
| $$ | $15–$35 |
| $ | under $15 |

Price categories reflect the cost of a three-course meal, not including drinks, taxes, and tip.

**A.J.'s.** A swaggering retro steak house.... *Tel 702/693-5000. Hard Rock, 4455 Paradise Rd. Reservations required. $$$*
**(see p. 62)**

**André's French Restaurant.** The perfect French bistro: country antiques, excellent food and wine, no attitude.... *Tel 702/385-5016. 401 S. 6th St. D not accepted. Jacket, reservations required. Closed Sun. $$$–$$$$*
**(see pp. 62, 74, 83)**

**Aqua.** Buzzing crowd enjoying sensational seafood.... *Tel 702/ 693-8199. Bellagio, 3600 Las Vegas Blvd. S. DC not accepted. Reservations required. $$$$*
**(see pp. 60, 71, 74, 77)**

**Aureole.** Charlie Palmer's superb regional American cuisine.... *Tel 702/632-7401. Mandalay Bay, 3950 Las Vegas Blvd. S. Reservations required. $$$$* **(see pp. 61, 63, 73)**

**Bally's Steakhouse.** Dark, smoky, clubby steakhouse.... *Tel 702/739-4111. Bally's, 3645 Las Vegas Blvd. S. Jacket required; reservation required for brunch. Closed Tue, Wed. $$$$* **(see pp. 67, 78)**

**Bellagio Buffet.** Gussied up like an outdoor marketplace, serving everything from calamari ceviche to crème brûlée.... *Tel 702/693-7223. Bellagio, 3600 Las Vegas Blvd. S. DC not accepted. $–$$* **(see pp. 65, 67)**

**Big Kitchen Buffet.** Lavish, classy buffet.... *Tel 702/739-4111. Bally's, 3645 Las Vegas Blvd. S. $* **(see p. 66)**

**Billy Bob's Steakhouse.** Big local hangout with a yippie-ai-oh-kai-ay feel.... *Tel 702/454-8031. Sam's Town, 5111 Boulder Hwy. $$$* **(see pp. 79, 81)**

**Bootlegger Ristorante.** A local-favorite Italian.... *Tel 702/736-4939. 5025 S. Eastern Ave. Lunch served Tue–Fri. Closed Mon. $$* **(see pp. 65, 70)**

**Burgundy Room.** Old-fashioned gourmet dining at throwback prices.... *Tel 702/477-3000. Lady Luck, 206 N. 3rd St. Closed Tue, Wed. Reservations required. $$$* **(see pp. 62, 65)**

**Café Lago.** Stylish 24/7 marine-themed eatery.... *Tel 702/731-7731. Caesars Palace, 3570 Las Vegas Blvd. S. Lunch served. No reservations. $–$$$* **(see pp. 63, 66, 68)**

**Carnival World Buffet.** Colorful surroundings, long lines, and fresh savory food from around the globe.... *Tel 702/247-7923. The Rio, 3700 W. Flamingo Rd. $*
**(see p. 65)**

**Celebrity Deli.** Reasonably priced New York-style delicatessen.... *Tel 702/733-7827. 4055 S. Maryland Pkwy. Lunch served. No dinner Sun. $–$$* **(see p. 69)**

**Charlie Palmer's Steakhouse.** Romantic yet masculine surroundings, primo prime beef.... *Tel 702/632-5120. Four Seasons, 3960 Las Vegas Blvd. S. Reservations required. D, DC not accepted. $$$$* **(see pp. 73, 79)**

**China Grill.** The best of the Orient filtered through a high-tech capitalist haze.... *Tel 702/632-7404. Mandalay Bay, 3950 Las Vegas Blvd. S. Reservations required. $$$ (cafe $$)*
**(see pp. 74, 82)**

**Chinois Las Vegas.** Wolfgang Puck's take on Chinese cuisine.... *Tel 702/737-9700. Forum Shops at Caesars, 3500 Las Vegas Blvd. S. Reservations required. Lunch served. $$–$$$$* **(see pp. 72, 75)**

**Circus Circus Buffet.** Jammed and fun as a school cafeteria—

with food barely a cut above.... *Tel 702/734-0410. Circus Circus, 2880 Las Vegas Blvd. S. $*     **(see pp. 66, 81)**

**Commander's Palace.** From the N'Awlins classic.... *Tel 702/892-8272. Desert Passage, 3663 Las Vegas Blvd. S. Lunch served. $$$–$$$$*     **(see pp. 64, 67, 73, 85)**

**Coyote Café and Grill Room.** Santa Fe import, a standard-bearer for nouvelle Southwestern.... *Tel 702/891-7349. MGM Grand, 3799 Las Vegas Blvd. S. Café open for lunch. Reservations required for Grill Room (not accepted for Café). $$$ (Café $$)*     **(see pp. 61, 85)**

**Delmonico Steakhouse.** Emeril Lagasse's top steak house.... *Tel 702/414-3737. The Venetian, 3355 Las Vegas Blvd. S. Jacket, reservations required. $$$$*     **(see pp. 59, 79)**

**Eiffel Tower.** Great views, pleasant music, and superb French classics.... *Tel 702/948-6957 or 702/946-7000. Paris, 3655 Las Vegas Blvd. S. Reservations required. $$$$*
**(see pp. 59, 71, 73, 83)**

**808.** Innovative Eurasian fare, postmodern Zen setting.... *Tel 702/731-7731. Caesars Palace, 3570 Las Vegas Blvd. S. Reservations required. Closed Tue–Wed. $$$–$$$$*
**(see pp. 60, 72, 75)**

**El Sombrero.** The oldest Mexican in the city.... *Tel 702/382-9234. 807 S. Main St. Lunch served. D, DC not accepted. $*     **(see pp. 68, 84)**

**Elements/Tremezzo.** Italian and steak-and-seafood siblings.... *Tel 702/785-9003. Aladdin, 3667 Las Vegas Blvd. S. Reservations required. $$$–$$$$*     **(see pp. 70, 77)**

**Emeril's New Orleans Fish House.** Superb seafood, but the place can get frenzied.... *Tel 702/891-7374. MGM Grand, 3799 Las Vegas Blvd. S. Reservations required. $$$–$$$$*
**(see pp. 60, 77)**

**Empress Court.** Hong Kong chefs and black-tie/china/crystal service.... *Tel 702/731-7731. Caesars Palace, 3570 Las Vegas Blvd. S. Reservations required. $$–$$$*
**(see pp. 71, 76)**

**Ferraro's.** Old-fashioned Italian classic.... *Tel 702/364-5300. 5900 W. Flamingo Rd. Lunch Mon–Fri. DC not accepted.* $$–$$$ **(see pp. 65, 71)**

**Festival Buffet.** Around the world for 900 cents.... *Tel 702/ 631-7000. The Fiesta, 2400 N. Rancho Dr.* $ **(see p. 66)**

**Fortune's.** Exquisite Chinese food.... *Tel 702/247-7923. Rio, 3700 W. Flamingo Rd. Reservations required. Closed Sun–Mon.* $$–$$$ **(see p. 76)**

**Francesco's.** A serene spot for delightful Italian food.... *Tel 702/894-7111. Treasure Island, 3300 Las Vegas Blvd. S. Reservations required.* $$$ **(see pp. 69, 78)**

**Garden Court Buffet.** Especially good Asian and Polynesian specialties.... *Tel 702/387-1896. Main Street Station, 200 N. Main St.* $ **(see p. 66)**

**Garduno's Cantina.** Feisty crowd and feistier margaritas.... *Tel 702/631-7000. The Fiesta, 2400 N. Rancho Dr., N. Las Vegas.* $ **(see pp. 67, 85)**

**Golden Nugget Buffet.** An ornate room that really doubles as a gourmet restaurant.... *Tel 702/385-7111. Golden Nugget, 129 E. Fremont St.* $ **(see pp. 66, 67)**

**Hamada of Japan.** Reliable sushi and teppan grill.... *Tel 702/733-3005. 598 E. Flamingo Rd.* $$ **(see p. 77)**

**House of Blues.** Un-hokey decor and fine Southern fare.... *Tel 702/632-7600. Mandalay Bay, 3950 Las Vegas Blvd. S. Lunch served.* $–$$ **(see pp. 67, 72, 86)**

**Hugo's Cellar.** Courtly relic for martinis and stolid Continental food.... *Tel 702/385-4011. Four Queens, 202 Fremont St.* $$$ **(see pp. 62, 71)**

**Huntridge Drugstore Restaurant/Tavern.** A drugstore counter, classic dive.... *Tel 702/384-3737. 1116-1122 E. Charleston Blvd. No credit cards. Lunch served.* $ **(see pp. 65, 68, 76)**

**Isis.** Egyptian theme, sultry ambience.... *Tel 702/262-4773.*

Luxor, 3900 Las Vegas Blvd. S. Jacket, reservations required. Closed Wed. $$$–$$$$ **(see p. 80)**

**Jazzed Café and Vinoteca.** Hepcat hangout with yummy Italian food.... Tel 702/798-5995, 2055 E. Tropicana Ave.; tel 702/233-2859, 8615 W. Sahara Ave. Tropicana branch closed Mon. D, DC not accepted. $$
**(see pp. 59, 69, 73)**

**Josef's Brasserie.** Like you're dining on the Boul-Mich.... Tel 702/732-3000. Desert Passage, 3667 Las Vegas Blvd. S. Serves lunch. DC not accepted. $$$ **(see pp. 77, 79, 83)**

**Kokomo's.** Lagoon-ish setting for steak and seafood.... Tel 702/791-7223. The Mirage, 3400 Las Vegas Blvd. S. DC not accepted. Lunch served. $$$ **(see pp. 72, 78)**

**La Barca Seafood Restaurant.** Hole-in-the-wall with great Mexican seafood.... Tel 702/657-9700. 953 E. Sahara Ave. Lunch served. Closed Mon–Thur. AE not accepted. $–$$
**(see pp. 78, 84)**

**Lawry's The Prime Rib.** Primo prime rib for meat connoisseurs.... Tel 702/893-2223. 4043 E. Howard Hughes Pkwy. Reservations required. $$$ **(see pp. 65, 80)**

**Le Cirque.** Soothing and sumptuous.... Tel 702/693-7223. Bellagio, 3600 Las Vegas Blvd. S. Jacket and tie, reservations required. DC not accepted. $$$$
**(see pp. 58, 71, 72, 74, 83)**

**Le Village Buffet.** Specialties from various regions of France.... Tel 702/946-7000. Paris, 3655 Las Vegas Blvd. S. $
**(see pp. 66, 81)**

**Lindo Michoacan.** Bona fide Mexican food.... Tel 702/735-6828. 2655 E. Desert Inn Rd. $$ **(see p. 84)**

**Lotus of Siam.** Authentic northern Thai cuisine.... Tel 702/735-3033. 953 E. Sahara Ave., #A-5. Lunch Mon–Fri. DC not accepted. $–$$ **(see p. 76)**

**Lutèce.** Top-drawer gourmet fare.... Tel 702/414-2220. The Venetian, 3355 Las Vegas Blvd. S. Reservations required. $$$$ **(see pp. 59, 78)**

**Manhattan of Las Vegas.** Swellegant Italian Rat Pack wannabe.... *Tel 702/737-5000. 2600 E. Flamingo Rd. Reservations required. $$$* **(see pp. 62, 70)**

**Mayflower Cuisinier.** Fine Asian-fusion dining.... *Tel 702/870-8432. 4750 W. Sahara Ave. Reservations required. Closed Sun. No lunch Sat. DC not accepted. $$$* **(see p. 75)**

**McCormick and Schmick's.** Mellow power-and-singles scene serving fresh seafood.... *Tel 702/836-9000. 335 Hughes Center Dr. Lunch Mon–Fri. $$$* **(see pp. 64, 77, 82)**

**Mediterranean Café and Market.** Casual spot for fine home-made Middle Eastern cuisine.... *Tel 702/731-6030. 4147 S. Maryland Pkwy. Lunch served. $–$$* **(see pp. 68, 86)**

**Michael's.** High-end but marvelous Continental.... *Tel 702/737-7111. Barbary Coast, 3595 Las Vegas Blvd. S. Reservations required. $$$$* **(see pp. 59, 65)**

**Mr. Lucky's.** Hippest 24-hour joint in town.... *Tel 702/693-5000. Hard Rock, 4455 Paradise Rd. $*
**(see pp. 59, 68, 81)**

**Mizuno's.** Zen ambience and superior teppan cooking.... *Tel 702/739-2713. Tropicana, 3801 Las Vegas Blvd. S. Reservations required. $$–$$$* **(see p. 77)**

**Mon Ami Gabi.** Simple, worthy bistro fare.... *Tel 702/946-7000. Paris, 3655 Las Vegas Blvd. S. Lunch served. No reservations for front room and patio. $$–$$$*
**(see pp. 63, 79, 83)**

**Napa.** A sublime dining experience.... *Tel 702/247-7923. The Rio, 3700 W. Flamingo Rd. Closed Sun, Mon. Reservations required. $$$$* **(see pp. 58, 60, 73)**

**Neyla.** Imaginative Near-Eastern fare.... *Tel 702/736-2100. MGM Grand, 3799 Las Vegas Blvd. S. $$$*
**(see pp. 61, 62)**

**Nob Hill.** Tribute to San Francisco.... *Tel 702/891–1111 or 702/891-7337. MGM Grand, 3799 Las Vegas Blvd. S. $$$* **(see pp. 61, 85)**

**Nobu.** Taking sushi to the next dimension.... *Tel 702/693-5090. Hard Rock, 4455 Paradise Rd. Reservations required.* $$$–$$$$ **(see pp. 75, 78)**

**Olio.** Trendoid Italian.... *Tel 702/891-7775. MGM Grand, 3799 Las Vegas Blvd. S. Lunch served.* $$–$$$$ **(see pp. 70, 72, 82)**

**Olive's.** Todd English fuses dishes from his acclaimed Olive's and Figs.... *Tel 702/693-8150. Bellagio, 3600 Las Vegas Blvd. S. Lunch served. No reservations.* $$$ **(see pp. 74, 82)**

**Osteria del Circo.** Le Cirque's younger, more festive sibling.... *Tel 702/693-8150. Bellagio, 3600 Las Vegas Blvd. S. Lunch served.* $$$ **(see pp. 69, 81)**

**Oxo/Spiedini.** Nouvelle steak house and Italian neighbor.... *Tel 702/869-8500 Spiedini, 702/869-2335 Oxo. Regent Las Vegas, 221 N. Rampart Blvd. DC not accepted. Reservations required.* $$$ **(see pp. 70, 72, 86)**

**P. F. Chang's China Bistro.** California-tinged Asian, notable more for its sexy scene than its food.... *Tel 702/792–2207. 4165 Paradise Rd.* $$ **(see pp. 59, 75, 82)**

**The Palm.** New York steak house clone.... *Tel 702/732-7256. Forum Shops at Caesars, 3500 Las Vegas Blvd. S. Lunch served. Reservations required.* $$$$ **(see pp. 64, 79)**

**Pamplemousse.** Serving French comfort food to star regulars.... *Tel 702/733-2066. 400 E. Sahara Ave. Closed Mon. Reservations required.* $$$ **(see pp. 62, 83)**

**Pharaoh's Pheast.** Acceptable food at $15 and under, amid excavations.... *Tel 702/262-4000. Luxor, 3900 Las Vegas Blvd. S.* $ **(see pp. 66, 81)**

**Picasso.** Mediterranean showcase for art and cuisine. Prix fixe tasting menus only.... *Tel 702/693-7223. Bellagio, 3600 Las Vegas Blvd. S. Closed Wed. Reservations required.* $$$$ **(see pp. 58, 60, 74)**

**Piero's.** Goodfellas-style hangout with inconsistent Italian food.... *Tel 702/369-2305. 355 Convention Center Dr.* $$$ **(see p. 70)**

**Pink Pony Café.** Kitschy but adorable.... *Tel 702/734-0410. Circus Circus, 2880 Las Vegas Blvd. S. $* **(see p. 68)**

**Pink Taco.** With-it crowd, nouvelle Mexican food.... *Tel 702/693-5000 and 702/693-5525. Hard Rock, 4455 Paradise Rd. $–$$* **(see pp. 72, 82, 84)**

**Pinot Brasserie.** Joachim Splichal's bistro cooking.... *Tel 702/414-8888. The Venetian, 3355 Las Vegas Blvd. S. Reservations required. $$$–$$$$* **(see pp. 73, 77, 83)**

**Postrio.** Another Puck import.... *Tel 702/796-1110. Venetian, 3355 Las Vegas Blvd. S. Lunch served. $$–$$$$*
**(see pp. 61, 74)**

**Prime.** Porterhouses, T-bones, and rib-eye steaks, with stylish culinary tweaks.... *Tel 702/693-7223. Bellagio, 3600 Las Vegas Blvd. S. Reservations required. $$$–$$$$*
**(see pp. 58, 63, 74, 79)**

**Pullman Grille.** Superb steaks and Victorian decor.... *Tel 702/387-1896. Main Street Station, 200 N. Main St. Reservations required. DC not accepted. Closed Mon–Wed. $$–$$$* **(see pp. 79, 80)**

**Raffles Café.** Striking round-the-clock cafe with innovative food.... *Tel 702/632-7777. Mandalay Bay, 3950 Las Vegas Blvd. S. $$* **(see pp. 68, 81)**

**Rainforest Café.** Kids love this Disney-fied ecological theme park.... *Tel 702/891-8580. MGM Grand, 3799 Las Vegas Blvd. S. Lunch served. $$* **(see pp. 74, 81)**

**The Range.** Strip views and New York strips.... *Tel 702/369-5084. Harrah's, 3475 Las Vegas Blvd. S. Reservations required. $$$* **(see pp. 62, 79)**

**Red Square.** A postmodern luxe vision of Russia.... *Tel 702/632-7407. Mandalay Bay, 3950 Las Vegas Blvd. S. Reservations required. $$$* **(see pp. 80, 82, 86)**

**Renoir.** Alex Stratta's gourmet artistry.... *Tel 702/791-7223. Mirage, 3400 Las Vegas Blvd. S. Reservations required. Closed Wed. $$$$* **(see pp. 58, 71)**

**Rosemary's.** Stylish New American.... *Tel 702/869-2251. 8125 W. Sahara Ave. No lunch Sat. Closed Sun. DC not accepted. $$–$$$* **(see pp. 61, 74, 85)**

**Rosewood Grille.** Handsomely appointed eatery.... *Tel 702/792-5965 and 702/7920-9099. 3339 Las Vegas Blvd. S. Reservations required. $$$–$$$$*
**(see pp. 60, 65, 78)**

**Royal Star.** Exquisite decor and dim sum.... *Tel 702/414-1888. Venetian, 3355 Las Vegas Blvd. S. Lunch served. DC not accepted. $$–$$$* **(see pp. 64, 76)**

**Sam Woo BBQ.** Shrine to Chinese barbecue. No English spoken.... *Tel 702/368-7628. 4125 W. Spring Mountain Rd. $–$$* **(see pp. 68, 76)**

**Samba Brazilian Steakhouse.** Sexy rodizio grill.... *Tel 702/791-7111 and 702/791-7223. The Mirage, 3400 Las Vegas Blvd. S. $$$* **(see pp. 72, 79, 84)**

**Second Street Grill.** Innovative Pacific Rim–tinged California cuisine.... *Tel 702/385-6277. Fremont, 200 E. Fremont St. Closed Tue. $$–$$$* **(see pp. 61, 75)**

**Sir Galahad.** Affordable prime rib dinner in medieval surroundings.... *Tel 702/597-7777. Excalibur, 3850 Las Vegas Blvd. S. Reservations required. $–$$* **(see pp. 74, 81)**

**Smith & Wollensky.** The Manhattan power-broker hangout's very authentic duplicate.... *Tel 702/862-4100. 3767 Las Vegas Blvd. S. $$$–$$$$* **(see pp. 74, 80)**

**Spago.** Designer pizzas by Puck.... *Tel 702/369-6300. Forum Shops at Caesars, 3500 Las Vegas Blvd. S. $$$*
**(see pp. 60, 64)**

**Stage Deli.** New York rip-off serving pastrami and pickles.... *Tel 702/893-4045. Forum Shops at Caesars, 3500 Las Vegas Blvd. S. Lunch served. $$* **(see p. 69)**

**Star Canyon.** Nouvelle Southwestern cuisine.... *Tel 702/414-3772. The Venetian, 3355 Las Vegas Blvd. S. Reservations required. DC not accepted. $$$* **(see pp. 80, 84)**

**The Steak House.** Elegant room, fabulous steaks.... *Tel 702/794-3767. Circus Circus, 2880 Las Vegas Blvd. S. Brunch Sun 9:30, 11:30, 12:30. Reservations required.* $$–$$$ **(see pp. 67, 78)**

**The Tillerman.** Serious seafood.... *Tel 702/731-4036. 2245 E. Flamingo Rd. No reservations.* $$$ **(see pp. 64, 77)**

**Trattoria del Lupo.** True Italian trattoria.... *Tel 702/632-7777 and 702/740-8522. Mandalay Bay, 3950 Las Vegas Blvd. S.* $$$ **(see pp. 64, 69)**

**Tsunami.** Futuristic Asian-styled food.... *Tel 702/414-1980. The Venetian, 3355 Las Vegas Blvd. S. Lunch served.* $$ **(see pp. 61, 75, 82)**

**Valentino.** Romantic Italian stunner.... *Tel 702/414-3000. The Venetian, 3355 Las Vegas Blvd. S. Closed lunch (PS Café open).* $$$$ **(see pp. 63, 70, 73)**

**Venetian.** Classic Italian.... *Tel 702/876-4190. 3713 W. Sahara Ave.* $$–$$$ **(see pp. 68, 71)**

**Viva Mercado.** Superior, health-conscious Mexican.... *Tel 702/435-6200. 4500 E. Sunset Rd.; tel 702/871-8826. 6182 W. Flamingo Rd. No reservations. DC not accepted.* $$ **(see p. 84)**

**Wild Sage.** Haute American food.... *Tel 702/944-7243. 600 E. Warm Springs Rd. Lunch served. DC not accepted.* $$ **(see pp. 67, 85)**

# Dining Downtown

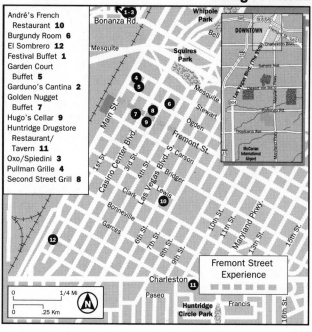

André's French
  Restaurant **10**
Burgundy Room **6**
El Sombrero **12**
Festival Buffet **1**
Garden Court
  Buffet **5**
Garduno's Cantina **2**
Golden Nugget
  Buffet **7**
Hugo's Cellar **9**
Huntridge Drugstore
  Restaurant/
  Tavern **11**
Oxo/Spiedini **3**
Pullman Grille **4**
Second Street Grill **8**

98

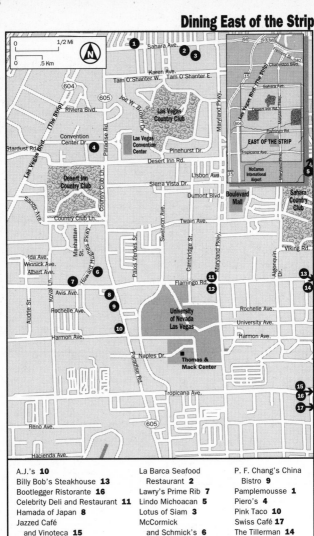

0    1/2 Mi

0    .5 Km

A.J.'s **10**
Billy Bob's Steakhouse **13**
Bootlegger Ristorante **16**
Celebrity Deli and Restaurant **11**
Hamada of Japan **8**
Jazzed Café
and Vinoteca **15**

La Barca Seafood
Restaurant **2**
Lawry's Prime Rib **7**
Lindo Michoacan **5**
Lotus of Siam **3**
McCormick
and Schmick's **6**
Mediterranean Café
and Market **12**
Mr. Lucky's **10**
Nobu **10**

P. F. Chang's China
Bistro **9**
Pamplemousse **1**
Piero's **4**
Pink Taco **10**
Swiss Café **17**
The Tillerman **14**

# Las Vegas Strip Dining

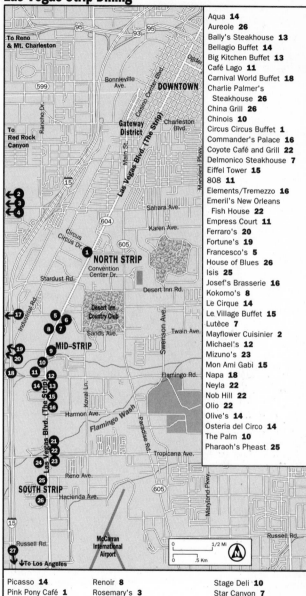

Aqua **14**
Aureole **26**
Bally's Steakhouse **13**
Bellagio Buffet **14**
Big Kitchen Buffet **13**
Café Lago **11**
Carnival World Buffet **18**
Charlie Palmer's
  Steakhouse **26**
China Grill **26**
Chinois **10**
Circus Circus Buffet **1**
Commander's Palace **16**
Coyote Café and Grill **22**
Delmonico Steakhouse **7**
Eiffel Tower **15**
808 **11**
Elements/Tremezzo **16**
Emeril's New Orleans
  Fish House **22**
Empress Court **11**
Ferraro's **20**
Fortune's **19**
Francesco's **5**
House of Blues **26**
Isis **25**
Josef's Brasserie **16**
Kokomo's **8**
Le Cirque **14**
Le Village Buffet **15**
Lutèce **7**
Mayflower Cuisinier **2**
Michael's **12**
Mizuno's **23**
Mon Ami Gabi **15**
Napa **18**
Neyla **22**
Nob Hill **22**
Olio **22**
Olive's **14**
Osteria del Circo **14**
The Palm **10**
Pharaoh's Pheast **25**

Picasso **14**
Pink Pony Café **1**
Pinot Brasserie **7**
Postrio **7**
Prime **14**
Raffles Café **26**
Rainforest Café **22**
The Range **9**
Red Square **26**

Renoir **8**
Rosemary's **3**
Rosewood Grille **6**
Royal Star **7**
Sam Woo BBQ **17**
Samba Brazilian Steakhouse **8**
Sir Galahad **24**
Smith & Wollensky **21**
Spago **10**

Stage Deli **10**
Star Canyon **7**
The Steak House **1**
Trattoria del Lupo **26**
Tsunami **7**
Valentino **7**
Venetian **4**
Viva Mercado **19**
Wild Sage **27**

# 3

# sions

Think of Vegas as the
real-life equivalent of
those virtual-
reality/IMAX/3-D
motion simulators:
nonstop, dizzying
excitement, with

sights and sounds assailing you from every angle. **The Strip** itself is one giant theme park. Hotels install attractions not only to keep guests on the property but to lure outside revenue as well; you can ride gondolas (indoors), zoom up the Eiffel Tower, or hurtle around the Statue of Liberty and Empire State Building on a roller coaster—and if that's too mundane, you can visit Atlantis and Star Trek. Everywhere you wander are serenading minstrels, tumbling acrobats, animatronic statues, resplendent fountains that kick-step like showgirls, buccaneers battling a British naval frigate, and volcanoes spewing lava dozens of feet into the air. Hotel lobbies are virtual zoos or jungles filled with exotic wildlife. Simple shops contain museums of memorabilia. Restaurants have black-clad, harnessed "angels" scaling wine towers or walls of fire encased within water. And those aren't even the official attractions. Though many Las Vegas attractions are designed to be interactive, they also offer the expected shrines to glitz and kitsch (like the **Liberace Museum**) and the gambling industry. Today, there are even prominent art collections as well as cutting-edge galleries. Some of the most glorious offerings are outside town, from the man-made splendor of **Lake Mead** and **Hoover Dam** to the ruddy desert terrain of **Red Rock Canyon**. And within an hour's drive, you can also tour the former atomic Nevada Test Site or a proposed radioactive dump facility, even snoop for military hardware and aliens near top-secret Area 51. But ultimately, is anything more otherworldly than what you find along that glowing Strip?

### Getting Your Bearings

All roads lead to **the Strip**, the long axle from which most main arteries emanate. The first time doing the Strip can be a profoundly disorienting experience. What other street's skyline includes an Egyptian pyramid, Italianate villa, Arthurian castle, Roman palace, and miniature versions of New York, Paris, and Venice—in many places linked by futuristic monorails? Driving it (with the infamous traffic jams) is daunting; walking can be downright dangerous at major intersections like Flamingo and Tropicana, where pedestrian overpasses were constructed. At least there's a shuttle that crawls along fairly reliably. The 3.5-mile-long Strip (officially **Las Vegas Boulevard South**) can be divided into lower (south) and upper (north) segments. The **southern section** begins near the airport at **Hacienda Avenue**, where you'll encounter such monsters as Mandalay Bay, Luxor, and

Excalibur and, across Tropicana Avenue, New York-New York and the MGM Grand. Continuing north, you hit Monte Carlo, Aladdin, and Paris. The lower section ends at **Flamingo Road**, site of the Bellagio, Caesars Palace, Bally's, and Barbary Coast hotels on each corner. Just to the west lie three more mega-properties, Rio, Gold Coast, and the Palms. The **upper section** roughly begins with the Caesars Forum Shops and, across the Strip, the seedy-Chinatown facade of the Imperial Palace. Proceeding north, you hit the Mirage, Treasure Island, Venetian, Stardust, Riviera, and Circus Circus. The uppermost limit is the halfheartedly Moorish Sahara (conveniently at Sahara Avenue).

Now you reach an unsavory netherland known as the **Stratosphere district** after the towering hotel of the same name. From here on, the Strip becomes a dingy, sordid lineup of quickie wedding chapels, bail bondsmen, sex emporia, seedy bars, tattoo shops, and at-your-own-risk motels that often rent by the hour. Turn east on Charleston Avenue, though, and you'll find the **Gateway district**, the southern fringe of Downtown, which is atmospherically skanky, scuzzy, and sleazy in a proto-boho SoHo sorta way. Galleries, thrift-chic shops, and coffeehouses are springing up, where grungeniks etch their bodies with graffiti and discourse knowledgeably on herbal remedies. Continue up Las Vegas Boulevard to reach **Downtown**, aka Glitter Gulch, a few square blocks of tourist area centered around Fremont Street.

The Strip is just that—a narrow swath through a sprawling town, though there are several other neighborhoods of interest off the Strip. Near the Convention Center and Las Vegas Hilton, a mini-area has sprouted along **Paradise Road**, which roughly parallels the Strip, anchored by the glittery Hard Rock Hotel. The UNLV campus lies just east (on trendy Maryland Parkway), as does the Liberace Museum, about a mile down on Tropicana Avenue. Even farther east is the **Boulder Strip,** along the Boulder Highway, home to many of the so-called locals' casinos. Proceed farther in any direction and a confusing grid of streets and cul-de-sacs with lookalike residential developments takes over. Like any other Sunbelt city growing too big for its britches, Las Vegas has a score of planned communities: the tony nouveau enclave **Green Valley** to the southeast (where Mike Tyson and Wayne Newton have spreads) and the even ritzier **Summerlin** on the other side of town. Drive through **Henderson** (the less exclusive area surrounding Green Valley) toward **Lake Mead** and **Hoover Dam**; continue northwest along the Summerlin route and

**DIVERSIONS** | **INTRODUCTION**

you'll hit the marvelous **Red Rock Canyon** and **Mount Charleston**, both enormous recreational areas.

# The Lowdown

**Where the hell am I?...** Ah, Las Vegas, City of Themes. At the **Eiffel Tower Experience**, passengers wait to board the elevators on a replica of the Pont Alexandre III that spans Paris's Seine River. At 50 stories, it's a half-size to-scale replica—and it's even the right rusty color. Riders may be too busy losing their Nathan's hot dogs to appreciate New York-New York's **Manhattan Express** roller coaster, but they do get a bird's-eye view of the Chrysler Building, the Empire State Building, the Statue of Liberty—in cars duplicating yellow cabs, no less. You board the **Venetian Gondolas** at the end of the Venetian's mall in Piazza San Marco; swept under the Bridge of Sighs, you traverse a "Grand Canal" surrounded by impeccably re-created Venetian neighborhoods (all except the squalor and foul water, that is), where glass blowers, jugglers, and sword swallowers stroll the narrow "alleys." Made by the oldest gondola firm in Venice, these boats are only a foot shorter than Venice's, but they cheat—there's a tiny whirring motor underneath (indistinguishable from the sounds of the slots in the casino below). Pharaohs, Sphinxes, obelisks, hieroglyphs, and other Egyptian symbols greet visitors on their way to the obsessively authentic **Luxor's King Tut Tomb and Museum**, where renowned Egyptologist Dr. Omar Mabreuck planted replica artifacts in the precise order they were found in the original tomb. Sorry, no animatronic mummies. Knights in shining armor, troubadours, even an animatronic dragon lurking beneath the drawbridge lure tourists to King Arthur's court in **Excalibur**'s public spaces.

**Freebie spectacles...** Ever wonder why traffic screeches to an abrupt halt on the Strip? It's usually the numerous free spectacles that stop cars in their tracks. In the **Treasure Island Pirate Battle**, the British frigate *HMS Britannia* and pirate ship *Hispaniola* skirmish on an elaborate re-creation of Robert Louis Stevenson's immortal Buccaneer Bay. Cannon fire, great stunt dives, a sinking ship (the pirates always win), and B-movie dialogue titillate audiences. Best views are from the excellent if pricey Buccaneer Bay Club, north end of Battle Bar, or outside on the plank bridge by the frigate-side rope railing (get there 30 to 45 minutes in advance). **Fountains at Bellagio** offers techno-wizardry, as 1,200 choreographed dancing fountains sway and spray under 51,000 colored lights. Programs vary from a frisky Frank Sinatra rendition of "Luck Be A Lady" to a tongue-in-cheek "Hey, Big Spender" (which should be the property's theme song). In **Lost City of Atlantis**, at Caesars Forum Shops, an animatronic Neptune (sounding suspiciously like James Earl Jones) shakes his trident at his rebellious, hard-bodied offspring Gadrius and Alia. Crowds clamor as the fountains play, mists swirl, lightning crackles, lasers shoot, winged birds cackle, and Atlantis sinks forever—or at least for an hour. When the **Mirage Volcano** erupts, it spews smoke, steam, flames, and simulated lava 100 feet into the air. A few times, errant sparks have set the nearby palm trees ablaze, which may be the only times this spectacle was really as impressive as it wants to be. Somewhat lamer, the **Excalibur Medieval Village/Fantasy Faire** features decent magicians, jugglers, and clowns on its Court Jester's Stage; knights ride unicorns, damsels in distress cry for help (usually because their long hair has snagged on someone's suit of armor), and a fearsomely bellowing animatronic dragon emerges from a murky moat, only to be chased off by Merlin. The gaudy, hokey **Fremont Street Experience** is essentially a five-block-long screen presenting neon "moving pictures" (dive-bombing jet fighters, dancing showgirls, and the like). At least it's helped to make Downtown safe, if somewhat sanitized. In Rio's **Masquerade Show in the Sky**, five parade floats (including a paddlewheel riverboat and a swan-winged gondola) circle the casino suspended from a ceiling track, with exotically appareled performers tossing off confetti, beads, and discount coupons while Elvis impersonators bounce off the walls and tap dancers spring like jacks-in-the-box up through the floor.

**Best shows for kids...** Kids clamor for shoulder perches at the **Treasure Island Pirate Battle**. The bombardment includes more explosions than all three *Die Hard* movies, and while the actors don't buckle the swash as well as Errol Flynn, they do many circus-worthy stunts. At the **Circus Circus Midway**, acrobats somersault, clowns cavort, and an indoor carnival tempts kids with free popcorn, face painting, and old-fashioned arcade games (skeeball,

Camel Chases, claw machines). Clown costumes and harlequins dangle from high wires while plastic ice cream cones jut from the walls, giving this "permanent circus" a slightly demented air. **Excalibur Medieval Village/Fantasy Faire** offers free stage shows, carnival games, wandering minstrels, Arthurian characters, and two Round Table–themed motion simulator rides (both real yawns, despite the input of George Lucas). But, no surprise, kids prefer the 51-foot-long fire-belching animatronic dragon, from the slimy green scales of his tail to his glowing yellow eyeballs and blood-red grin. The four-story, multimedia **M&M's World** verges on surreal, starting with the exterior's 40-foot gyrating yellow bag dispensing M&Ms. Animatronic spokescandies shout like Don Rickles, kids "graduate" from the interactive M&M's Academy, and a 3-D movie chronicles the Vegas misadventures of "Red" and "Yellow." It ends in the inevitable logo shop, but the M&Ms in 21 colors sure beat Ritalin™. A free shuttle bus leads on from here to the related **Ethel M's Chocolate Factory** for free tours of the facility started a century ago by Ethel Mars (yes, as in Mars™ bars—not to mention, Snickers™, Milky Way™, and Three Musketeers™).

**Thrill rides...** **Stratosphere**'s Big Shot launches riders 160 feet straight up the outside of the tower in 2 startling seconds to nearly 1,100 feet above the Strip with four G's of force from the thrust. You float for an instant at the apex, then the seat practically drops out from under you; your teeth and butt clench, your head flattens, and you're trying to remember your chiropractor's phone number. It lasts only 12 seconds, but it's a pure adrenaline rush. **Adventuredome**, the 5-acre indoor amusement park at Circus Circus, has several rides for thrill addicts: Canyon Blaster, the world's only indoor double-loop, double-corkscrew rollercoaster (with a 90-foot peak and speeds up to 55 mph); Chaos, which spins riders at a vertiginous 12 rpm as it does back flips and almost collides with Canyon Blaster; and the Inverter, which twirls you 360 degrees both clockwise and counterclockwise, 50 feet above the concrete—with only a T-bar and harness to hold on to. New York-New York's **Manhattan Express** careens through the New York skyline, whipping past the Empire State and Chrysler buildings, ascending to a maximum height of 203 feet. At one point it seems as if you'll kamikaze-dive 144 feet into the valet entrance on the Strip at nearly 70 mph (wusses, be forewarned, it's the second plunge). Next come 540-degree spirals, camelback hills, 180-degree twist-and-dive drops, and high-banked turns before diving back through the casino roof. Wheee! A rocket-shaped elevator ascends to vertiginous heights at **AJ Hackett Bungy**: Even the most valiant have wobbly legs after playing human rubber band, plunging 171 feet. If you feel really daring, do it at night, when it's like swan-diving into a vacuum surrounded by psychedelic colors. Just beware of the jaw-dropping cost. **Flyaway Indoor Skydiving** simulates a 35-foot free fall in a 21-foot-high wind tunnel. An airplane propeller sends 120-mph blasts of air upward, suspending you for 15 thrilling minutes. (There's also a 20-minute training session.) One drawback: The padded suit makes you look (and walk) like the Michelin Man. **Wet 'n' Wild**'s thrill rides are all wet—like Royal Flush, which propels you down a steep enclosed chute into a giant toilet bowl where you swirl at 45 mph before being whooshed headfirst into a 10-foot pool. On Sahara's **Speed: The Ride**, thrill-seekers catapult out of a rocket bay at 35 mph, plunge down a mist-filled underground tunnel, then blast through the surface to be flung through the Sahara's marquee and up to the top of a 224-foot tower—then repeat, only *backwards* this time. A little game of chicken, anyone? On certain weekend evenings, the **Las Vegas Motor Speedway** opens its track to any street-legal car for "Test and Tune" drag racing. The speedway also offers three racing academies, where even a half-day course provides the ultimate booming, vrooming thrill.

**Overrated…** The $12.50 admission charge to the tiny **Bellagio Gallery of Fine Art** is outrageous, considering how many notable works are already displayed for free in Bellagio's public spaces and restaurants. The **Venetian Gondolas** glide along a Grand Canal that's a quarter-mile long—and only 3 feet deep. *Gondolieri* in striped shirts and red bandannas say "It's-a real nice, no?" and sing those classic Venetian standards "That's Amore" and "O Solo Mio." ("This is the equivalent of playing a Smurf in a kiddie park," confided one disgruntled boater.) Despite its lofty perch 106 floors above Las Vegas, **Stratosphere**'s High Roller ride is no-thrills, with speeds maxing out at 35 mph. Riders are strapped in, with limited views (best after dark to experience any sensation) for a tame ride twice around the top of the tower. The insipid dialogue in **Lost City of Atlantis** is barely audible over the sounds of hissing steam and rumbling thunder—but never fear, the insistent pitch on surrounding screens for the adjacent 3-D motion simulator **Race for Atlantis** comes through loud and clear. The tilting chariot ride of Race for Atlantis is not worth the long wait in line; even worse, you've got to wear a visor that looks like a cross between fighter-pilot goggles and Elton John's eyewear. The discounted combo ticket is the best deal at **Star Trek: The Experience,** though the visual effects are hardly enterprising and the dialogue and plot are moronic. Upon exiting, avoid the callow kids in Starfleet costumes offering free theme merchandise—if you apply for a *Star Trek*™ Mastercard™. **Bellagio Conservatory** would be a serene garden retreat if it weren't jammed with folks clicking away on disposable cameras. Siegfried and Roy do a good deed by promoting ecological awareness through the **Secret Garden and Dolphin Habitat,** but their thickly accented audio tour is an unintentional hoot: "Just like a snowflake, ze skin of each tiger isss diffy-rent." Their white kitties also occupy the Mirage's free **Tiger Habitat,** but it's hard to spot them against the white background there—and all that white-on-white enhances the cats' comfort so much, it lulls them to sleep. Downtown, the **Fremont Street Experience** sound-and-light shows are followed by commercials for buffets and shows before the overhead canopy returns to plain old mesh. Plus, you get a neck-ache trying to take everything in above you. Despite the technical wizardry, it's basically a high-wattage attraction for the dim-witted. Alas, the fabled **Mirage Volcano**'s lava sprays look like mere flumes of colored water spitting fire into the Mirage Lagoon, and the deafening soundtrack recalls a bull elephant in heat.

**Au naturel...** At the **Bellagio Conservatory**, ponds, bridges, wrought-iron gazebos, arbors, and trellises duplicate an exquisite Edwardian garden, albeit one underneath a sculpted green copper skylight. Autumn showcases actual fall foliage, pumpkins, colossal cornucopias; spring features delicate cherry and apple blossoms; holidays bring extras like a 32-foot Christmas tree (decorated by Martha Stewart) and poinsettias and mistletoe everywhere. But nature's not enough in Vegas;

seven-time Tony Award–winner David Hersey designed lighting that would subtly reflect the changing seasons and spotlight each individual flower. **Ethel M's Chocolate Factory** includes a 3-acre Botanical Cactus Garden, where more than 300 species, from prickly pears to vaulting saguaros, flourish. On the UNLV campus, the **Marjorie Barrack Museum** includes fascinating displays on desert flora and fauna and a surprisingly lush 1.5-acre garden featuring plants that thrive on little or no water. Or venture out to see the real thing at **Red Rock Canyon Natural Conservation Area** (abbreviated by locals to Red Rock), a rugged wilderness of Crayola™-colored rocks, aromatic purple sage, bighorn sheep, and towering Ponderosa pines.

**Lions and tigers and bears, oh my...** Siegfried & Roy's trademark White Himalayan tigers are extinct in the wild, but not at the Mirage lobby's **Tiger Habitat**, which features a rotating cast (the tigers all take their turns between hanging out at Siegfried & Roy's home or performing in their act). Fake concrete palms and a fountain in the pool lend a truly authentic Vegas touch. While you're here, check out the enormous saltwater aquarium behind the hotel's registration desk, complete with menacing sharks and gliding rays. Siggy and Roy's pets are also part of the Mirage's **Secret Garden and Dolphin Habitat**, a twofold outdoor attraction that showcases white tigers, the white lions of Timbavati, Bengal tigers, and for diversity's sake, one snow leopard, panther, and Asian elephant in an exquisitely landscaped tropical sanctuary. Not to be outdone, the **MGM Grand Lion Habitat** plays up its own trademark; several big cats here are direct descendants of the first MGM mascot, Metro. The 5,345-square-foot habitat is cleverly designed, with glass walkways that allow the lions to prowl, stalk, and stretch above and below you. Even the **Las Vegas Museum of Natural History** has live animals ranging from turtles to tarantulas, scorpions (which glow under UV light) to snakes, not to mention the eggs of 35 bird species. But the majority of the exhibits at this temple of taxidermy are fossils, including sabre-toothed cats and ancient crocodiles, and wonderfully posed dioramas of civets, caracals, coyotes, even African water chevrotain in impeccably rendered natural habitats from around the world. Feeding time is fascinatingly gross at the Mojave Desert reptile room at **Marjorie Barrack**

**Museum**, home to frisky if frightening-looking gila monsters, iguanas, rattlers, and Western whiptail lizards.

**Under the sea...** Mandalay Bay's remarkable **Shark Reef** displays approximately 2,000 specimens from over 100 species, from crocs to sea turtles, petite blue damselfish to 12-foot nurse sharks. The ingenious design creates total sensory immersion: You explore an ancient tropical city being claimed by the sea (the water level "rises" as you proceed), from an aboveground ruined temple to the deck of a sunken wooden ship in shark-infested waters. Best is the tank featuring iridescent moon jellies bathed in black light; the effect is like watching a living lava lamp. Acrylic tunnels simulate a diver's-eye view, culminating in the 1.3-million-gallon shark tank where dozens of shark species glide menacingly above, around, and below you. And just to remind you that there are slithery predators on land as well, there's an open-air exhibit of Burmese pythons, three of the world's 12 golden crocodiles in captivity, and terrifying water monitors. One good thing about the **Lost City of Atlantis**: its 50,000-gallon saltwater backdrop hosting over 100 species, including puffers, flounder, rays, and sharks. Frolicking around in four huge connecting saltwater pools, the playful bottlenose dolphins of the Mirage's **Secret Garden and Dolphin Habitat** enrapture visitors; underwater and poolside observation areas allow maximum viewing.

**Kids' favorite theme parks...** **Adventuredome** is an amazing climate-controlled 5-acre park enclosed by a 150-foot-high pink glass dome. Kids of all ages will find something to do: traditional rides like a carousel, Ferris wheel, and bumper cars; Sega arcade; vicious rides that would make adults lose their hot dogs; animatronic dinos stuck in tar pits; continuous circus acts; mini-golf; hair-braiding; and removable tattoo booths. Older kids will like the Xtreme Zone's climbing wall, "rad bungee" (you do flips on a special trampoline while harnessed), and Lazer Blast for team laser tag (way cool in the black-light room). The family that sprays together stays together at **Wet 'n' Wild**, a 15-acre water park right on the Strip: the ideal place to cool off in the Las Vegas summer swelter. There are cannon-shot chutes, lazy rivers, sunbathing areas with cascading waterfalls, video and arcade games, snack bar, swimwear shop, even pockets of green space where families picnic. **Stratosphere**'s Strat-O-Fair transports kids back to the future with its 1964 World's Fair "Googie" decor; a vintage 1958 Ferris wheel provides spectacular Strip views from its 80-foot apex, while the "Little Shot" catapults smaller kids 20 feet. The park also offers "Hyper-Bowl" (a virtual bowling game with a 10-foot 3-D screen) and the world's only "Hover Crash" (futuristic bumper cars).

**Theme parks for grownups...** Star Trek: The Experience is not just a ride but an entire environment. Cross Space Bridge from the Hilton into a neon 24th-century universe replicating the *Deep Space Nine* promenade, patrolled by Ferengi and Klingons; the SpaceQuest casino features lightbeam-activated slots and porthole-shaped TV monitors creating the illusion of orbiting Earth, and Quark's Bar and Restaurant, patterned after a Cardassian mess hall, serves HamBORGers and Romulan Ale. Props, costumes, cast photos, and Trek timelines fill the witty "History of the Future Museum." As for the "ride": You're beamed aboard the starship *Enterprise* and interact with the crew on the bridge; a red alert sounds, you're abducted by Klingons, a Turbolift takes you to the shuttle bay (ignore the worn hotel carpeting here). Klingon blasts rock the bay and you quickly board a 27-seat shuttlecraft on a mission to rescue Captain Picard from the Borg and repair a rift in the time-space continuum. Sahara's **Las Vegas Cyber Speedway** promises "the most realistic simulated race car experience available." You sit in stock cars mounted on six-axis hydraulic motion bases, then burn virtual rubber on the Las Vegas Motor Speedway or the Strip. You can communicate with your pit crew during the race; computer-generated reports list your average speed and your finishing position. The complex also features truck and car races in two 3-D theaters, plus the adjacent NASCAR Café, with real autos mounted everywhere (including the world's largest, "Carzilla," a 34-by-12-foot Pontiac Grand Prix) and servers dressed as grease monkeys. It serves as launch pad for **Speed: The Ride**, a hypodermic of pure adrenaline sufficiently scarifying to be a stunt on *Fear Factor*. There's a macho edge to the fun at **Gameworks**, developed by Universal Studios, Dreamworks SKG, and Sega Enterprises; it features everything from old-fashioned pinball machines (with updated themes) to air, land, sea, and outer space virtual-reality games, not to mention an imposing climbing wall. Tamer stuff includes pool tables, air hockey, and classic video games (Missile Command™, Pac Man™). More than an arcade, it attracts plenty of grownups, including the likes of Carmen Electra, David Schwimmer, Will Smith, and Gillian Anderson. Keeping the adult factor strong, The Loft is known for liberal happy hours, live weekend entertainment, and cushy nooks for making out. The make-out mood is also high at the romantic **Fountains at Bellagio**, where couples lucky enough to snag patio seats at the bar swoon to the waters' choreographed splashing and spraying, accompanied by Pavarotti, Sinatra, Lionel Ritchie, and of course, Gene Kelly warbling "Singin' in the Rain." For just $9.95, you can don a wild costume and fling petals and party favors from a hanging parade float in **Masquerade Show in the Sky**; less exhibitionistic types can just boogie away in the adoring crowds on ground level. **Madame Tussaud's Celebrity Experience** waxes glorious over Vegas excess, showcasing more than 100 American icons in five themed interactive environments. The "Las Vegas Legends" showroom features Strip legends such as Sinatra, Tom Jones, and Wayne Newton; Paul Newman and Joanne Woodward greet visitors to a classic Vegas chapel adorned with photos of other celebrities who got hitched here.

**Honeymoon in Vegas...** Las Vegas bills itself not only as the "Entertainment Capital of the World," but the "Marriage Capital of the World" as well, with approximately 120,000 couples getting hitched here annually. You can plan a wedding months in advance (hotels specialize in one-stop matrimonial shopping; see Accommodations for top choices) or you can say your vows on the fly in a drive-up chapel or hovering in a helicopter above the Strip ("I do; Roger and out," responded one blushing bride over the propeller noise). Elvis, Captain Kirk, or King Arthur can perform the ceremony. You can even kneel before your future master/mistress in an S&M dungeon, where black leather is accessorized with white lace cat-o'-nine-tails. A civil ceremony costs $25, while elaborate themed weddings run $1,000 and up. No blood test (or marital counseling) is required, and there's no waiting period. A license (one is issued every 6.5 minutes) costs $35; just show up at the **Marriage License Bureau** (tel

702/455-3156, 200 S. 3rd St., 1st floor; open Mon-Thur 8am-midnight, Fri and Sat 24 hours) with government-sanctioned picture ID. **A Little White Wedding Chapel** (tel 702/382-5943, 1301 Las Vegas Blvd. S.) is one of the more venerable chapels (celebs have included Judy Garland, Bruce Willis and Demi Moore, Michael Jordan, and Sinatra). It was also the first to offer drive-through service (the $80 Limo Lovers and Liplockers special includes a single red rose and a garter). A mere $45 includes limo service from your hotel, nondenominational minister (slip him/her money separately), and free witness. You can get married in the Cherub Chariot underneath a canopy of chubby angels and twinkling stars, enjoy a dignified wedding in a gazebo surrounded by fountains, or soar in a floral hot air balloon accommodating up to 14 guests ($500 and up), called "The Little Chapel in the Sky." The most tranquil is **Little Church of The West** (tel 702/739-7971, 4617 Las Vegas Blvd. S.), open for business since 1942. Elvis Presley and Ann-Margret staged a happy ending here in *Viva Las Vegas*, and movie-mad Japanese have invaded in droves ever since. Real-life celebrity hitchings include Dudley Moore, Judy Garland, Bob Geldof, Zsa Zsa Gabor, Cindy Crawford, and Mickey Rooney (who married all eight of his wives here, starting with Ava Gardner). The faux-pine cabin has a certain rustic charm, with an adorable steeple and bell tower, delightful garden, and, inside, cedar-paneled tower, candelabras, and lace curtains. **Graceland Wedding Chapel** (tel 702/474-6655, 619 Las Vegas Blvd. S.) is equally historic, even spanning generations (both 1950s Latin heartthrob Fernando Lamas and C-action-movie king son Lorenzo Lamas); Jon Bon Jovi is the most notable recent guest. Norm "Elvis" Jones performs roughly 40 Elvis weddings a week, finishing with a 15-minute concert. Graceland has a long-running rivalry with **Viva Las Vegas Wedding Chapel** (tel 702/384-0771, 1205 Las Vegas Blvd. S.), where owner Ron DeCar (a singer and Elvis impersonator at the Tropicana for 12 years) conducts approximately 10 to 15 *Blue Hawaii*–inspired weddings weekly, with hula girls accompanying the bridesmaids. But Viva Las Vegas offers other movie-themed weddings as well: disco ceremonies with polyester-clad John Travolta minister, *Godfather*-style weddings, and *Beach Blanket Bingo* bashes. The carpet is exchanged for artificial turf for sports fans who want to tackle each other. There's even a gothic package, complete with Grim Reaper pronouncing "Till Death Do You Part" in a darkened candlelit chapel. Viva Las Vegas is one of many chapels to provide themed weddings for Trekkies (and Trekkers), but only the full-scale attraction **Star Trek: The Experience** can transport beaming couples to the bridge of the *Enterprise*, replete with flickering control panels and Star Fleet officers. They'll even customize; weddings in full Klingon makeup and regalia are particularly popular, staffers confide.

**Neon dreams...** Neon art may be the great Las Vegas contribution to American culture. The most spectacular example is the **Fremont Street Experience**, a five-block pedestrian mall semi-enclosed by a 90-foot vaulted steel-mesh canopy sprinkled with more than two million computer-controlled bulbs (with 35 computers, it's amazingly complex, with fiber optics as sophisticated as spy satellites) and a concert-quality half-a-million-watt sound system. There are several different "shows." For more of a historical perspective, walk through the open-air **Neon Museum**, which rescued such classics as the horse and cowboy from the Hacienda (1967), the flickering conflagration from the Flame Restaurant (1961), and the lamp from the original Aladdin (1966). A couple of blocks down Fremont (off 1st St.) are the legendary Downtown glowing icons: Vegas Vic and Vegas Vickie. Vic waves his arm in welcome while puffing a cig, resembling a cross between Howdy Doody and the Marlboro Man. Sultry Vickie looks like she's trying to get his attention across the street, kicking up her heels as if to say, "Wanna good time, stranger?"

**Kidding around...** Relics of Las Vegas's attempt to market itself as a family destination are still scattered around town. The best is the outstanding **Lied Children's Museum**, set in the architecturally innovative Las Vegas Library, where you can become a human battery, stand in a giant bubble, play disc jockey at KKID radio, check out conditions in the Las Vegas Valley at a real weather station, or harness excess kid power (aka hyperactivity) into a lightning spark. Parents will really appreciate the Every Day Living area, where young visitors earn a "paycheck," use the ATM machine in the bank, and shop for groceries. It's not all fossils and stuffed animals at the **Las Vegas Museum of Natural History**: Five robotic dinos include a 35-foot T-Rex and cute Troödons, and the

Young Scientist Center offers such interactive displays as "Whose Foot Is It?" (comparing animal tracks) and Dig A Fossil (mini T-Rex bones). In the Learning Center, kids can dissect owl pellets and cow eyes: gross but fun. **Shark Reef** also supplies delightfully disgusting details on the displayed species (betcha never knew moon jellyfish have four horseshoe-shaped genitals). At the vast "touch tank," youngsters feel up sea cucumbers, sting rays, sea urchins, and horseshoe crabs. **Circus Circus Midway**'s performers include veterans of such companies as the Moscow Circus, Ringling Brothers, and the Big Apple Circus: not just high-wire walkers, trapeze artists, and clowns, but delightful trained dog-and-cat acts (using rescued abused or abandoned animals) and cyclists who defy the laws of gravity and physics. Kids who love animals can admire the big cats at **MGM Grand Lion Habitat** (just don't let them talk you into the $20 lion cub photo op) and **Secret Garden and Dolphin Habitat**, which also has elephants, a lovely outdoor setting, and eight show-Flippers. Adults have been known to shove kids out of the way, it's so much fun.

**For high-tech kids...** Different "zones" at **Gameworks** offer more than 300 games of all types (including multiplayer and virtual reality), as well as a 75-foot climbing rock and Internet access for playing games with contestants as far afield as England and Japan. You can duke it out with a range of nasty cinematic aliens, race at Indy, free-fall three stories, or bobsled down an icy, precipitous course. Supervise your kids: Some of the games are graphically violent. In the IMAX 3-D motion simulator ride **Race for Atlantis**, you're "chosen by the gods" to race a daunting field of competitors in "fighter chariots" and retrieve a magic ring that will determine the fate of the sea-world. The flocks of birds, dragons, dolphins, and weapons are startlingly realistic—3-D spears and shrapnel seem to fly straight at you. Zooming and twisting through canyons, you'll feel like you're in the climactic scene of *Star Wars*. **Adventuredome**'s ReBoot is the first IMAX motion ride created solely with computer-generated images. Wickedly up-to-date, it rockets you into cyberspace where you battle a vicious virus, Megabyte, and its sidekicks, Hack and Slash. The ensuing chase feels astonishingly authentic as you smash through walls, tumble down stairs, and ride stormy seas.

Jimmy, a twisted Claymation™ clown, is the star of Adventuredome's other IMAX motion-simulator ride, Fun House Express. As Jimmy's hostage, you'll drop through a trap door, careen off the track into the air, land in near-G-force whirligigs, and end up sliding down his long pink tongue. Clowning around, indeed.

**Kitsch collections...** Don't miss the **Liberace Museum**, which houses Mr. Showmanship's elaborate bejeweled costumes, bejeweled cars, bejeweled pianos, and bejeweled candelabras. The collection of rare and antique pianos includes a diamond-studded, gold-plated, 7-foot Baldwin covered in rhinestones, but that is counterpointed by George Gershwin's Chickering grand or a Boesendorfer played by Liszt, Schumann, and Brahms— there *was* a quiet, introverted, tasteful pianist somewhere inside the feathers, furs, and rhinestones. Cars range from sublime (one of only seven Rolls Royce Phantom V Landau limos, worth over $1 million) to the ridiculous (the red-white-and-blue Rolls Royce commissioned for his Bicentennial salute, with matching feathered cape and hot pants). The setting abounds in velvet screens, gilt mirrors, crystal, and marble statues of naked men, and a family photo room features a "royal portrait" of his mother surrounded by cherubs and cupids. Not included are his death from AIDS and covert gay lifestyle (including orgies at his home). Ask about his private life and the sweet old ladies, keepers of the flame, blurt "Oh, ohhh no. No, I can't answer that." Sorry, there's only one velvet painting of the King at the **Elvis-a-Rama Museum**, but it's still a must for fans, beginning in a pitch-black room where a spotlighted 3-D portrait of Elvis eerily talks about performing. Horns blare and the museum doors swing open to unveil an 80-foot-long mural of The King striking various iconic poses. Aficionados could spend days studying all the memorabilia on display: gold records; handwritten lyrics; costumes—gold lamé, natch, alongside spangled white jumpsuits; cars (Liberace might have coveted the purple Cadillac); a 1959 full-dress Army uniform; and original wardrobe items from *King Creole*, *Clambake*, and *Fun in Acapulco*. And who could resist a free 30-minute concert with an Elvis impersonator in the '50s-style soda shop/cafe? Animatronic Elvii welcome you at **Madame Tussaud's Celebrity Encounter**, where you can interact with the waxwork celebs in various multimedia environments. Many stars personally sat for their casts; the modelmakers uncannily captured Michael Jackson in black fetishistic gear, a beatific-looking Shirley MacLaine, the smarmy smile of David Copperfield, and the grin of Eddie Murphy. The Tropicana's **Casino Legends Hall of Fame** is more fun than it sounds—artifacts from 738 casinos (550 of which no longer exist), including old menus, showgirl costumes, vintage movie posters (*Viva Las Vegas*, *Vegas Vacation*), and cancelled checks made out to performers ($406 to Tony Bennett in 1952 from El Rancho; $7,000 to Eartha Kitt in 1954). Car lovers will be astounded by the **Imperial Palace Auto Collections** (fittingly located in the Imperial Palace's parking facility). Classics include cars of presidents (Truman, Eisenhower, JFK), dictators (Hitler, Mussolini), and celebrities (Elvis's powder-blue 1976 Cadillac Eldorado, Liberace's 1981 cream Zimmer with candelabra, and Sammy Davis Jr.'s 1972 Stutz). Oddities include Howard Hughes's eccentric 1954 Chrysler (with an air-purification system in the trunk for the germ-phobic titan), Al Capone's 1930 V-16 Cadillac, a 1965 Batmobile (for the TV series), a 1947 Tucker (one of only 51 produced), and even the steel armor–plated Range Rover Popemobile for the Pope's 1982 U.K. trip. There are taxis (including a 1908 French model), fire engines, old Harleys, dump trucks, motorized rickshaws, tractors, army vehicles, delivery vans, racing cars, and a 1925 Studebaker paddy wagon. More than 350 vehicles are displayed—and every irreplaceable gem is for sale, if you can afford it. **Star Trek: The Experience**'s History of the Future Museum includes costumes (including Uhura's, Janeway's, and Worf's uniforms), authentic props (phasers, tricorders, and Data's original arm), full-scale starship models (Enterprise, Birds of Prey), cast member photos, and fun factoids. Unlike Liberace's shrine, **Elvis-a-Rama Museum** offers true insight into the human being, not just the legend. Compare Elvis's bank deposit slip for his first professional performance—$240—to the 1969 American Express application listing his annual income as $3 million; read his 1959 letter to then-girlfriend Anita Wood accusing her of cheating ("Darling I pray you haven't let your loneliness, passions and desires make you do something that would hurt me."), coincidentally just as Priscilla Beaulieu was entering the picture. Who ain't nothin' but a hound dog, El?

**Show me the cheese: gift shops...** The disappointingly tasteful **Elvis-a-Rama Museum** finally gets good and tacky in its gift shop, with Elvis mouse pads and temporary tattoos. The **Liberace Museum** shop comes through in high camp style with red-white-and-blue spangled vests, James Dean ties (hmmm?), candelabras, and Liberace piggy banks, dolls, and fridge magnets in several resplendent costumes. **M&M's World** purveys numerous logo items, from ties and T-shirts to teacups, calculators to cuff links to cocktail dresses (gotta have that slinky $2,500 number covered with sequined M&M's, Snickers, and Twix wrappers). The Deep Space Nine Promenade shops at **Star Trek: The Experience** pry open the wallets of Trekkers with the world's largest collection of Trek merchandise and memorabilia. Yes, you too can have Vulcan ears, tribbles, Ferengi masks, a gold-plated communicator, or a $3,000 duplicate of the captain's chair.

**History lessons (why not?)...** More often than not in Vegas, the past is no more than a springboard for hotel themes. Witness **Luxor's King Tut's Tomb and Museum**, which re-creates the boy pharaoh's tomb with hundreds of items, from the guardian statues and the fabled sarcophagus itself to vases, beds, and basketry, all reproduced using the same gold leaf, linens, pigments, tools, and original 3,300-year-old Egyptian methods. There's even one authentic stone fragment. **Casino Legends Hall of Fame** contains the world's largest collection of gambling-related objects, from Marilyn Monroe and Joe DiMaggio's marriage license and a pair of Cassius Clay's boxing gloves to mobster photos, videos of casino demolitions, matchbooks, dice, chips (over 13,000), and swizzle sticks. Hall of Fame inductees, each with individual display, are enshrined in different sections: "Headliners" (the Rat Pack, Liberace, Wayne Newton, Shecky Greene, Engelbert Humperdinck), "Gamblers" (Amarillo Slim, Jay Sarno), and "Visionaries" (Benny Binion, Howard Hughes, Carl Icahn, Steve Wynn). UNLV's **Marjorie Barrack Museum** explores the culture of the area's natives and early settlers with breathtaking collections of Southern Paiute baskets, Navajo textiles, Hopi kachinas, Guatemalan *huipils* (blouses), and ceremonial masks from the Americas. Out at the **Hoover Dam**, visitor center exhibits detail the dam's arduous five-year construction (amazingly completed ahead of schedule), along with Ripley-like factoids (didja know that Lake Mead could cover the state of Pennsylvania in a foot of water, or that all the concrete in the dam could pave an entire cross-continental highway?).

**Thumbs up from the galleries...** Though locals joke that there's more active culture in the nearest frozen yogurt shop, Las Vegas's arts scene is blooming like a delicate cactus flower in the desert. The initial impetus came from Steve Wynn, who opened the **Bellagio Gallery of Fine Art** with a flurry of press releases pompously comparing Wynn to great art patrons of the past like the Medicis, Henry Clay Frick, or Andrew Mellon. Though Wynn took most of his collection when he sold Mirage Resorts (locals speculate that it might resurface in his "reinvention" of the Desert Inn), the Bellagio space now hosts a parade of prestigious smaller exhibits, ranging from "safe" (The Phillips Collection of Impressionist and Post-Impressionist Masterworks) to idiosyncratic (Steve Martin's eclectic modern art collection, with audio commentary by the actor/director). Its thunder has been stolen by the Venetian's fall 2001 unveiling of the **Guggenheim-Hermitage Las Vegas** (nicknamed the "Jewel Box") and the whopping-big **Guggenheim Las Vegas**, both designed by superstar Pritzker-prize-winning architect Rem Koolhaas. The Guggenheim-Hermitage is a collaborative alliance between two great museums whose holdings complement one another perfectly; biannual shows feature 20 artworks from each institution, many never before seen in the United States. The initial installation, "Masterpieces from the Hermitage and Guggenheim Collections," highlights important works by Monet, Cézanne, Gauguin, Bonnard, Renoir, Matisse, Picasso, Picabia, Leger, Chagall, and Kandinsky. The facility's controversial design features walls armored in Cor-Ten steel, upon which paintings are attached with magnets, like giant post-its®. The seven-story **Guggenheim Las Vegas** may be the world's most technologically advanced museum: One entire end wall doubles as a multimedia screen, and the hinged 70-foot-high roof opens to reveal a 120x70-foot skylight (when closed, the two panels wittily re-create Michelangelo's Sistine Chapel frescoes). The massive facility focuses on blockbuster traveling exhibitions, beginning with the Frank Gehry–designed installation "The Art of

the Motorcycle," with over 120 bikes and related memorabilia. The local arts scene boasts its own, less expensive
contributions. The aggressively contemporary building
design (blazingly white, monumental, with curves and
angles like the Frank Lloyd Wrong school of architecture)
of the Sahara West Library and Fine Arts Museum
reflects the solemn agenda of the **Las Vegas Art Museum**
within, which presents nationally renowned artists as well
as major international exhibits such as a comprehensive
Chagall retrospective. Affiliated with the Smithsonian,
the museum's permanent collection includes seminal
works by Salvador Dalí, Alexander Calder, Red Grooms,
Robert Indiana, and more. The **Marjorie Barrack
Museum**'s spacious, beautifully laid out front galleries
highlight contemporary visual arts, often by visiting
UNLV artists. Current works are the stock-in-trade of the
**The Arts Factory**, the brainchild of commercial
photographer Wes Isbutt, who bought a block-long run-
down 1944 warehouse to set up a mini-Soho/artists' com-
mune. There are nearly 20 tenants, with a long waiting
list; some are exhibit spaces, some ateliers closed to the
public, but you never know who might be smoking outside and let you in. Contemporary Arts Collective (tel
702/382-3886, Room 102) often shows members' work
in a variety of media; the Nevada Institute of Contemporary Art (tel 702/434-2666, Room 101) is an adventuresome small facility with rotating exhibits, mostly touring
shows; the George L. Sturman Fine Arts Gallery (tel
702/384-2615, Room 204) is an eccentric, jam-packed
grab bag—Disney animation cells, early Christos like
wrapped phone books, Calder mobiles, thrones from
Cameroon, Hockneys, De Koonings, Dürer etchings, and
Milton Avery and Ansel Adams photos. The *pièces de
résistance* are shoes collected from various artists, from
Chihuly to Rauschenberg.

**Rev your motors...** Sahara's **Las Vegas Cyber Speedway**
outraces the competition with 7/8-scale, amazingly
detailed NASCAR Winston Cup–style cars that sit in
service bays replicating pit areas. In a simulated version of
the Las Vegas Motor Speedway (or down the Strip), you
"race" fellow drivers, competing in actual time; the thrum
and hum is surprisingly realistic. Take turns at speeds
approaching 200 mph, screech around corners, blow tires,
get clipped by other cars: It's literally heart-pounding

(those with cardiac or respiratory problems are not allowed). But if you want to feel genuinely pumped, the **Las Vegas Motor Speedway** hosts occasional drag racing for any cars that pass tech inspection, as well as three racing programs: Champ Ride, the Derek Daly Performance Driving Academy, and the Richard Petty Driving Experience. Courses range from 3 hours to 3 days. Riding shotgun with a professional instructor, even neophytes can burn rubber up to 165 mph around the banked track; longer courses graduate you to driving solo laps, checkered flags and all.

**For your viewing pleasure...** The quickest way to see all the lights on the Strip is via chopper with **Sundance Helicopters**. Its nighttime tours offer eye-level views of the ironwork of the Eiffel Tower at Paris, the roller coaster atop the Stratosphere, and fly-bys of the Fountains at Bellagio and the Mirage volcano. Sundance's pilots enjoy angling the aircraft for better views, providing a nice adrenaline rush. If you'd rather keep your feet on solid ground, the 1,149-foot **Stratosphere Tower** is the tallest freestanding observation tower in the United States (it was originally supposed to be taller, but the FAA objected) with 360-degree panoramic views. Mind you, you can get the same view with a sunset drink or dinner at the **Top of the Tower** bar and restaurant (see Nightlife). The **Eiffel Tower Experience** may not be the real thing (three legs actually break through the Paris's casino ceiling), but 50 stories is still enough to out-Strip most other contenders.

**Away from the Strip...** If you hanker after greenery, drive to **Mount Charleston**, a cool respite no matter what the time of year. Climb through several distinct ecosystems to the 11,218-foot summit for splendid panoramic views of the valley; the Desert View Trail (7 miles down NV 158) is where locals repaired to watch the mushrooming atomic explosions in the 1950s. A raft of recreational opportunities, from golf to skiing, is available. Ask at one Visitors Center (see Hotlines) for a hiking trail map. **Red Rock Canyon National Conservation Area** is a brilliant red splash of sandstone, its bacon-like striated exposed rocks revealing more than 600 million years of geological history. The phenomenal terrain features arches, natural bridges, 3,000-foot cliffs, sandstone boulders, and peaks in a striking palette of colors. Ponderosa

DIVERSIONS | THE LOWDOWN

pines tower, bighorn sheep and desert tortoises wander through, and you may stumble on ancient petroglyphs, arrowheads, and pottery shards of the Anasazi and Paiutes who called the area home centuries ago. There's a 13-mile driving loop (beware of feeding cute but rabid wild burros), but hiking is the best way to appreciate the terrain (be alert for scorpions and snakes). The similar, less trammeled **Valley of Fire State Park** is named for the fiery red sandstone sculpted by wind and rain over the eons into spectacular domes, spirals, and beehives (kinda like the hairdos of some senior citizens back in Vegas). The boulders and pinnacles similarly range in color from deep red to white, with pink, lavender, burnt orange, sienna, and russet highlights. There are also areas of fossilized logs that rival the Petrified Forest.

**Head for the lake...** If you're feeling parched, head to **Lake Mead/Hoover Dam**, a haven for water sports less than 40 miles away. Drive out State Highway 167, aka North Shore Road, past stunning desert scenery—rugged dark mountains, ruddy sandstone outcroppings, gaping canyons, and bluffs reflected in the lake. Turnoffs lead to warm springs and beaches (those past Callville Bay Marina toward Echo Bay are sandier and less crowded). As a bonus, there are many secluded coves, accessible only by long hikes or boat, for anglers and sunbathers (including some that are unofficially nude or gay). Created by the dam, Lake Mead is the largest man-made lake in the Western hemisphere, with an amazing 550 miles of shoreline; you can sail, jet-ski, water-ski, river-raft, even scuba-dive; fishermen pull in bass (both striped and large-mouth), bluegills, catfish, and crappie. Equipment and so forth can be obtained from **Lake Mead Resort and Marina** (tel 702/293-3484), **Las Vegas Bay** (tel 702/565-9111), and **Callville Bay Marina** (tel 702/565-8958). Ranger-led hikes (from wetlands to vividly hued eroded sandstone formations) and bird-watching expeditions are organized at the **Lake Mead Visitors Center** (tel 702/293-8990 or U.S. 93 at NV 166). **Lake Mead Cruises** (tel 702/293-6180) operates a Mississippi-style paddle wheeler, the *Desert Princess*, a delightful ride through the Black Canyon, past the colorful rock formation nicknamed Arizona's Painted Pots, up to Hoover Dam itself; the dinner cruises are the most spectacular, as you gaze upon the Dam lit up at night. **Guided tours of Hoover Dam**

(tel 702/294-3522; admission charged) prowl around the dam's working parts, descending into its bowels where futuristic turbine engines quake. Hoover Dam towers an imposing 726 feet above Black Canyon; spanning 1,244 feet, the dam is every bit the engineering marvel it's built up to be. Despite a few Art Deco and Spanish Mission elements, its starkness harmonizes with the desert setting—its honest grandeur puts the pompous palaces of the Strip to shame.

**Par for the course...** The magnificent desert setting, year-round play, and the high percentage of corporate and convention visitors make Las Vegas a golfing mecca, with dozens of courses. Peak season is from October to May, when top courses schedule tee times up to 2 months in advance. (If you're fool enough to play at high noon in summer, you'll be pleased to hear that greens fees plunge dramatically then.) The **Desert Inn Golf Club** (tel 702/431-4653, 3145 Las Vegas Blvd. S.), has hosted the PGA Tour, the Senior PGA Tour, and the LPGA Tour, and is perennially ranked among *Golf Digest*'s top 75 courses. Pending a rumored last-minute reprieve, this historic course will be demolished in early 2002 to make room for Steve Wynn's re-imagined D.I. If this does come to pass, the 7,015-yard, par-72 **Bali Hai Golf Club** (tel 702/450-8000, 5160 Las Vegas Blvd. S.) will be the only golf course on the Strip. To match the development's South Seas theme, the Bali Hai course is verdantly landscaped: 7 acres of water, an island green, 2,500 palm trees, over 100,000 tropical plants and flowers, and transition areas accented with blinding Augusta white sand and black volcanic rock outcroppings. Sharp doglegs, ever-present water hazards and sandtraps, and undulating greens require pinpoint positioning. The gorgeous clubhouse—filled with Asian handicrafts, carved dark wood moldings, and bamboo—includes a Wolfgang Puck–managed gourmet restaurant, Cili (Balinese for "prosperous"), which fuses Eastern and Western cuisine. The par-72, 7,322-yard **Rio Secco Golf Club** (tel 702/889-2400, 2851 Grand Hills Dr., Henderson) is primarily for guests of the Rio Suites Hotel and Casino; proles can prowl it for $250 and up. Designed by Rees Jones, this is a heartbreaker, with treacherously curvaceous greens; the front six holes snake through a canyon, and the middle six skitter along the plateau, while the back six range along a dry riverbed. Averaging around $125, prices at the Bobby Weed/Raymond Floyd–designed, 7,063-yard, par-71 **Tournament Players Club at the Canyons** (tel 702/256-2000, 9851 Canyon Run Dr., Summerlin) are more than fair. There's a lot of desert to clear before reaching those emerald greens, with arroyos and rocky outcroppings posing as very scenic hazards. The 7,261-yard, par-72 **Reflection Bay Golf Club** (tel 702/740-4653, 75 Monte Lago Blvd.) is the first Jack Nicklaus–designed course in Nevada, primarily for use of guests at the Lake Las Vegas Resort. It features an unusual water hazard for Las Vegas: five holes straddling 1.5 miles of lakefront beach. The aquatic theme is carried through with a 4-acre lake on holes one and 10 as well as three major waterfalls, ranging between 25 and 40 feet. Nicklaus made superb use of the terrain's natural contours, incorporating the hump of swales and dip of arroyos on the arid, hilly back nine. The **Angel Park Golf Club** (tel 702/254-4653, 100 South Rampart Blvd.) is the town's most complete facility, with two full courses and a 12-hole, par-3 course and 18-hole putting course lit for night play (you can tee off at 6am and play through midnight). Designed by Arnold Palmer, the two 18-hole courses, the 5,438-yard Mountain and 5,751-yard Palm, are both short, placing a premium on shot placement rather than power. Mountain is known for its narrow fairways, tiered greens, and tricky uneven lies, while the Palm incorporates nasty features like natural canyons as bunkers. The Cloud Nine par-3 course has 12 holes modeled after (in)famous holes around the globe (in the Las Vegas spirit of appropriating everything from somewhere else), including the "Double Green" from St. Andrews, the "Postage Stamp" from Royal Troon, and "Island Green" from the Tournament Players Club at Sawgrass. The Cloud Nine fee is just $25 to $40 (compared to $100 and up on the two full courses). The par-72, 7,029-yard **Royal Links Country Club** (tel 888/427-6682, Vegas Valley Rd. at Nellis Blvd.) goes even further, with a Perry Dye–designed course simulating the look of famed Scottish, Irish, and British courses (not only Royal Troon's "Postage Stamp" but also St. Andrews' nefarious "Road Hole," where you must clear a section of old wall with blind tee shots). The clubhouse is patterned after a Scottish castle and contains collections of golfing monuments and memorabilia; the single-malt selection at the bar is predictably well above par. The city's oldest course, the par-72, 6,319-yard **Las Vegas Golf Club** (tel 702/646-3003, 4300 W. Washington Ave.) can be ragged around the edges and brown in spots, but the rates are the lowest around, with a year-round rate (including cart) of $29.75 for tourists. The austerely beautiful, Johnny Miller–designed **Badlands Golf Club** (tel 702/242-4653, 9119 Alta Dr.) has two courses: the original 18 holes, a hellacious drive through natural washes, canyons, and arroyos that favor the straight shooter, and the newer nine-hole Outlaw course, which has fewer desert obstacles to shoot past. Two pluses are a raft of reduced rates ("twilight tees" after 2pm are as low as $39) and golf carts equipped with Skyline, a satellite system that calculates distances and offers tips. Of course, there's also the ultra-exclusive Tom Fazio–designed Shadow Creek Country Club in North Las Vegas, which former Mirage Resorts chairman Steve Wynn underwrote to the tune of $40 million so he could play in peace with his buddies (like Michael Jordan and former president George Bush). MGM/Mirage Resorts guests can now experience its mystique and exceptional natural beauty on a limited basis, but greens fees are astronomical.

**Rockin' it...** Thousands of climbers from around the globe get a grip at **Red Rock Canyon**, making it one of the top five climbing areas in the United States, with dozens of moderate and tough ascents. The sandstone boulders and 3,000-foot cliffs provide endlessly diverse features, holds, iron nubbins, ledges, and cracks. There are so many side canyons that even on the busiest days, you can claim your own turf. The ultimate macho climb is the 7,068-foot ruddy sandstone peak Mount Wilson. There are several outstanding indoor climbing facilities in town, but only at **Gameworks** can you get your rocks off on the world's tallest freestanding rock-climbing structure—75 feet, with more than 900 holds. It attracts lots of exhibitionists who scale the heights in front of passersby on the Strip.

**Parking it....** There are more than 60 parks in the greater Las Vegas area, many offering pools, tennis courts, soccer and baseball fields, and paths for biking and in-line skating. Leagues, tournaments, and various cultural events are held throughout the year—call the **Las Vegas Department of Parks and Leisure Activities** (tel 702/229-6297) and the **Clark County Parks and Recreation Department** (tel

702/455-8200) for activities and schedules. Joggers, cyclers, and bladers appreciate **Sunset Park** (2601 E. Sunset Rd.) for the paths snaking through copses of trees and past limpid ponds; it's also a smash with tennis players for its eight courts, all lit for night play—just be prepared to wait (and wait...). Players sometimes hold courts until they drop from heat exhaustion. Fortunately, reservations are accepted, including round-robin play to prevent too much hogging. **Lorenzi Park** (3300 W. Washington Ave.) serves up a completely unpretentious tennis experience; the courts are well-maintained and usually crowd-free. **Floyd Lamb State Park** (9200 Tule Springs Rd.) comes up aces in the natural beauty department, with ponds stocked with trout, peacocks strutting about like showgirls, phenomenal fossil remains of Pleistocene critters such as giant sloths and woolly mammoths, and an extensive wetlands area filled with mallards, teals, and bullfrogs. For getting away from it all within city limits, you can't do better for picnicking, hiking, and fishing.

# The Index

**Adventuredome.** America's largest indoor theme park, under an enormous pink dome.... *Tel 702/794-3939. 2880 Las Vegas Blvd. S. Open daily, hours vary (usually 10am–6pm Mon–Thur, 10am–midnight otherwise). Admission free; ride tickets $3–5, or buy an unlimited rides pass.* **(see pp. 106, 115)**

**AJ Hackett Bungy.** Pleasant, efficient instructors do much to alleviate the terror of jumping off a 171-foot tower. And hey, you get a free T-shirt (the video's another $20).... *Tel 702/385-4321. 810 Circus Circus Dr. 11am–8:30pm daily (till 10:30pm Fri, Sat). Admission charged.* **(see p. 107)**

**The Arts Factory.** A cutting-edge compound with numerous

exhibition spaces, mostly high-quality.... *Tel 702/434-2666 or 702/383-3133. 101–3 E. Charleston Blvd. Gallery hours vary; most closed Mon.* **(see p. 120)**

**Bellagio Conservatory.** A remarkable three-story glass-domed botanical garden, where the flowers change seasonally at a cost of $5 million annually (a 90,000-square-foot greenhouse behind the hotel nourishes the various varietals).... *Tel 702/693-7111. Bellagio, 3600 Las Vegas Blvd. S. Open 24 hours daily. Free.* **(see p. 108)**

**Bellagio Gallery of Fine Art.** Showcases top-notch visiting collections from around the globe.... *Tel 702/693-7111. Bellagio, 3600 Las Vegas Blvd. S. 9am–midnight daily. Reservations required. Admission charged.* **(see p. 119)**

**Casino Legends Hall of Fame.** Collection traces the development of gambling in Nevada from its 1931 inception to the present.... *Tel 702/739-2222. Tropicana, 3501 Las Vegas Blvd. S. 7am–9pm daily. Admission charged.* **(see pp. 117, 118)**

**Circus Circus Midway.** Dazzling circus acts, decor, and ambience.... *Tel 702/734-0410. Circus Circus, 2880 S. Las Vegas Blvd. S. 11am–midnight daily. Free.* **(see pp. 105, 115)**

**Eiffel Tower Experience.** A half-sized replica for those who've never experienced the real thing.... *Tel 702/946-7000. Paris, 3655 Las Vegas Blvd. S. 10am–10pm daily (except during high winds). Admission charged.* **(see p. 121)**

**Elvis-a-Rama Museum.** With almost $4 million worth of Presley's personal effects, the largest collection outside Graceland.... *Tel 702/309-7200. 3401 Industrial Rd. 10am–7pm daily. Free shuttle from Strip hotels. Admission charged; children under 12 free.* **(see pp. 116, 117, 118)**

**Ethel M's Chocolate Factory.** Where Ethel Mars started her cottage industry a century ago. Don't miss the wonderful cactus gardens. Shuttle buses from M&M's World.... *Tel 702/458-8864. 2 Cactus Dr., Henderson. 8:30am–7pm daily. Free.* **(see pp. 106, 109)**

**Excalibur Medieval Village/Fantasy Faire.** From the animatronic dragon to the arcade and stage shows, it's cut-rate, but free free free.... *Tel 702/597-7777. Excalibur, 3850*

*Las Vegas Blvd. S. Stage acts 10am–10pm daily, dragon battle 6pm–1am. Free.* **(see pp. 105, 106)**

**Flyaway Indoor Skydiving.** A remarkably effective simulation of skydiving.... *Tel 702/731-4768. 200 Convention Center Dr. 10am–7pm daily (till 5pm Sun). Admission charged.*
**(see p. 107)**

**Fountains at Bellagio.** After-dark sight-and-sound show sends geysers of water 240 feet in the air out of Bellagio's 8-acre lake.... *Tel 702/693-7111. Bellagio, 3600 Las Vegas Blvd. S. Every half hour, dusk–midnight. Free.* **(see pp. 105, 112)**

**Fremont Street Experience.** Sound-and-light extravaganzas on the canopy of this five-block-long pedestrian promenade.... *Tel 702/678-5777. 425 Fremont St. Hourly, dusk–11pm (till midnight Fri, Sat). Free.* **(see pp. 105, 108, 114)**

**Gameworks.** This 47,000-square-foot entertainment experience offers hardcore games, a climbing wall, drinks, music, and food.... *Tel 702/432-4263. Showcase Mall, 3785 Las Vegas Blvd. S. 10am–2am daily. Admission free; games vary in price.* **(see pp. 111, 115, 125)**

**Guggenheim/Hermitage Museum.** Masterpieces from St. Petersburg's Hermitage and the Guggenheim Foundation in a postmodern setting....*Tel 702/414-1000. Venetian, 3355 Las Vegas Blvd. S. 10am–11pm daily. Admission charged.* **(see p. 119)**

**Guggenheim Las Vegas.** Huge, splashy art museum showcasing blue-chip traveling exhibits.... *Tel 702/414-1000. Venetian, 3355 Las Vegas Blvd. S. 10am–11pm daily. Admission charged.* **(see p. 119)**

**Imperial Palace Auto Collections.** An astonishing collection of motorized vehicles.... *Tel 702/731-3311. Imperial Palace, 3535 Las Vegas Blvd. S. 9:30am–11:30pm daily. Admission charged.* **(see p. 117)**

**Lake Mead/Hoover Dam.** The big dam and the big lake it created.... *Tel 702/293-8367 or 702/294-3522. 30 miles SE of Las Vegas on US Highway 93. From Las Vegas go southeast on I-515, which turns into US-93. 8am–5:45pm daily. Admission charged.* **(see p. 122)**

**Las Vegas Art Museum.** Eclectic exhibits by nationally and internationally renowned artists.... *Sahara West Library, 960 W. Sahara Ave. 10am–5pm Tue–Sat, 1–5pm Sun. Admission charged.* **(see p. 120)**

**Las Vegas Cyber Speedway.** Testosterone test-driving for guys and gals alike in a heavily themed environment, including the NASCAR Café.... *Tel 702/737-2111. Sahara, 2535 Las Vegas Blvd. S. 10am–10pm daily (till 11pm Fri–Sat). Admission charged.* **(see pp. 111, 120)**

**Las Vegas Motor Speedway.** Rev your motors for real, either pitted against other amateurs, or with pro instructors at this world-class facility.... *Tel 702/644-4444 (800/BE-PETTY for Richard Petty Driving Experience; 888/GO-DEREK for Derek Daly Performance Academy). 7000 Las Vegas Blvd. N. Reservations required. Hours and prices vary.* **(see pp. 107, 121)**

**Las Vegas Museum of Natural History.** Surprisingly fun stop, with several environments, ranging from old-fashioned dioramas to state-of-the-art interactive displays.... *Tel 702/384-3466. 900 Las Vegas Blvd. N. 9am–4pm daily. Admission charged.* **(see pp. 109, 114)**

**Liberace Museum.** Camp out at this shrine to Mr. Showmanship.... *Tel 702/798-5595. Liberace Plaza, 1775 E. Tropicana Ave. 10am–5pm Mon–Sat, 1–5pm Sun. Admission charged.* **(see pp. 116, 118)**

**Lied Children's Museum.** Wow! Cool! Geared to the emotional, intellectual, and physical perspective of a child, with more than 100 hands-on displays in its 22,000 square feet.... *Tel 702/382-3445. Las Vegas Library, 833 Las Vegas Blvd. N. 10am–5pm Tue–Sat, noon–5pm Sun, closed Mon. Admission charged.* **(see p. 114)**

**Lost City of Atlantis.** One of the best animatronic shows, which isn't saying much. Neptune gets pissy with his offspring and sinks Atlantis in retribution.... *Tel 702/893-4800. The Forum Shops at Caesars, 3570 Las Vegas Blvd. S. 10am–11pm Sun–Thur (till midnight Fri, Sat). Alternates on hour and half hour with Festival Fountain of the Gods Animatronic show. Free.* **(see pp. 105, 108, 110)**

**Luxor's King Tut's Tomb and Museum.** Exact reproductions of items found in King Tutankhamen's tomb by the 1922 Howard Carter expedition.... *Tel 702/262-4555. Luxor, 3900 Las Vegas Blvd. S. 9am–11pm daily (till 1am Fri, Sat). Admission charged.* **(see pp. 104, 118)**

**M&M's World.** Four stories devoted to 3-D movies, commercials, bad M&M murals, tastings, and sassy animatronics.... *Tel 702/736-7611. Showcase Mall, 3785 Las Vegas Blvd. S. 9am–midnight daily. Free.* **(see pp. 106, 118)**

**Madame Tussaud's Celebrity Encounter.** Not just a wax museum, but a multimedia interactive extravaganza done with Vegas pizzazz.... *Tel 702/367-1847. The Venetian, 3355 Las Vegas Blvd. S. 10am–8pm daily. Admission charged.* **(see pp. 112, 116)**

**Manhattan Express.** Prepare to lose your spare change on this "twist and shout" coaster through the New York-New York skyline. Lines are long, especially on weekends, for the 5-minute ride.... *Tel 702/740-6969. New York-New York, 3790 Las Vegas Blvd. S. 10:30am–10:30pm daily (till midnight Fri, Sat). Admission charged.*
**(see pp. 104, 106)**

**Marjorie Barrack Museum.** This UNLV secret gem displays everything from gila monsters to ceremonial dance masks to provocative modern art.... *Tel 702/895-3381. 4505 S. Maryland Pkwy. 8am–4:45pm Mon–Fri, 10am–2pm Sat, closed Sun. Free.* **(see pp. 109, 118, 120)**

**Masquerade Show in the Sky.** It's Carnival time, as gargantuan floats circle the ceiling and performers shimmy.... *Tel 702/252-7777. Rio, 3700 W. Flamingo Rd. Every 2 hrs, 4–10pm Thur–Mon. Closed Tue, Wed. Free to watch; $9.95 to participate.* **(see pp. 105, 112)**

**MGM Grand Lion Habitat.** Multilevel glass enclosure and "see-through" walkway allows you to view the majestic cats.... *Tel 702/891-1111. MGM Grand, 3799 Las Vegas Blvd. S. 11am–10pm daily. Free.* **(see pp. 109, 115)**

**Mirage Volcano.** Three-story volcano, flames, fake lava, gaping crowds.... *Tel 702/791-7111. Mirage, 3400 Las Vegas Blvd. S. Every 15 minutes, dusk–midnight (canceled during windy periods). Free.* **(see pp. 105, 108)**

**Mount Charleston.** Skiing, hiking, horseback riding and golf in pristine forest.... *Tel 702/872-7098 (park), 702/872-5462 (ski area), 702/872-5408 (lodge and stables). State Highway 156, 36 miles north of Las Vegas. Free.* **(see p. 121)**

**Neon Museum.** An admirable attempt to resurrect old signs from the neon boneyard.... *No telephone. Fremont St. between 3rd and Main streets. 24 hours daily. Free.* **(see p. 114)**

**Race for Atlantis.** A giant-screen IMAX 3-D motion-simulator thrill ride, projecting everything from sea dragons to spears on an 82-foot-diameter dome.... *Tel 702/893-4800. Forum Shops at Caesars, 3500 Las Vegas Blvd. S. 10am–11pm daily (till midnight Fri, Sat). Admission charged.*
**(see pp. 108, 115)**

**Red Rock Canyon National Conservation Area.** Just 20 miles from town, a dazzling repository of neon-colored rock formations, rich wildlife, and recreational activities.... *Tel 702/363-1921. Route 159 (head west from the Strip on W. Charleston Blvd.). Visitors center open 8am–4:30pm daily; loop accessible 7am–dusk. Admission $5 per car.* **(see pp. 109, 121, 125)**

**Secret Garden and Dolphin Habitat.** All about glorious animals and the efforts of Siegfried & Roy to conserve the environment.... *Tel 702/791-7111. Mirage, 3400 Las Vegas Blvd. S. 11am–5:30pm daily, Secret Garden closed Wed. $10 ($5 Wed Dolphin Habitat only). Children under 10 free.*
**(see pp. 108, 109, 110, 115)**

**Shark Reef.** A dramatic aquarium experience that really puts you underwater with the predators....*702/632-4555. Mandalay Bay, 3950 Las Vegas Blvd. S. 10am–11pm daily. Admission charged.* **(see pp. 110, 115)**

**Speed: The Ride.** Nasty fun for daredevils, lasting 45 seconds— or an eternity.... *Tel 702/737-2111. Sahara, 2535 Las Vegas Blvd. S. 10am–10pm daily, until midnight Fri. and Sat. Admission charged. Over 54 inches only.* **(see pp. 107, 111)**

**Star Trek: The Experience.** Pricey ride, but worth trek-king to for the nifty museum and futuristic environment.... *Tel 702/732-5111. Las Vegas Hilton, 3000 Paradise Rd. 11am–11pm daily. Admission charged.*
**(see pp. 108, 111, 114, 117, 118)**

DIVERSIONS | THE INDEX

**Stratosphere Tower/Strat-O-Fair/Thrill Rides.** An observation tower, the world's highest roller coaster, futuristic midway, and a truly scarifying G-force ride. Rides often closed due to high winds or inclement weather.... *Tel 702/380-7777. Stratosphere, 2000 Las Vegas Blvd. S. 10am–1am daily (till 2am Fri, Sat). Admission charged to Tower; rides additional.* **(see pp. 106, 107, 111, 121)**

**Sundance Helicopters.** The longest view tours of Vegas. Like all the heli-companies, they also offer weddings and Grand Canyon tours ($299).... *Tel 702/736-0606. Tours take off two blocks east of Mandalay Bay.* **(see p. 121)**

**Tiger Habitat.** Royal Himalayan White Tigers playing, swimming, and usually sleeping right inside the Mirage lobby.... *Tel 702/791-7111. Mirage, 3400 Las Vegas Blvd. S. 24 hours daily. Free.* **(see pp. 108, 109)**

**Treasure Island Pirate Battle.** "Pirate-technic" naval battle on block-long Buccaneer Bay—the town's best freebie spectacle.... *Tel 702/894-7111. 3300 Las Vegas Blvd. S. Every 90 minutes 4–11:30pm daily. Free.* **(see pp. 104, 105)**

**Valley of Fire State Park.** Nevada's first state park is an exceptionally gorgeous expanse of wind-carved red sandstone.... *Tel 702/397-2088. I-15, 60 miles northeast of town. 8:30am–4:30pm daily.* **(see p. 122)**

**Venetian Gondolas.** 236,000 gallons of water simulate the Grand Canal, which sits above the casino. The fleet of 40 gondolas, like everything else in Vegas, is certified authentic.... *Tel 702/414-4500. Venetian, 3355 Las Vegas Blvd. S. 10:30am–10:30pm daily. Admission charged.* **(see pp. 104, 107)**

**Wet 'n' Wild.** Water park with thrill rides, beach, lazy river, and pool for more serene pastimes.... *Tel 702/737-3819. 2601 Las Vegas Blvd. S. 10am–8pm daily May–early Oct. Admission charged.* **(see pp. 107, 110)**

# Las Vegas Diversions

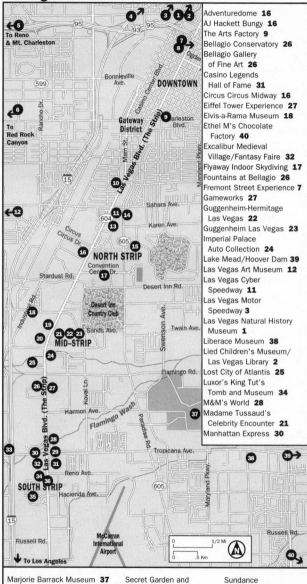

Adventuredome **16**
AJ Hackett Bungy **16**
The Arts Factory **9**
Bellagio Conservatory **26**
Bellagio Gallery
  of Fine Art **26**
Casino Legends
  Hall of Fame **31**
Circus Circus Midway **16**
Eiffel Tower Experience **27**
Elvis-a-Rama Museum **18**
Ethel M's Chocolate
  Factory **40**
Excalibur Medieval
  Village/Fantasy Faire **32**
Flyaway Indoor Skydiving **17**
Fountains at Bellagio **26**
Fremont Street Experience **7**
Gameworks **27**
Guggenheim-Hermitage
  Las Vegas **22**
Guggenheim Las Vegas **23**
Imperial Palace
  Auto Collection **24**
Lake Mead/Hoover Dam **39**
Las Vegas Art Museum **12**
Las Vegas Cyber
  Speedway **11**
Las Vegas Motor
  Speedway **3**
Las Vegas Natural History
  Museum **1**
Liberace Museum **38**
Lied Children's Museum/
  Las Vegas Library **2**
Lost City of Atlantis **25**
Luxor's King Tut's
  Tomb and Museum **34**
M&M's World **28**
Madame Tussaud's
  Celebrity Encounter **21**
Manhattan Express **30**

Marjorie Barrack Museum **37**
Masquerade Show in the Sky **33**
MGM Grand Lion Habitat **29**
Mirage Volcano **20**
Mount Charleston **5**
Neon Museum **8**
Race for Atlantis **25**
Red Rock Canyon National
  Conservation Area **6**

Secret Garden and
  Dolphin Habitat **20**
Shark Reef **36**
Speed: The Ride **14**
Star Trek:
  The Experience **15**
Stratosphere,
  Strat-o-Fair, Tower
  and Thrill Rides **10**

Sundance
  Helicopters **35**
Tiger Habitat **20**
Treasure Island
  Pirate Battle **19**
Valley of Fire
  State Park **4**
Venetian Gondolas **21**
Wet 'n' Wild **13**

# 4

# nos

Forget the PR
blather about Las
Vegas becoming
an upscale
destination—sure,
they're importing
world-class

restaurants, shows, and shops, installing artworks, and fabricating increasingly tasteful surroundings, but local shorthand still refers to all those "resorts" and "hotel/casinos" as casinos, plain and simple. The extracurricular activities may generate a higher percentage of revenue than before, but the focus remains on gambling—or gaming, as government officials and corporate execs prefer to call it.

Las Vegas itself is one big casino. The incessant warbling of slot machines greets you upon deplaning at McCarran International Airport. Video poker machines earn 7-Elevens more income than cigarette, coffee, and Slurpee sales combined. You can monkey around with a full electronic deck while grease monkeys pump your gas. Even hair salons are a beehive of gambling activity.

But the epicenter of this bizarre universe is the casino floor. Bugsy Siegel's fabled subterranean tunnels and escape routes at his original Flamingo are nothing compared to the mazes of **Caesars Palace**, the **MGM Grand**, **Circus Circus**, **Riviera** (arguably the most maddening layout), and the other major casinos, and there's a method to the madness: The more disoriented you become, the higher the odds you'll be sucked into the adrenaline high. Oxygen is reputedly pumped into the rooms to reinvigorate gamblers. There are no clocks or windows, lighting remains the same 24 hours a day, and trompe l'oeil skies with fleecy clouds are painted on the ceilings to create the illusion of endless daylight, to counteract claustrophobia and cabin fever. Colorful theme tie-in chips make you forget you're playing for real money. Such distractions as cocktail waitress cleavage and rounds of free drinks help keep players woozily rooted in place. All perfectly innocent, of course (and I've got a piece of the Brooklyn Bridge replica at New York-New York to sell you).

Not all casinos are alike. They run the gamut from redneck to blueblood. There are the "high roller" casinos, like **Bellagio**, **Venetian**, **Ceasars Palace**, **Aladdin**'s London Club, and **Mirage**. Millions are won and lost in private salons; decor is suitably grand. Then there are the mid-range casinos that offer the same facilities, as well as high-stakes rooms. Grimier and grittier Downtown is the province, mostly, of low rollers and old-time gamblers in ancient, smoky, claustrophobic casinos. One term you'll hear often is locals' hotels/locals' casinos (**Boulder Station**, **Texas Station**, **Palace Station**, **Sunset Station**, **Green Valley Station**, **Fiesta**, **Reserve**, **Santa Fe**, **Orleans**, **Gold Coast**, **Suncoast**, **Sam's Town**, **Arizona Charlie's West**, **Arizona Charlie's East**, and **Terrible's**), off-

Strip properties patronized by savvy locals for their regular prize giveaways, higher bonus points, faster comps, and better paybacks on more machines. All major venues feature the usual complement of games: blackjack, baccarat, craps, roulette, keno, and several variations on poker. Most also have some version of the Racing and Sports Book, an area filled with video monitors broadcasting every conceivable sporting event; you place your bets at the windows or from your seats.

Slots and poker are omnipresent. Believe it or not, slots used to be looked down on as being "for the wives," as they'd say in the '60s; typical pit bosses contemptuously referred to players as "worms." Now every slot area has an impressive SUV or Porsche on display for the winning. Look for "progressive slots" (where several machines in the house or connected casinos build up the stakes for higher payouts—like a lottery on speed). Regular players may join a casino's Slot Club or get a player's reward card; these function much like frequent-flyer programs, letting you accrue points at slots or table games to get cash back, special discounts, or VIP invitations. The "Player's Edge" column in the *Review Journal*'s Friday "Neon" section gives the skinny on the week's best bonus points deals. And always ask at registration about the casino "fun book," which offers coupons for everything from two-for-one dinners and discounted show tickets to free single plays at the tables (to ensure your money remains on site). As Anthony Curtis, publisher of the local casino bible, *The Las Vegas Advisor*, quips, "Gambling without a fun book is like sex without a condom."

If you gamble wisely and within your limits, the casinos provide unparalleled people-watching: poker-playing sharks with the cold-eyed, mind-numbing intensity of serial killers; big-assed, big-haired 25-cent slotniks, robotically feeding the maws of machines; and pinching, leering conventioneers. It's a glorious living theater—at times, of the absurd.

### The Rules, and the Odds

The Las Vegas Convention and Visitors Authority and similar organizations put out booklets describing each game and explaining the rules, as well as etiquette (e.g., when to tip dealers, when not to touch your cards). Many casinos offer free helpful "gambling lessons" daily—they do have a vested (or invested) interest, after all. The flip side of this is that pamphlets on addiction are omnipresent, and dealers aren't allowed to seat obviously addicted players (provided they can identify them).

The best advice is simply to study the rules, watch the

good players, don't get swept up in the endorphic excitement, and gamble sensibly *within your means.* As Kenny Rogers sang, "You gotta know when to fold 'em." And remember: There's no such thing as a sure system (or, lord help us, ESP hunches and lucky silver dollars). Some people swear that there are favorable slot positions (usually by the entrance station, on the theory that they serve as a lure), aka "loose slots." Don't bet on it.

## Gambling terms

*The casinos have a language of their own, as well. "Virgins" are first-time players, while "voyeurs" watch and wander. A "break in" isn't an attempt to rob the house: It's a novice dealer. "Steamers" are players who quickly increase their bets while winning, "chasers" those who raise their bets when losing (which could lead to their becoming "degenerates"—people who gamble to their detriment). "The grind" refers to low-end betting. "Niece" is self-evident: the young woman accompanying an older man. A tip is a "toke" (probably short for token). A "George" is a generous tipper (clearly old slang, since it refers to the president on the one-dollar bill). A "stiff" (aka "DOA") is someone who doesn't tip. A "whale" is a player with a million-dollar-plus credit line, as are Adnan Khashoggi, Bruce Willis, and Dennis Rodman. There are perhaps 250 whales worldwide, most of them obscure Saudi princes, Japanese CFOs, South American playboys, and former dictators' right-hand men.*

Casino-favoring odds are built into the rules of each gambling activity (tellingly, they're termed "negative-expectation propositions"). You can beat the slots, the roulette wheel, or the video-poker machine short-term, but continue playing, and the house advantage will catch up with—and surpass—you. It's simple mathematics and statistics. Games requiring little skill usually offer the worst odds. Keno leads the pack, followed by roulette, wheel of fortune, slots and video poker, and certain craps situations. If you play perfectly (and not even computers do that), the best odds are when the house advantage is 0.5 percent (blackjack) to 1.4 percent (craps). Compare that to 5.26 percent for double-zero roulette and 20 percent for keno.

Sure, some casinos truthfully advertise higher payouts on slots. Yes, there is a statistical advantage in the increasingly rare single- and double-deck blackjack game (that is, if you're Dustin Hoffman in *Rain Man*, or experienced enough to count cards surreptitiously). True, roulette odds decrease significantly from 1:38 to 1:37 when the double zero is eliminated (though the payout—this is where the house edge comes in—is $2 less). On video-poker machines, payoffs vary from machine to machine; look for those offering at least 6:1 for flushes and 9:1 for a full house (the norm is 5:1 and 8:1).

When all else fails, don't cheat. You'd be surprised how many idiots think they can get away with covertly substituting cards or pilfering a few chips from their inattentive neighbor. Dealers, pit bosses, and floor managers are ever vigilant. And see those elegant opaque black mirrors in the ceiling? That's the "eye in the sky," a security camera broadcasting and videotaping all activity upstairs in the casino manager's lair. Even if you're caught innocuously adding a few chips to your bet pile, expect judges to be stonily unsympathetic (after all, casinos make generous contributions to their campaign coffers).

## Getting Comped

Almost any casino bar with video poker serves a free beer or well drink if you give the bartender a ten and ask for a roll of quarters. (You can then wander off, ostensibly to play machines elsewhere in the casino, cashing in the quarters later. If they catch on, go to a different casino.) Or sit down in a Race and Sports Book, peruse a Racing Form, and look serious; waitresses will serve you, rarely checking whether you bet or not. This sometimes works in the keno area; a few casinos comp drinks while you place even $1 keno bets.

To qualify for a free dinner, let alone a room, you generally have to gamble at a $5 table for four to eight hours. Even experienced gamblers are likely to lose several hundred dollars in that amount of time (hey, at least that $9.95 buffet is all-you-can-eat).

The locals' hotels usually offer better deals; several Downtown properties will comp a weeknight room for guaranteed play of as little as $200. If you planned on gambling large amounts anyway, say chips of $25 or higher, ask the dealer for a rating card. Whenever you sit at a table, you hand over the card, the dealer enters how much you bet, and you accrue points toward fabulous "free" prizes. The magic words when the suits approach are "Can I do anything for you?" Bingo! You're comped. If you feel you've wagered a small fortune and casino staffers don't approach you, ask what level of play merits freebies—or find a friendlier casino (with less snob appeal). You needn't look the part of the high roller; long gone are the days (or rather nights) when dinner jacket and evening gown were practically de rigueur. You could probably wear a diaper and slippers as long as you can back up your credit-card slips.

Nonetheless, you can probably forget about those legendary V.I.P. suites. To rate those you must be at least a "premium gambler," guaranteed to wager $100,000 to $500,000.

They comprise fewer than 5 percent of gamblers, yet they account for nearly 30 percent of the town's $9 billion annual casino revenue.

# The Lowdown

**Friendliest pit staff...** Local casinos survive on repeat business and high volume; staffers often form relationships with customers, rather like the folks at "Cheers," where everybody knows your name. These include **Palace Station, Sunset Station, Texas Station, The Fiesta, Orleans**, the **Gold Coast**, and best of all, **Sam's Town**. Dealers are friendly, but the crowds are very savvy: a wonderful opportunity to watch and learn how to improve your odds. Patrons at Mardi Gras–themed **Harrah's** are practically encouraged to behave like Bourbon Street revelers; the eager-to-please staffers manage to be both refreshing and terrifying. At **Hard Rock**, the ultra-cool dealers (the men sporting goatees and single earrings) have been known to high-five big winners, while the comparatively nondescript **Bally's**—the most relaxed, least pumped-up mega-casino—has unruffled dealers who suit the almost calm atmosphere. They're particularly friendly at the crap tables, where they offer pointers during slow periods. **New York-New York** is a Disney-fied version of the Big Apple, which means that you won't be mugged in the Central Park–themed casino (you'll have to lose your money the old-fashioned way, at the tables), and the dealers are as polite and cheerful as, well, Disney tour guides.

**Cheekiest waitress costumes...** Cocktail server costumes can make or break Las Vegas casinos and have accordingly been the sticking point in some labor negotiations. Cocktail waitresses at the **Rio** lost the battle against skimpy costumes yet won the wage war: tit for tat. The thong-cut outfits they almost wear, not to mention seemingly unsupported décolletage, are marvels of engineering skill; no wonder Rio often hosts Larry Flynt in his gold wheelchair. **Orleans** adopted similar diamond/harlequin-patterned outfits that hike up into what can appear to be very uncomfortable positions. Red-and-black satin get-ups with provocatively plunging fringe neck- and hemlines earn **Texas Station** the "Debbie Does Dallas" prize. Me-Tarzan-you-Jane awards go to **The Reserve**, where the zebra-print outfits suggest a bordello at the foot of Mt. Kilimanjaro. **Mandalay Bay** waitresses are hardly demure geishas, wearing red-green-and-gold slit numbers that scream Suzie Wong. **Monte Carlo**'s mademoiselles have a touch of class sprinkled with Gallic naughtiness (significant cleavage); their outfits are fetishistic French-maid black lace with jade and scarlet brocade. The **Hard Rock**'s cocktail waitresses sport leopard-skin hot pants and leather bras—they look like they could strangle a mike and bring a crowd to its feet. **Caesars Palace** waitresses are perfectly coiffed, manicured, and made up, and barely clad in white, gold-embossed togas cinched with Gucci-esque gold belts. And Caesars is almost equal opportunity in this rather chauvinistic town: Gals have a chance to leer at the armor-bedecked "centurions" and "gladiators" standing guard.

**For nickel-and-dimers...** Downtown, **Lady Luck** teems with seniors fresh off the tour buses and honeymooners in RVs who feel lucky just being in Las Vegas. After a recent renovation, it's a brightened-up dump; motherly waitresses push drinks carts around, pouring liberally, and lots of freebies and constant promotions draw a knowledgeable local crowd as well as visitors. The **Gold Spike** boasts most of the town's remaining penny slots. Seniors fight over the coveted seats, and it's so smoky you wish those unsubstantiated claims that casinos pump oxygen through the room were true. **Slots A Fun** is a wild and wonderful cross between a sordid downtown bus depot and a honky-tonk arcade. Maybe it's the 99¢ half-pound hot dogs and 75¢ Heinekens. Or the wall of fame displaying Polaroids of big winners. Or the smell of stale beer and sweat. Don't discount it automatically: It's phenomenal for people-watching. The somewhat run-down **Palace Station** delivers nickel slots and 50¢ roulette and dollar blackjack tables aplenty. Among the heavy hitters, **Excalibur** has supplanted **Circus Circus** as the big cheese in town. This is where the Simpsons might go on vacation (it's certainly animated enough), with plenty of ye olde slot-o-philes with jangling fanny packs. Despite **Barbary Coast**'s plush turn-of-the-century look, it has a rep as a grind joint (low-end betting), with plenty of retirees hoping to augment their Social Security checks.

**Casinos Royale...** **Caesars Palace** defines swank. For all its occasional excess, it walks the high wire between kitsch and true luxe. Mirrors and marble columns galore; a restrained color scheme of ivory, gold, black, and white; and staffers clad in togas and tuxes define the Las Vegas experience. The **Las Vegas Hilton** is glittery and old-fashioned, with stained glass, Italian marble columns, and seemingly more Austrian crystal chandeliers than Vienna's Schoenbrunn Palace. **Aladdin's** goes ultra-posh with its 35,000-square-foot, self-contained branch of the London Club, an international gaming operator. Though most of the club is private, mere mortals can savor its suave, sophisticated ambience by eating at the art-filled restaurant or sipping premium liquors in its two elegantly appointed bars. Downtown, **Golden Nugget** is arguably the only casino that merits being called classy, with understated ambience and marble and brass decor reminiscent of a select European resort. In Summerlin, the **Regent**'s "European style" casino has oak wainscoting, cerulean walls, and an inner circle of table games topped by a magnificent dome. The Race and Sports Book resembles a gentleman's club, with cushy sofas and paintings of athletic events. Two smaller domes crown the two *salons privés*, with Axminster-style carpets, hand-carved wood columns, and comfy club chairs at the tables.

**Most witty theme...** The **Mirage**'s straw ceilings, lush creepers, tropical carpets, carved overhead jungle, and separate thatched areas provide the right exotic note. Fondling the perky breasts of the two bronze mermaids at its entrance supposedly grants good fortune (they certainly look impeccably polished). The **Venetian** is lavish but tasteful, with ornate tilework, Greco-Roman friezes, marble columns with gilded capitals, and molded ceilings adorned with hand-painted frescoes. **Texas Station** earns five Lone Stars for its clever design: Miniature oil derricks pumping above slot carousels; brick columns with friezes of bucking broncos and cattle brands; and Stetsons, horseshoes, harnesses, and antique Texan flags and maps dangling throughout. **New York-New York** conjures up Central Park: (fake) autumn trees, footbridges over a meandering stream, street lamps, and clever murals of the skyline. Tuxedo-backed chairs at the tables and yellow-cab change carts are other whimsical touches. **Paris** includes winding cobblestone pathways, Art

Nouveau Metro signs, fountains, cast-iron street lamps, a replica of the Pont Alexandre III, and a miniature Seine. Cocktail waitresses dress up as pert gendarmes in red-trimmed royal blue uniforms. *Très charmant.*

**Old-style flavor...** **Barbary Coast** epitomizes the bordello theme so prevalent in older Las Vegas casinos: a stunning $2-million stained-glass skylight, acres of red velour, and satellite-sized crystal globe chandeliers. The dealers even wear red garters on their arms. The classic **Caesars Palace** strikes the ideal balance between glitz and ritz that one expects of Sin City. Its Palace Casino is nominally higher end, the Forum lower. The high-energy Sports Book, traditionally where all the heavy betters and bookies hang out, particularly epitomizes old-time gambling adrenaline. **Stardust** combines Las Vegas grime with long-gone glitz: Gum-cracking cigarette girls patrol the premises like in a '40s film noir, while liquid crystal balls and mirrored columns scream the Studio 54 of the '70s. Downtown, **Binion's Horseshoe** is for serious gamblers, even at the low-end tables, where everyone looks gruff and dyspeptic. Talking (especially at the poker and blackjack tables) is kept to a minimum. The legendary home of the World Series of Poker, it has a classic Runyonesque feel.

**Over the top (even by Vegas standards)...** **Circus Circus** has toned down its glaring colors and busy decor, but it's still surreal. Since the Big Top area, with arcades and free circus acts, sits above the main casino, trapeze artists actually somersault mere feet above a few tables. Like a trailer-park version of Camelot, **Excalibur** dresses uncomfortable-looking staffers as troubadours, wizards, jesters, and fair damsels. It's a hallucinogenic vision of garish stained glass, faux-stone walls, heraldic banners, and neon scenes of knights slaying dragons. **Luxor**'s entrance *is* impressive, a temple gateway bookended by imposing statues of Ramses, but the clutter inside—Egyptian statues, hieroglyphs etched like graffiti on the walls, replicas of artifacts from the Temple of Karnak—seems incongruous amid the slots and gaming tables. The **Las Vegas Hilton**'s Space Quest casino, bathed in a bluish light, looks like it was created from spare parts of the Enterprise. **Aladdin**'s refreshingly bright, high-ceilinged design is overwhelmed by the loony *Arabian Nights* motif: Filigreed flying carpets dangle from walls and ceilings, a gaudy 36-foot-long Aladdin's lamp periodically emits smoke, and cocktail servers dress like extras from *I Dream of Jeannie*. A giant Lucky the Leprechaun greets guests downtown at **Fitzgerald's;** inside there's a genuine piece of the Blarney Stone (which, naturally, looks fake) to rub for good luck. Alas, it's not as deliriously kitschy as it used to be, but the ceiling is stamped with gold, and shamrocks are stenciled all over the walls.

**Don't live up to their billing...** On the Strip, the **Monte Carlo**, despite its superficial elegance, is soulless and second-rate. It strives for a Continental air, with stained-glass and mirrored ceilings, but disco blares, and there are $1 minimums during the week—no wonder the big spenders have deserted it. **Bellagio** is supposed to be the last word in posh, but its casino is actually rather crass and brassy, trimmed with orange and yellow or garishly striped awnings with equally glaring fringe. Expansions, razings, and renovations have completely obliterated all traces of the legendary Bugsy Siegel at the **Flamingo Hilton**, leaving only a migraine-inducing decor that includes blinding neon and mirrors everywhere. The **MGM Grand** offers state-of-the-art interactive slots and the latest trendy table games, and it mostly junked its blaring Cecil B. DeMille-on-Prozac decor in favor of more restrained, Art Deco touches. But the world's largest casino (four football fields long) is difficult to negotiate. Pseudo-exotic **Mandalay Bay** incorporates thatching, potted plants, Buddhas, Asian plaster moldings, and lagoons and lotus ponds in its casino, but the hip crowd really stays here for the high-tech, high-energy dining and entertainment venues. The **Tropicana** has an amazing stained-glass-and-mirror canopy ceiling (including cavorting topless angels as showgirls), but it's totally incongruous amid the otherwise Polynesian jungle of bogus palms, thatching, and loud umbrella-drink colors. The **Rio,** just off the Strip and frequently expanded, hasn't kept up its Carnival theme beyond some token masks; if any casino had a right to go full-blown gaudy and bawdy, this is the one.

**Worth leaving the Strip to see...** The **Hard Rock** wittily incorporates its signature musical motifs (guitar-handled slots, piano-shaped roulette tables, saxophone chandeliers); its memorabilia collection changes more often than the Billboard Top 100, but you might see a set of the Doors' drums, an Elvis jumpsuit, a Madonna bustier, or a jewel-encrusted Elton piano. There's such a high celeb-spotting quotient, gambling almost seems incidental. **Orleans** admirably re-creates the Big Easy: Grillwork balconies, masks, and plaques from various Mardi Gras crewes dangle from the walls, and Zydeco music keeps things hopping. **The Reserve**, with its safari theme, is well over the top, yet carries it off with sheer brio. The wittiest touches are the hippo wading pool, the crashed airplane whose pilot's scorched hand makes a wrong turn signal, and cavorting simians in outlandish dresses and pearls climbing the bamboo walls of the Funky Monkey Bar. **Sunset Station** features two distinct interior designs, one in Mediterranean Revival (a "village" with barrel tile roofs, balconies, and flowered shutters), the other favoring gem colors like amethyst and turquoise, with sinuous grotto-like walls studded with colored glass mosaic work. Three casinos Downtown almost double as museums: **Main Street Station** with its Victorian stained glass galore and architectural features from famous buildings around the world; the gilded-and-mirrored **Golden Nugget,** which displays the world's two largest gold nuggets; and colorful throwback **Binion's Horseshoe**, where hard-living founder Benny Binion's gun collection includes an 1869 Winchester rifle and original Smith and Wesson 32-caliber (when asked how many guys he'd killed, Benny supposedly responded laconically, "Just those who deserved it").

**High-roller havens...** Casinos provide semi-private rooms in little nooks for high-stakes gamblers (technically, they can't deny access to other players, but they find a way to make them uncomfortable). Many high-roller rooms are separated from the main action only by a velvet rope or marble railing, allowing you to steal covert peeks. **Caesars Palace** has several rooms with $1,000 minimum tables—tricked out in marble, velvet, and silk, they're opulent without seeming decadent (although the fawning staff seem like they'd peel their customers' grapes upon command). The intimate baccarat rooms are almost European in feel; hands of $100,000 and more are not uncommon. The action in the semi-private rooms at the **MGM**

**Grand** draws fat cats. The poker rooms at the **Mirage** are fabled for their killer jackpots and attitude. Other *salons privés* here are awash in Empire and Regency splendor. The snob appeal of **Bellagio** draws moneyed Young Turks to its private areas; even in the carefully segregated slots area, the ka-chings can't quite drown out the beepers and ringing cell phones. The Race and Sports Book features individual monitors and buttery reclining chairs; the poker salon is particularly impressive, from the luxuriantly padded swivel chairs to the murals depicting masked commedia dell'arte characters. At the equally intimate, but hardly hushed **Hard Rock**, Gen-Xers and younger boomers can flaunt their money in congenial surroundings—hey, any place that welcomes Dennis Rodman on a regular basis automatically becomes a big gambling spot (or a big gamble—your call). Traditionally the favored spot for high-profile conventions, the **Las Vegas Hilton** offers baccarat and high-roller sections cushioned with silk-swathed walls and velvet upholstery. The enormous Sports Book is ultra-luxe and high-tech (the video wall alone is second only in size to NASA's). Blackjack aficionados know it offers the most beneficent rules in town. Deep-pocketed big-biz types also like the **Venetian**, with its lavish re-creations of Venice's landmarks and high guest-room prices helping to keep the riffraff out. The otherwise low-roller **Stratosphere** has upped the ante with high-stakes blackjack, craps, and double-zero roulette: $3,000 minimum bets can escalate to a maximum $100,000, depending on the game and initial bet. At **Aladdin**'s London Club, there's a $10 million chip, the world's highest denomination, and the rock-bottom bet is $200. The **Rio** lures many high rollers off the Strip thanks to its superb restaurants and popular disco, Club Rio.

**Best bets... Fiesta** advertises itself as the "Royal Flush Capital," with the most players earning that 800-1 payoff. **Excalibur** offers Circus Bucks, a progressive slot machine whose jackpot starts at $500,000 (all for a $3 pull), and the Sword in the Stone, a free pull for $10,000. **Stratosphere**'s return on slots and video poker ranks among the Strip's highest. **Bally's** offers incentives such as "Push Your Luck Blackjack" (add a tie bet to your regular bet; tie four hands and your name could be drawn for $25,000), $1 million free pulls daily, and free scratch cards for prizes.

**Aladdin** is known for loose progressive dollar slots and plentiful 9/6 video poker. **Harrah's** offers the innovative "Play an Hour on Us" for first-time Gold Slot Club members: After one hour of tracked play on quarter or higher machines, you're compensated for losses up to $100. Allegedly a higher percentage of slots at **Fitzgerald's** offer cars as prizes than anywhere else in town, but plenty of others also offer cars as slot prizes: a BMW at the **Monte Carlo**, Mustang convertibles or Harleys at **Caesars**, and the occasional Lincoln Town Car or Caddy at the **Flamingo Hilton. Slots A Fun,** one of the last domains of the penny slot, also boasts nickel progressive slots and several single-deck blackjack games. At **Orleans**, poker tables offer occasional "bad-beat" jackpots awarded to losers with the biggest hands. Locals are keen on the cozy keno lounge at **Gold Coast**, whose gimmick is "Freeno": Register your six favorite numbers and hang around the casino in hopes of winning $100 to $500. A mere $2 for the Gold Coast's popular progressive game can net several hundred thousands of dollars when the meter ticks high enough. The odds of hitting your numbers remain constant no matter where you play keno, but **The Reserve** tames the beastly keno advantage with a Zero-Catch Pays policy on dollar bets—even if none of your numbers hit, you still win. Aficionados claim the video poker and slots machines here are the town's loosest. **Main Street Station** gives players who hit jackpots of 125 coins or more a scratch card worth $5 to $5,000 and its 20X odds on craps are among the town's highest.

## The Index

**Aladdin.** The themed casino is Moor for your money; the London Club exudes European elegance.... *Tel 702/785-5555. 3667 Las Vegas Blvd. S.* **(see pp. 142, 143, 146, 147)**

**Bally's.** A less-is-more casino that doesn't take itself too seri-

ously.... *Tel 702/739-4111. 3645 Las Vegas Blvd. S.*
(see pp. 140, 146)

**Barbary Coast.** Decorated like Jed Clampett's Beverly Hills mansion, it's often packed due to its strategic Strip location.... *Tel 702/737-7111. 3595 Las Vegas Blvd. S.*
(see pp. 141, 143)

**Bellagio.** Enormous and bustling, and an odd blend of old and new money.... *Tel 702/693-7111. 3600 Las Vegas Blvd. S.*
(see pp. 144, 146)

**Binion's Horseshoe.** Overflowing with character, and characters.... *Tel 702/382-1600. 128 Fremont St.*
(see pp. 143, 145)

**Caesars Palace.** Everything on a grand scale, from the classical statues to the cocktail waitresses' breasts.... *Tel 702/731-7110. 3750 Las Vegas Blvd. S.*
(see pp. 142, 143, 145, 147)

**Circus Circus.** Still the most surreal experience in town, especially while gambling under the Big Top area.... *Tel 702/734-0410. 2880 Las Vegas Blvd. S.* (see pp. 141, 143)

**Excalibur.** This low-rent Arthurian casino entertains boisterous crowds.... *Tel 702/597-7777. 3850 Las Vegas Blvd. S.*
(see pp. 141, 143)

**The Fiesta.** Locals' casino with possibly the most promotions and giveaways in town.... *Tel 702/631-7000. 2400 N. Rancho Dr.* (see p. 140)

**Fitzgerald's.** The Emerald Isle theme is blessedly less aggressive now; great spot for learning the games or scoring deals.... *Tel 702/388-2400. 301 E. Fremont St.* (see pp. 144, 147)

**Flamingo Hilton.** It's big, it's brash, and it draws plenty of package tour groups.... *Tel 702/733-3111. 3555 Las Vegas Blvd. S.* (see pp. 144, 147)

**Gold Coast.** Locals come here for keno and bingo bargains, as well as an excellent slot club and variety of machines.... *Tel 702/367-7111. 4000 W. Flamingo Rd.* (see pp. 140, 147)

CASINOS | THE INDEX

**Gold Spike.** Decor is like an alcoholic uncle's 1960s ranch house; come here for penny slots.... *Tel 702/384-8444. 400 E. Ogden Ave.* **(see p. 141)**

**Golden Nugget.** The class act Downtown—a handsome clientele and stylish digs.... *Tel 702/385-7111. 129 E. Fremont Ave.* **(see pp. 142, 145)**

**Hard Rock.** Youthful vibes and undeniable coolness.... *Tel 702/693-5000. 4455 Paradise Rd.*
**(see pp. 140, 141, 144, 146)**

**Harrah's.** By far the nicest middle-level casino, from attentive staffers to festive surroundings.... *Tel 702/369-5000. 3475 Las Vegas Blvd. S.* **(see pp. 140, 147)**

**Lady Luck.** Utterly lacking in any style—even trashy—but the most generous spot Downtown.... *Tel 702/477-3000. 206 N. 3rd St.* **(see p. 141)**

**Las Vegas Hilton.** An exceptional blend of old-style dash-and-flash and contemporary convenience.... *Tel 702/732-5111. 3000 Paradise Rd.* **(see pp. 142, 143, 146)**

**Luxor.** Despite the Ra! Ra! ancient Egypt theme, one of the better mid-level casinos in town.... *Tel 702/262-4000. 3900 Las Vegas Blvd. S.* **(see p. 143)**

**Main Street Station.** Filled with antiques and old-time deals. *Tel 702/387-1896. 200 N. Main St.* **(see pp. 145, 147)**

**Mandalay Bay.** Swank choice for the Gen-Xer with flash and cash.... *Tel 702/632-7777. 3950 Las Vegas Blvd. S.*
**(see p. 141)**

**MGM Grand.** The Hollywood-themed casino offers everything under the stars.... *Tel 702/891-1111. 3799 Las Vegas Blvd. S.* **(see p. 145)**

**Mirage.** A seductive combination of tropical languor and pulsating action.... *Tel 702/791-7111. 3400 Las Vegas Blvd. S.* **(see pp. 142, 146)**

**Monte Carlo.** Nickel slots mar the classy pretensions of this

CASINOS | THE INDEX

otherwise attractive room.... *Tel 702/730-7777. 3770 Las Vegas Blvd. S.* **(see pp. 141, 144, 147)**

**New York-New York.** Witty Manhattan-themed decor.... *Tel 702/740-6969. 3790 Las Vegas Blvd. S.*
**(see pp. 140, 142)**

**Orleans.** *Laissez les bons temps rouler* at this exemplary locals' casino.... *Tel 702/365-7111. 4500 W. Tropicana Ave.*
**(see pp. 140, 145)**

**Palace Station.** Ba-da-bing Bingo and inviting service keep this railroad-themed casino on track.... *Tel 702/367-2411. 2411 W. Sahara Ave.* **(see pp. 140, 141)**

**Paris.** Magnifique upper-middle-brow-roller casino.... *Tel 702/946-7000. 3655 Las Vegas Blvd. S.* **(see p. 142)**

**Regent.** Posh but not pretentious, it lures a well-shod suburban Summerlin crowd.... *Tel 702/869-7777. 221 N. Rampart Blvd.* **(see p. 142)**

**The Reserve.** Tongue-in-cheek gone-ape decor.... *Tel 702/558-7000. 777 W. Lake Mead Dr.*
**(see pp. 141, 145, 147)**

**Rio All-Suite Casino Resort.** Bustling, huge, slightly impersonal, but wildly popular with a range of gamblers.... *Tel 702/252-7777. 3700 W. Flamingo Rd.*
**(see pp. 140, 144, 146)**

**Sam's Town.** Old West decor and warm ambience mark this solid locals' casino.... *Tel 702/456-7777. 5111 Boulder Hwy.* **(see p. 140)**

**Slots A Fun.** A premier low-stakes (and high-amusement) facility, dirt-cheap in more ways than one.... *Tel 702/734-0410. 2880 Las Vegas Blvd. S.* **(see pp. 141, 147)**

**Stardust.** Popular for its many promotions and state-of-the-art Sports Book.... *Tel 702/732-6111. 3000 Las Vegas Blvd. S.*
**(see p. 143)**

**Stratosphere.** Wide spectrum of games and gamblers.... *Tel 702/380-7777. 2000 Las Vegas Blvd. S.* **(see p. 146)**

**Sunset Station.** A Mediterranean theme and the friendly vibe common to locals' casinos.... *Tel 702/547-7777. 1301 W. Sunset Rd.* **(see p. 145)**

**Texas Station.** Locals' spot to lasso a Texas-sized welcome.... *Tel 702/631-1000. 2101 Texas Star Lane.*
**(see pp. 140, 141, 142)**

**Tropicana.** A solidly middle-American crowd comes here, despite the fancy decor touches.... *Tel 702/739-2222. 3801 Las Vegas Blvd. S.* **(see p. 144)**

**Venetian.** High-glamour stakes, with remarkable duplication of Venetian art and architecture.... *Tel 702/733-5000. 3355 Las Vegas Blvd. S.* **(see pp. 142, 146)**

shop

# 5

## ping

Las Vegas no longer peddles only fuzzy dice, Elvis clocks, and rhinestone-studded apparel. From glitzy to ritzy, Las Vegas sells it all.

If you want flash and trash—appliqué, beads, feathers, sequins, bejeweled cowboy boots—you've come to the right place. But today's Las Vegas also offers leading department stores like Saks and Neiman Marcus, as well as hot-shot designer boutiques like Armani and DKNY. You can parade in Prada or get versed in Versace. **Forum Shops at Caesars** enjoys the highest average annual sales per square foot of retail space in the country ($1,200, which is triple the figures elsewhere). As of late 1999, total retail revenue along the 4-mile Strip exceeded $18 billion (more than New York's and San Francisco's combined). At this rate, the sounds of cash registers could almost drown out those of slot machines. Most major productions, theme restaurants, and hotels sell logo merchandise. And don't forget the kitsch souvenirs on tap at such attractions as Liberace Museum, M&M's World, Siegfried & Roy's Secret Garden and Dolphin Habitat, and Star Trek: The Experience (see Diversions). Most malls also offer animatronic and laser shows, motion-simulator rides, live pianists—anything to turn you upside down and shake those pockets loose of whatever the casinos didn't.

### Target Zones

Shopping areas, by and large, are clustered in mega-malls and hotel arcades, particularly along the Strip (**Las Vegas Boulevard South**). The only streets that offer a variety of stores are **South Maryland Parkway** (anything appealing to college kids and Gen-Xers—retro threads, indie CDs) and **South Rainbow Boulevard** (the interior-design drag, with dozens of galleries, furniture stores, and home accessories shops). Representing the "new" (or merely nouveau) upscale Vegas, **Via Bellagio** (Bellagio, tel 702/693-7111, 3600 Las Vegas Blvd. S.) is easily the most opulent shopping environment. The barrel-vaulted grand hallway contains chandeliers, potted palms, Axminster-style rugs, inlaid marble, an arched skylight of wrought iron and etched glass, and a gilded dome. Even the bathrooms have gold-plated fixtures. Prada, Chanel, Armani, Moschino, Hermès, Tiffany, and Gucci all showcase their latest lines. The **Bellagio Lobby Shops** (tel 702/793-7111) showcase more specialized boutique retailers, including renowned jewelers (Jay Strongwater, Steven Lagos, Barry Kieselstein-Cord) and glass artists (Dino Rosin, Dale Chihuly), at equally mind-boggling prices. Via Bellagio's inspiration was probably **Appian Way** (tel 702/731-7110, 3570 Las Vegas Blvd. S.), the elegant marble-floored arcade in Caesars

Palace dominated by its 18-foot replica of Michelangelo's *David;* upscale retailers include Cartier, Ciro, Godiva, and Marshall Rousso. But for the longest time, **Forum Shops at Caesars** (tel 702/893-4800, 3500 Las Vegas Blvd. S.) was THE discriminating destination, and it still houses both upscale (Dior to Dunhill to DKNY, Estée Lauder to Lalique to Polo Ralph Lauren) and populist (NikeTown, Guess?, Warner Brothers, Disney, Banana Republic, Virgin Megastore) among its nearly 100 outlets. The restaurants range accordingly, from Caviarteria, The Palm, and Wolfgang Puck's Chinois and Spago to Planet Hollywood. The celeb-sighting quotient is high (best vantage point: the "outdoor" patio of Bertolini's restaurant by the main fountain). The Forum Shops at Caesars patented the concept of shopping as entertainment, offering thundering, smoke-billowing animatronic shows like Lost City of Atlantis, IMAX motion-simulator rides, and a 50,000-gallon saltwater aquarium with hundreds of tropical fish with regular feedings by scuba divers (see Diversions). The design combines the streets of ancient Rome with Milan's La Scala arcades, underneath a "sky" ceiling that passes from sunrise to sunset every hour. Another high-end contender is the Venetian's **Grand Canal Shoppes** (tel 702/414-4500, 3355 Las Vegas Blvd. S.), a setting of "neighborhoods" lining both sides of the Grand Canal, with genuine marble balconies and cobblestone streets (the brick "exteriors" are cleverly retouched stucco). Extravagantly costumed street performers (jesters, harpists, magicians, jugglers) circulate. Big-name stores include Ann Taylor, Davidoff, Mikimoto, Burberry, and Lladro; it's a foot fetishist's paradise with Jimmy Choo (the late Princess Diana's preferred shoemaker), Ludwig Reiter, Rockport, Cesare Paciotti,and Kenneth Cole. The restaurants (see Dining) are the most superlative grouping of any mall in town. Specialty shops import exquisite Venetian crafts (Ripa di Monti's stunning antique and contemporary Italian art glass; Il Prato's delightful commedia dell'arte marionettes and papier-mâché masks). Attractions include the wildly popular gondola rides (see Diversions) and "Theaters of Sensation" adventure 3-D motion simulators. Paris's **Le Boulevard** district (tel 702/967-4111, 3655 Las Vegas Blvd. S.) provides a similar "authentic" ambience, albeit on a humbler scale, with street performers, cobblestone walkways, winding alleys, and mansard-roofed facades from various Parisian *arrondissements.* Virtually all the shops tend toward the oh-so-Gallic, including a wine-and-cheese emporium (La Cave) and lingerie store (La

Vogue). You can even buy Arc de Triomphe replicas (Les Mémoires), *Madeline* merchandise alongside haute kiddie couture (Les Enfants), or Toulouse-Lautrec posters (L'Art de Paris). **Fashion Show Mall** (tel 702/369-0704, 3200 Las Vegas Blvd. S.) plugs along in its own quietly tasteful way. There are plump couches, fake palms, enormous picture windows, marble floors, a high-quality food court, even a pianist on a grand playing classical, jazz, pop, and (ugh) lots of Andrew Lloyd Webber. It features higher-end department stores like Saks Fifth Avenue and Neiman Marcus, and such retailers as Bally, BCBG, Betsey Johnson, and The Body Shop. Construction on a million-square-foot expansion (the first segment to be completed in fall 2002, the second in fall 2003) has driven out several long-standing stores and restaurants; eventually the mall will have nearly 2 million square feet, including a tri-level Nordstrom, Bloomingdale's Home, and Lord & Taylor. Aladdin's **Desert Passage** (tel 702/862-0710, 3663 Las Vegas Blvd. S.), besides an impressive array of restaurants and nightlife venues (see Dining and Entertainment) including Bice, Commander's Palace, Josef's Brasserie, and Blue Note Jazz Club, has 130-plus stores ranging from international players (L'Occitane, Betsey Johnson, Hervé Leger, Hugo Boss, Tommy Bahama, Mont Blanc) to more individual boutiques (Jeanne Lottie's fanciful accessories, Joan Vass's fancy knitwear) and a U.N. of global home furnishings outlets like Sur La Table, African Odyssey, and Bernard K. Passman. A main rotunda, lined with Moorish arches, leads to seven themed sections, evoking the ancient Mediterranean spice routes stretching from India to Morocco. (One of them, Merchant's Harbor, replicates a North African wharf with the sounds of crying gulls, Persian rugs hanging from "balconies," and a 155-foot freighter docked in water.) Arches, parapets, onion domes, and minarets emerge from faux sandstone, and fountain-filled tiled plazas re-create souks with acrobats, belly dancers, henna artists, and "urchins" providing rides on Arabian "pedi-carts."

Needless to say, every major Strip hotel has a shopping arcade where you can pick up apparel, gifts, logo items, T-shirts, electronics, cosmetics, toys, etc. Among the most notable are **The Tower Shops** (Stratosphere, 2000 Las Vegas Blvd. S.), with 40 stores in themed environments (Paris, New York, Hong Kong, etc.); the **Masquerade Village Shops** (Rio All-Suite Casino Resort, 3700 W. Flamingo Rd.), with 26 retailers like Nicole Miller and

Speedo; **Street of Dreams** (Monte Carlo, 3770 Las Vegas Blvd. S.) where Anne Klein, Bulgari, and Cartier start off the ABCs; and **Star Lane Shops** (MGM Grand, 3799 Las Vegas Blvd. S.), including stellar names such as El Portal (with Coach, Dior, and Fendi leather goods and luggage). Circus Circus, Luxor, and Excalibur maintain their kitsch themes throughout the shopping areas and are fun for that reason alone.

Away from the Strip down in Henderson, **Galleria at Sunset** (tel 702/434-0202, 1300 W. Sunset Rd.) is the usual lower-middle-class outpost, handsomely designed in Southwestern style with terra-cotta stonework, cascading fountains, skylights, and interior landscaping. The duplex mall features 130 outlets like Dillard's, JC Penney, Robinson's, Mervyn's, The Disney Store, Gap, Eddie Bauer, The Limited, B. Dalton Bookstore, Ann Taylor, and Caché. **Meadows Mall** (tel 702/878-4849, 4300 Meadows Lane), offers 144 stores, anchored by Macy's, Dillard's, Sears, and JC Penney. Families especially enjoy its intricately embellished carousel, indoor oasis pool, live entertainment, and five themed courts, including "Natural History" (with "fossilized" floor complete with desert animal tracks). **Boulevard Mall** (tel 702/732-8949, 3528 S. Maryland Pkwy.), Nevada's largest shopping center, features more than 140 stores and an elaborate food court. Here you'll find comfortably familiar names like Macy's, Sears, Dillard's, Marshalls, The Disney Store, Payless, Gap, Radio Shack, Lane Bryant, Bath & Body Works, and Victoria's Secret.

## Bargain Hunting

Sorry, folks, this is not the place for endless white sales, though summer predictably offers numerous discounts. But you could scout Maryland Parkway, close to UNLV, for secondhand and cheaper stores. And the farther you get from the Strip and Glitter Gulch, especially at the locals' casinos, the better your chances of finding reasonably priced items. **Belz Factory Outlet World** (tel 702/896-5599, 7400 Las Vegas Blvd. S.) features more than 140 outlets, such as Saks Off Fifth, Calvin Klein, Fila, Royal Doulton, Esprit, Levi's, Reebok, and Waterford. For those who don't mind a trek, **Fashion Outlet Las Vegas** (tel 702/874-1400, at Exit 1 off I-15 in Primm, 30 minutes south of the Strip) offers more than 100 designers; shop here for Banana Republic, Kenneth Cole, Brooks Brothers, Coach, Lacoste, Tommy Hilfiger,

Benetton, Versace, Gap, J. Crew, Guess?, Jhane Barnes, Burberry, Polo Ralph Lauren, Williams-Sonoma, and Escada.

### Hours of Business

Most hotel shopping arcades remain open daily until 10 or 11pm, sometimes later on weekends. The major malls, especially those with dining and entertainment options, are open until at least midnight. Freestanding stores, especially off the Strip, cling to more old-fashioned hours, usually opening at 9 or 10am and closing anywhere from 5 to 7pm.

# The Lowdown

**Best for kids...** At the Forum Shops, **FAO Schwarz** knows how to put on a show. A 48-foot, smoke-spewing Trojan horse guards the entrance; then you dart past animatronic mini-rhinos and Star Wars storm troopers. The toy selection is huge; there's even a private high-roller room where prices run $3,000–$30,000. Also at Forum Shops, **NikeTown**, full of sports relics and interactive displays, will lift the spirits of any tyke or teen with its selection of Air Jordans and other overpriced sneakers. **Ron Lee's World of Clowns** sells Warners Brothers and Disney characters, as well as its own line of clown figurines; they don't clown around, throwing in a factory tour, rides on a glorious antique carousel, and a museum displaying clown costumes, props, and posters going back to Barnum's era. At **Build-A-Bear Workshop,** you customize your own fuzzy-wuzzy teddy or assorted other animal pals, dogs to frogs. After stops at the "Stuff Me," "Fluff Me," and "Dress Me" stations, your cuddly pal comes to life, whereupon "Name Me" computers create a birth certificate. Tots adore it. Illusionist stores are a dime a dozen in Vegas, but **Houdini's Magic Shop** not only sells everything from collapsible black top hats to Houdini handcuffs, it also stages magic shows and provides free private instruction for each trick purchased. The Grand Canal Shoppes outpost is the best, where the Houdini Museum showcases autographed pictures, letters, and Houdini's own handcuffs and straitjacket.

**Tackiest *tchotchkes*...** **Bonanza Gifts Shop**, which

advertises itself as the world's largest souvenir store, isn't as tacky as it should be. Roulette ashtrays, money lollipops (in various denominations), Area 51 merchandise featuring lime-green aliens, and sparkling dice pencil sharpeners are the best of the bad lot, along with the requisite Elvis memorabilia. At **Gambler's General Store**, a leading casino supplier, chips come in 17 neon colors (lime, aqua, hot pink) and over 120 symbols (dollar signs to astrological signs, palm trees to presidents). They'll even emboss them with gold monograms. And don't neglect those birthstone dice earrings and Vegas ties. **Houdini's Magic Shop** also peddles novelties that take the cheesecake: aliens pickled in jars, Area 51 badges, "living arms," even that old favorite, the rubber chicken. Or for a remembrance of Sin City, how about **Slightly Sinful**'s T-shirts reading "Peter Gun...Stick 'em up and spread 'em"?

**Souvenirs with panache...** Downtown, **Gambler's General Store** sells the truest Vegas souvenirs: gambling books and computer programs, chips, cards, craps tables, even video poker and roulette wheels and slot machines (for private use only; every state has different regulations, so ask before buying). Purchase authentic pieces of Vegas history at the **Casino Legends Hall of Fame** gift shop—vintage ashtrays, matchbooks, postcards, shot glasses, framed menus, card decks, and dice from over 200 Sin City hotels, many long closed, like the Apache, El Rancho Vegas, Landmark, Thunderbird, and Dunes.

**Campier than thou...** The Forum Shops has two art galleries that have to be seen to be believed: **Galleria di Sorrento**, which often has outrageous themed art shows, and **Galerie Lassen**, starring marine artist Lassen's oh-so-spiritual images of Hawaiian beaches and playful whales spouting off. There's a 2,700-gallon aquarium at the entrance, life-size sculptures of dolphins and sharks suspended from the ceiling, custom-painted cars, like a 1993 black Lamborghini Diablo, and a video wall projecting soothing sea images. Or, for a Vegas memento, how about a genuine showgirl wig from **Serge's Showgirl Wigs**? It features Raquel Welch's and Dolly Parton's collections, as well as several Elvis stylings, all hanging lovingly from beautifully chiseled face dummies mounted on columns.

Prices range from $150 to $1,500. (Check the phone listings for cheaper shops advertising "real human hair from $29.95," and hairstyles for the "transvestite/transsexuals set.") At Excalibur's **Dragon's Lair** you can buy real swords, halberds, shields, even a suit of armor hewn in Toledo, Spain. The kiddies will have to settle for miniature dragons and sorcerers. The **N'Awlins Store** (no, not in the Orleans, instead at the Rio) sells Cajun hot sauce, Mardi Gras masks, and voodoo items like *gris-gris* love potions, Dambala snakes, and dolls bristling with pins. At the Stratosphere, **Cleo's** features hand-crafted foot jewelry (dubbed "shoewels") as well as thumb rings, beaded anklets, toe rings, boot jewels, and waist chains.

**For collectors...** **Gallery of Legends** sells autographed balls, photos, and clothes (all new—no dirty uniforms or frayed jockstraps) from superstars like Michael Jordan, Jeff Gordon, Joe Montana, Muhammad Ali, and especially baseball stars, from Babe Ruth to Barry Bonds. They also carry signed albums by Aerosmith and ZZ Top; signed guitars from The Dead and The Stones; the requisite Rat Packer stuff (signed photos, chips, cards); and even the occasional TV prop (green scrubs taken right from *E.R.*'s operating room—no stage blood—and signed by the entire cast). The Tropicana's **Casino Legends Hall of Fame** sports an immense selection of books and videos celebrating Vegas's colorful past, from mobsters to musical greats. The Grand Canal Shoppes' **In Celebration of Golf** includes a re-creation of an old Scottish clubhouse, an art gallery (all golf images), animatronic figures, a display of antique golfing memorabilia, and an indoor golf simulator. It has a vast stock of apparel, books, and decorative objects, even a golf concierge arranging tee times. A special room of **Albion Book Company** displays the first issue of *Sports Illustrated*, editions of *National Geographic* dating back to the early 1900s, and first editions of books dating back to the early 1600s, most for sale. Funnies fanatics love **Alternate Reality**, where the latest Marvel or DC books are secondary to works by the industry's real superheroes: artists like Chris Ware, Evan Dorking, Robert Crumb, Dame Darcy, Roberta Gregory, and Frank Miller. Patrons at the **Ré Society Gallery** can watch printmakers run a rare 8-ton 19th-century French lithography press to re-create vivid vintage posters, from

Alphonse Mucha's voluptuous Art Nouveau goddesses to the angular designs of Deco maestros like Erté. Ré also produces prints, plates, and mugs depicting past and present celebrities (Judy Garland, Andy Warhol, Marilyn Monroe—and Drew Carey).

**Books and record deals...** Downtown, the **Gamblers Book Shop** offers thousands of titles on gambling history, table game strategies, even volumes about Las Vegas and Nevada history. Clerks even offer their tips on handicapping. **Get Booked** caters to the gay/lesbian population with CDs, jewelry, alternative-lifestyle books and posters, and catty/chatty local gossip. **Dead Poet Books** is slightly musty, smells of old hand-tooled leather, and stocks first editions of classics and arcane authors, with everything from metaphysical cookbooks to military memoirs. The 6,000-square-foot **Albion Book Company** holds 100,000 tomes (including valuable first editions), rare magazines, even sheet music. Among Maryland Parkway's many hip record stores, **Big B's** adventuresome selection satisfies anyone's jones for indie labels, new and recycled, and they often beat the behemoths' prices. Its friendly staff's encyclopedic knowledge of obscure titles is like something out of the movie *High Fidelity*.

**Retro-fitting...** Whether your fashion passion runs toward "Ralph Kramden" bowling shirts or "Jack Lord" Hawaiian shirts, sequined show costumes or studded rancher's boots, it's at **The Attic** somewhere. This Downtown shop's decor is delectably retro hippie, with zebra carpeting and plush crushed-velour seating areas. **Retro Vintage Clothing** displays owner Melina Crisostomo's unerring eye—antique Victorian lace, 1930s Chanel evening wear, Oscar de la Renta tailored business suits, and plenty of accessories, such as gloves, purses, and kooky classic sunglasses. **Valentino's** caters to the Swing Era revival, with everything from 1920s rhinestone anklets to 1940s zoot suits, pink Springolator mules to pencil skirts. For the ultimate in retro bijoux, scope out Tiffany's and Gucci's Via Bellagio neighbor, **Fred K. Leighton**, renowned for estate and antique jewelry, including items from the Duchess of Windsor's collection and Art Deco masterpieces from Cartier, Van Cleef &

Arpels, and Boucheron. At **Buffalo Exchange** you can find funky '70s stuff like tan suede leisure shoes and red platform shoes, along with hundreds of jeans, some rather grotty, but some fun, like bell-bottoms with hand-stitched peace symbols.

**Haute couture...** The **Armani** boutique at Via Bellagio displays clothing fetishistically for maximum impact. Skirts and shirts float in glass cubicles like astronauts in space station compartments. Mannequins sport TVs for heads. Translucent walls are lit from within, imparting an otherworldly glow to the suits, dresses, blouses, and trousers arrayed on single metal rods. Hunt down tiny **Ice** in the Forum Shops: Owner Dottie Chanin collects one-of-a-kind delights from her various international forays—silver, shawls, sweaters, and hand-painted silk and cut-velvet scarves. Also in the Forum Shops you'll find **Shauna Stein**, which scouts all the fashion shows in New York, Paris, and Milan for hot looks from Oldham to Valentino, and the over-the-top sequined and beaded bags of **Judith Leiber. Bernini** carries exquisite high-end Italian suits and accessories from Brioni, Moschino, Gianfranco Ferré, and Zegna; the original Appian Way shop is the ritziest, getting first dibs on exclusives like 22K gold-striped suits.

**Clubbier wear...** **Jeanne Lottie**'s fun, funky bags designed by Jane Ip are often "inspired" by Kate Spade, Prada, Gucci, and Vuitton (the graffiti-style handbags are dead ringers), but Ip's idiosyncratic eye also gets free play (hologram butterfly bags, clutches composed of faux newspaper front pages, purses appliquéd with orange shells). Also in the Desert Passage shops, **Soco**, the younger, trendier division of France's legendary Le Tanneur leather goods house, offers innovative nylon net and glacé leather totes and briefcases, embroidered with silhouettes in raffia to (faux) reptile skin—playful yet sleek fashion statements. The store also sells chic small leather goods, including shoes from a 16th-century Venetian footwear house. **Stash** carries such young hipster labels as Lucky Brand and Bisou Bisou, but specializes in explosively hued garments (hot pink studded tees) and band-wear like beaded jeans and faux-python slacks.

**To beautify your home...** **Unika** sells cool postmodern, old-fashioned items: distressed armoires, desks, and wine cabinets; marvelous earthenware urns and raku vases; and fanciful wrought-iron lamps. Mandalay Bay's **Bali Trading Company** imports the best that Indonesia and the South Pacific have to offer: hand-crafted teak chests, shadow puppets, batiks, hand-woven textiles like Ikat wall hangings, even sarongs. **Amen Wardy Home** at the Forum Shops is like no home on earth: Austrian glassware, ceramic cachepots, exotic wood armoires and screens, and hand-painted dishes. Even the wax fruit looks good. **Showcase Slots and Antiquities** offers antique video poker and slot machines galore, including a 1949 Jennings Sun Chief (the first lighted model), as well as vintage nostalgia items like jukeboxes, neon signs, and barber poles. Amid the rows of booths at **Red Rooster Antique Mall**, you'll find everything from china to clothes to cabinets. You could find something truly special: It's a fine line between antiquarian and junk maven. Alongside its vintage clothes, **The Attic** carries love-child-era furnishings such as chartreuse-and-purple mushroom stools, leopard-print lampshades, and 1950s TVs and radios. **Centaur Galleries** is a treasure trove of Russian arts and crafts: soulful icons dating from Peter the Great's reign to the Bolshevik revolution, as well as lacquered boxes and paintings. The gallery also carries wildlife sculptures in bronze or frosted glass and stacks of master prints by Picasso, Braque, Chagall, Dali, and Renoir: It's like ransacking the attic of a wealthy eccentric uncle.

**Forbidden delights...** What trip to Sin City would be complete without a naughty souvenir? **Slightly Sinful** offers boas, G-strings, even schoolgirl uniforms for those who want to play striptease at home; men, too, have a choice of Chippendales-style glitter. Let's not forget lingerie and evening wear for all fetishes, edible undies, and other sexual accessories from videos to vibrators. **Bare Essentials** carries "sexy theme costumes," often with strategic holes, as well as more traditional lingerie, provocatively voguish clubwear, and men's thongs that leave little to the imagination. **Paradise Electro Stimulations** is serious about stimulating your erogenous zones, with its plugs, dildos, and vibrators in every conceivable shape and size.

# The Index

**Albion Book Company.** Prized first editions and mint-condition used books.... *Tel 702/792-9554. 2466 E. Desert Inn Rd., Suite G.* **(see pp. 160, 161)**

**Alternate Reality.** Cool, colorful comics corner.... *Tel 702/736-3673. 4800 S. Maryland Pkwy.* **(see p. 160)**

**Amen Wardy Home.** Wild, wacky, wonderful home decor.... *Tel 702/734-0480. Forum Shops at Caesars, 3500 Las Vegas Blvd. S.* **(see p. 163)**

**Armani.** Faboo fashion.... *Tel 702/893-8327. Via Bellagio, Bellagio, 3600 Las Vegas Blvd. S.* **(see p. 162)**

**The Attic.** Vintage couture to retro home furnishings.... *Tel 702/388-4088. 1018 S. Main St.* **(see pp. 161, 163)**

**Bali Trading Company.** Superlative collection of South Seas items.... *Tel 702/632–7777. Mandalay Bay, 3950 Las Vegas Blvd. S.* **(see p. 163)**

**Bare Essentials.** Vegas's largest store for naughty apparel.... *Tel 702/247-4711. 4029 W. Sahara Ave.* **(see p. 163)**

**Bernini.** Upscale Italian men's fashions.... *Tel 702/893-7786. Appian Way, Caesars Palace, 3570 Las Vegas Blvd. S.* **(see p. 162)**

**Big B's.** Eclectic playlist at great indie record store.... *Tel 702/732-4433. 4761 S. Maryland Pkwy.* **(see p. 161)**

**Bonanza Gifts Shop.** World's largest souvenir shop.... *Tel 702/385–7359. 2460 Las Vegas Blvd. S.* **(see p. 158)**

**Buffalo Exchange.** Retro store with a few funky finds.... *Tel 702/791–3960. 4110 S. Maryland Pkwy.* **(see p. 162)**

**Build-A-Bear Workshop.** Where kids can create teddies from scratch....*Tel 702/836-0899. Desert Passage, 3663 Las Vegas Blvd. S.* **(see p. 158)**

**Casino Legends Hall of Fame.** Vintage Vegas artifacts, including Rat Pack memorabilia....*Tel 702/739-5444. Tropicana, 3501 Las Vegas Blvd. S.* **(see p. 160)**

**Centaur Galleries.** Eclectic artworks for sale....*Tel 702/737-0004. Fashion Show Mall, 3200 Las Vegas Blvd. S.* **(see p. 163)**

**Cleo's.** A foot fetishist's fantasy.... *Tel 702/385-6924. Tower Shops, Stratosphere, 2000 Las Vegas Blvd. S., #44.* **(see p. 160)**

**Dead Poet Books.** Model used bookstore.... *Tel 702/227-4070. 3858 W. Sahara Ave.* **(see p. 161)**

**Dragon's Lair.** Ersatz Camelot weaponry.... *Tel 702/597–7777. Excalibur, 3850 Las Vegas Blvd. S.* **(see p. 160)**

**FAO Schwarz.** Huge high-end toy store.... *Tel 702/796-6500. Forum Shops at Caesars, 3500 Las Vegas Blvd. S.* **(see p. 158)**

**Fred K. Leighton.** Rare goodies culled from famous estates.... *Tel 702/693-7050. Via Bellagio, 3600 Las Vegas Blvd. S.* **(see p. 161)**

**Galerie Lassen.** 7,000-square-foot shrine to the art of Christian Riese Lassen.... *Tel 702/631-6900. Forum Shops at Caesars, 3500 Las Vegas Blvd. S.* **(see p. 159)**

**Galleria di Sorrento.** How's this for garish: a $7,000 4-foot-tall, 1-inch-wide cartoon canvas of a hippo with a bird of prey hitching a ride.... *Tel 702/369-8000. Forum Shops at Caesars, 3500 Las Vegas Blvd. S.* **(see p. 159)**

**Gallery of Legends.** Memorabilia, from jocks to rockers.... *Tel 702/471-8300. Desert Passage, 3663 Las Vegas Blvd. S.* **(see p. 160)**

SHOPPING | THE INDEX

**Gambler's Book Shop.** A virtual library on gambling....*Tel 702/382-7555. 630 S. 11th St.* **(see p. 161)**

**Gambler's General Store.** One-stop shopping for gambling paraphernalia.... *Tel 702/382-9903. 800 S. Main St.*
**(see p. 159)**

**Get Booked.** Books, CDs, coffee, and light cruising for gays and lesbians.... *Tel 702/737-7780. 4640 Paradise Rd.* **(see p. 161)**

**Houdini's Magic Shop.** Disappear for hours in this magical shop.... *Tel 702/798-4789 (general); 702/796-0301 (Venetian branch). Grand Canal Shoppes branch, 3355 Las Vegas Ave. S.* **(see pp. 158, 159)**

**Ice.** Unique high-end design items....*Tel 702/696-9700. Forum Shops, 3500 Las Vegas Blvd. S.* **(see p. 162)**

**In Celebration of Golf.** A virtual golf museum, with memorabilia including trophies and autographed photos.... *Tel 702/733-5000. Grand Canal Shoppes, Venetian, 3355 Las Vegas Blvd. S.* **(see p. 160)**

**Jeanne Lottie.** Stunning high-concept handbags....*Tel 702/836-3288. Desert Passage, 3663 Las Vegas Blvd. S.*
**(see p. 162)**

**Judith Leiber.** Glitzy handbags.... *Tel 702/731-7110. Forum Shops at Caesars, 3500 Las Vegas Blvd. S.* **(see p. 162)**

**N'Awlins Store.** *Gris-gris* dolls, masks, and Cajun spices.... *Tel 702/252–7777. Rio All-Suite Casino Resort, 3700 W. Flamingo Rd.* **(see p. 160)**

**NikeTown.** You know you want to pay too much for that logo sweatshirt. Just do it.... *Tel 702/650-8888. Forum Shops at Caesars, 3500 Las Vegas Blvd. S.* **(see p. 158)**

**Paradise Electro Stimulations.** Everything motorized to stimulate your love muscles. Call for appointments.... *Tel 702/474-2991. 1509 W. Oakey Blvd.* **(see p. 163)**

**Ré Society Gallery.** Classic posters re-mastered on site, plus pop-culture images.... *Tel 702/792-2278. Paris, 3655 Las Vegas Blvd. S.* **(see p. 160)**

SHOPPING | THE INDEX

**Red Rooster Antique Mall.** Endless selection of old stuff, wildly varying in quality.... *Tel 702/382–5253. 307 W. Charleston Blvd.* **(see p. 163)**

**Retro Vintage Clothing.** Funky and classic vintage clothes and accessories.... *Tel 702/877-8989. 906 S. Valley View Blvd.* **(see p. 161)**

**Ron Lee's World of Clowns.** Top doll manufacturers, with tour and museum connected to shop.... *Tel 702/434-1700. 330 Carousel Pkwy.* **(see p. 158)**

**Serge's Showgirl Wigs.** The ultimate in showgirl paraphernalia.... *Tel 702/732-1015. 953 E. Sahara Ave., Suite A-2.* **(see p. 159)**

**Shauna Stein.** Haute couture for truly discriminating women.... *Tel 702/893-9786. Forum Shops at Caesars, 3500 Las Vegas Blvd. S.* **(see p. 162)**

**Showcase Slots and Antiquities.** Classic pieces of Americana.... *Tel 702/740-5722. 4305 S. Industrial Rd., Suite B-110.* **(see p. 163)**

**Slightly Sinful.** Leather, lace, and spangles for the sexually playful.... *Tel 702/387-1006. 1232 Las Vegas Blvd. S.* **(see pp. 159, 163)**

**Soco.** Cutting-edge accessories.... *Tel 702/836-0830. Desert Passage, 3663 Las Vegas Blvd. S.* **(see p. 162)**

**Stash.** Playful neo-retro fashions.... *Tel 702/804-1640. 9410 W. Sahara Ave.* **(see p. 162)**

**Unika.** Tasteful yet fun furnishings and accessories.... *Tel 702/258-0773. 1238 S. Rainbow Blvd.* **(see p. 163)**

**Valentino's.** Vintage threads.... *Tel 702/383-9555. 906 S. 6th St.* **(see p. 161)**

SHOPPING | THE INDEX

# 6

# tlife

"In this town," wrote Hunter S. Thompson, "they love a drunk. Fresh meat." Wine bars, beer bars, martini bars, vodka bars made from ice, cigar bars, oxygen bars, singles bars, bare-all bars: You name it, you'll find a watering hole of your choice. And of course, there are the casino lounges, many offering free shows as a break between gambling and eating. Meanwhile, most of the top restaurants (see Dining) have zoo-like singles-bar scenes, discos, and even after-hours clubs.

In Las Vegas, beefy ranchers and red-faced insurance salesmen will always ogle cocktail waitresses and topless dancers. Leather-skinned divorcees still tap long varnished nails while listening to lounge lizards in piano bars. But the possibilities have expanded exponentially; the Strip's new glam image brings in younger, trendier travelers, and dress codes and attitude are making inroads. Corporate sharks of both sexes enact mating rituals in sleek microbreweries and cigar bars. Underage candy ravers clutching dolls, pacifiers, and stuffed animals trance dance in deserted warehouses splashed with graffiti. Ponytailed neo-hipsters and navel-pierced goth chicks frequent coffeehouses showcasing obscenity-laced poems of existential despair. The club scene here was more sock hop than hip-hop a mere six years ago, but newly trendoid Las Vegas now appropriates the night-crawling frenzy of New York and L.A.

Casinos have been aggressively importing famed nightlife mavens, from club promoters to international DJs. David Rabin and Will Regan from Manhattan (Lotus) and L.A.'s Brad Johnson (Sunset Room) jumpstarted the craze with the Venetian's smash **V Bar**. New York-New York replicated Manhattan's **Coyote Ugly**, where 35 sassy female bartenders perform bar-top stunts. Bellagio entered the sweepstakes in January 2002 with the Euro-elegant **Light**, a collaboration between film producer/Planet Hollywood co-creator Keith Barish, his son Chris, and Andrew Sasson of Southampton's trendy Jet East; from the candlelit entrance to the Baccarat crystal and sterling silver ice buckets, this tony newcomer has attracted celebs like Tobey Maguire, David Spade, Gisele Bundchen, Rachel Hunter, and Luke and Owen Wilson. Aladdin signed up bicoastal impresario Mark Fleischman to launch a new incarnation of his Manhattan supper club **Tatou**, which will include a four-story glass box entrance spitting fire onto the Strip, a lobby waterfall, and DJs on a fog-and-flame-spewing hydraulic ball swooping over the dance floor. Michael Morton (brother of Hard Rock founder Peter Morton) introduced several venues at The Palms, including **Nines Steakhouse** (with its sizzling designer 'tini/sake and champagne/caviar bars), the rooftop

**Ghostbar**, **Skin Bar** (with late-night pool parties), and the impressive **Rain** dance club. The Palms also reincarnated Paris's soigné Buddha Bar as the sumptuously decadent, Indochinese-inspired **Little Buddha** (its *pièce de resistance*: a remarkable "river" sushi bar). Cindy Crawford's hubby, Rande Gerber, created two fabulous venues for the Green Valley Ranch Station Casino: the minimalist **drop bar**, already one of the town's most sophisticated watering holes; and **Whiskey Sky**, a vision of dramatically lit lucite surfaces spilling into an 8-acre infinity pool area with Gerber's trademark pillow-strewn mattresses and reservation-only "opium dens."

Showrooms have been converted into nightclubs even at the locals casinos, notably Sunset Station's multi-facility **Club Madrid** (where weekends often feature the band of former Madonna dancer Louie Louie, with its percussive powerhouse pop) and **Sam's Town Live!**, which removes its steel bleachers on weekends to create a partly open-air nightclub with retro bands, DJs, and dancers.

## Sources

Most freebie rags (see Sources in Entertainment) offer lounge act listings and the occasional coupon. You'll also find nightlife suggestions in *NEON*, the *Las Vegas Review Journal*'s weekend arts section (also accessible online at *www.lvrj.com*), as well as *City Life* and *Las Vegas Weekly*. The catch-all website for conventional conventioneer fare is *www.lvshowbiz.com*. Another option is the gushy but reasonably comprehensive *www.ilovevegas.com*. Both *www.lvlocalmusicscene.com* and *www.sincitysounds.com* exhaustively catalog the music scene, including the best places to buy—or wear—vinyl. The edgy websites *www.five-one.com* and *www.indievegas.com* carry info and links to everything from raves to body art studios. Another good source for alternative venues is **Liquid 303 Records** (tel 702/383-3285, 320 E. Charleston Blvd., #105). For those who want a sneak peak at the girlie show action, try *www.stripclubreview.com*.

## What It Will Cost

Nearly every watering hole offers some kind of entertainment. Covers and minimums vary according to venue and act. Generally, discos and nightclubs charge a $10 to $20 cover for men, $5 for women (local women free, according to the "men are boobs, women have boobs" philosophy of marketing). Most local bars have a $5 cover for their acts. Classier casino lounges levy a one- or two-drink minimum. Name performers, wherever they roost, will up the ante anywhere from $20 to $50. The strip clubs (whether topless or fully bared) usually charge a $10 cover and/or a two-drink minimum (exceptions are "fantasy rooms" and private booths in nude clubs, which may charge $15 or $20). Lap dances invariably run $20, no matter how high-toned or sleazy the venue. They're pretty tame—no touching or solicitation is allowed.

### Liquor Laws and Drinking Hours

The drinking age here is 21, and it's strictly enforced—if you look at all youthful, expect to be carded on and around the Strip approximately every 20 steps. Anything remotely resembling a dance place has a draconian 21-and-over code as well. Note that with one exception, totally nude joints aren't permitted to serve alcohol (which means that, ironically, an 18-year-old can gain entrance to nude but not topless bars).

The city also has remarkably tough drunk-driving laws (given the traffic nightmares and dangerous intersections, that's understandable). Stern local law officers straight from central casting make you feel like you're about to be trapped in a Turkish prison for 20 years. On the plus side, several non-casino bars and clubs offer free cab service back to your hotel if you're sloshed to the gills.

Clubs usually don't open, or at least don't start hopping, before 10pm. Lounges and bars usually remain open 24 hours, except for coffeehouses and some non-casino venues. Most bump-and-grind joints open by noon; you can "lap" up the action until 4am, if not all through the night. Liquor flows 24/7.

### Drugs

Yes, they exist. Yes, they're illegal. But they're plentiful, especially at raves and anywhere the younger set congregates. Allegedly, it's easy to score vitamins X (MDMA, aka Ecstasy) and K (Keta-mine, an equine tranquilizer), and rumors abound that there's plenty of cocaine-dealing in the bathrooms of some strip clubs and discos. As one local jokes, that could be why they're all furnished with either stainless steel or black porcelain fixtures.

# The Lowdown

**Big throbbing dance clubs...** Before the club craze finally hit Las Vegas, dance venues were cheesy approximations of big-city-slicker discos. Now fashion fascists increasingly patrol the scene, and the thugs at the door are as self-important as they are in New York and L.A. On the Strip, the three-level **Club Utopia** is as goth as Vegas gets. It not only draws leading DJs from New York, Miami, and London, it has spawned its own famed spin-meisters like Robert Oleysyck and DJ Speedy. The music is techno, tribal, progressive house, trance, funk, electronica, and rave; the lighting system is the city's wildest, and the trappings include fire-eaters and illuminated go-go cages. In numerous dark corners, multiply pierced couples redefine liplock. The Rio's much more refined **Club Rio** has brass railings, crystal globes, cushy booths, and a stalactite chandelier, but otherwise, it's extremely high-tech, with laser lighting, superior sound, and video banks on either side. A canny mix of canned dance music draws a dressed-up crowd of attractive folks hoping to meet other attractive folks. The Luxor's glitzy **Ra** is an eye-catching blend of barely clad go-go girls, sweeping lasers, and a pretty crowd gyrating to a sensational techno/ska/house mix; scenes of ancient Egypt alternate epileptically with the latest videos on giant screens. Top '80s bands and rappers like Doug E. Fresh and Run DMC occasionally play; visiting megawatt DJs, from Paul Oakenfeld to John Dyweed, blast progressive house, trance, and electronica at Wednesday's *Pleasuredome*, while resident spinners Duane King, Warren Peace, and McKenzie keep the house hip-hopping on *Mecca Fridays* and *Sultry Saturdays*. Trendoid quotient: two cigar lounges, a raw bar, and strong-Armanied dudes in headsets enforce dress codes at the door. Tri-level **Studio 54**, at the MGM Grand, not only displays the trademark moon of the original, but pays homage with a big crystal ball, leopard-print upholstery, cocktail waitresses in blue-spangled hot pants, and framed photos of regulars from the old 54, like Andy Warhol, Liza Minnelli, Halston, Liz Taylor, and Truman Capote. House DJs and high-energy retro acts like Kool & the Gang help clueless twentysomethings keep the beat with model wannabes and their sugar granddaddies. Nearby at **Baby's**, the Hard Rock's ultra-glam underground nightclub, a thousand gorgeous people sweat discreetly to the tunes spun by resident DJs "The Funkler" (aka Mike Fuller) and Robert Oleysyck. Psychedelic images of '60s happenings strobe on translucent walls, and tiny dance areas are interspersed with nooks where there's plenty of heavy petting on plush leather sofas. Venetian's **C2K** compensates for an awkward layout (four semicircular levels woven with industrial cat tracks) by importing globally renowned theme-night promoters like San Francisco's Spundae, London's Gatecrasher, and San Diego's Sinurgey. Go-go girls and boys shimmy everywhere, while the stylishly underdressed crowd's gyrations are displayed on large monitors. East of the Strip, well-heeled thirty-something professionals hang at **The Hop/Glo**'s popular after-hours bashes, especially Wednesday's *Twisted*, a scintillating "SIN" (Service Industry Night), where the town's sexiest bartenders and dealers let loose. The mixes, from top DJs like Speedy and Adam Webb, range from trance to deep house to rave. At the Rain part of The Palms' multilevel **Ghostbar/Rain**, fire plumes, fog, and showers spray a bamboo dance floor that virtually floats in a moat with dancing jets and fountains, while lasers, neon strobes, and music videos flicker over two-story waterwall projection screens.

**Dancing cheek to chic...** Posh and intimate, the Las Vegas Hilton's **The Nightclub** has blue and mauve strobe lights, frosted-glass panels, and lasers; its featured acts range from resurrected stars (Sheena Easton, a revelation) to assured dance/funk bands (Forward Motion, A51, Groove City). The top level of Mandalay Bay's **rumjungle** is a sizzling little club; the DJ booth sits right above the *churrascaria* where Brazilian barbecue turns on a spit, and the dance floor adjoins the fire pits. Live entertainment leans toward the exotic, with dancers, aerialists, acrobats, and percussionists prowling the walkway in neon-accented animal prints; occasionally there's live samba, reggae, or jungle trip-hop—the world's two largest conga drums are built right into the floor. After performances, **House of Blues** at Mandalay Bay converts into a stylish club, with laser beams sweeping the folk art trappings for an almost psychedelic effect: Alice on acid. The motto is "diversity, unity, love, and energy breed"; the music is whatever's terminally hip at the moment. **Seven**, a haunt for the *Ocean's Eleven* cast while shooting, is a handsomely retro restaurant/club with a sunken dance floor, inside/outside sushi bar, and patio with smashing Strip views. Each room vibrates to a different style of music, from trance to hip-hop. During poolside *Hush* evenings at **Sky Lounge**, the Strip's neon signs teasingly glimmer in the rooftop pool, while partyers luxuriate on giant "beds" or dance to the lounge/down-tempo spins of

Mike Fuller and Adam Cantrell. At the Barbary Coast, underground **Drai's** is transformed from a tony Provençal/Pacific Rim eatery into an after-hours club with long lines, extreme door 'tude, and 200 folks stuffed into an un-air-conditioned room to groove on the super trance, progressive, deep house spinning of resident DJs Adam Webb and Chris Johnson. The sizzling mix at **Gipsy**, the big gay dance club on Paradise, favors '80s trash disco, neo-disco, and Euro dance music. The dirtiest dancing is on Monday Latin nights, hosted by the lovely if foul-mouthed Miss Cha Cha. West of the Strip, neo-futuristic **Breathe Oxygen Bar** has become party central for the Vegas rave underground, dispensing herbal martinis and smoothies and holding alt events every couple of weeks (including performance art so cutting-edge it draws blood). The DJ spins a righteous funk/soul/house/acid jazz mix Thursdays through Saturdays at Venetian's **V Bar**, while a well-connected crowd grooves in the post-modern warehouse setting.

**Boogie nights...** Resplendent in pimp chic—towering Afro wigs, bell-bottoms, and platform shoes—Jungle Boogie rotates among the big clubs, including the Monte Carlo's **Monte Carlo Brew Pub**, which combines hunkered-down microbrewery coziness with a high-tech dance floor. **Armadillo Lounge**, at Texas Station, crosses *Saturday Night Fever* with Southwestern chic on *Disco Inferno* Thursdays, when the leisure suits and capri pants are favored in desert pastels. Rocking cover band Love Shack shimmies in weekends to perform its spot-on versions of '80s icons from Devo to Depeche Mode to the B-52's (complete with beehive wigs). **House of Blues** also revisits the '80s, with *Flashback Fridays*, bringing out of the woodwork all sorts of Karma Chameleons in spiked moussed hair and skinny ties; the *Groove Factory* punches in on Saturdays, with DJ Justin Hoffman's bass-heavy house tracks and phat hip-hop-happening remixes.

**Best people-watching...** The parking lot of Paradise Road's **Gordon Biersch Brewing Company** tells it all: a sea of beemers and Range Rovers. Local models of both sexes, sleekly handsome as the exposed-brick decor, prowl with their designer Nokias at the ready. **Baby's** packs a plethora of Pretty Young Things into its retro-groovy underground space at the Hard Rock, waited upon by a bartending crew in black leather bustiers, hot pants, and studded collars and bracelets. The exhibitionist crowd at **Club Utopia** displays enough body piercings to lend new meaning to the term "chain gang"; look for girls in lavender minis and matching mohawks alongside boys with long lank hair and kohl-rimmed eyes. The ogling quotient is high at **The Beach**, where staff and clientele alike parade in muscle Ts, halter tops, and cutoffs as if auditioning for *Temptation Island* or *Blind Date*. Watch for Hot Body contests and Jell-O shot games. **Gipsy** attracts a stand-and-pose ME-lieu: young guppy crowd, a dazzling array of well-stilettoed transvestites, and several curious or unconcerned hets. For maximum eye-popping, keep an eye out for fashion shows of sexy couture or "What would you do for $500?" evenings.

**Drinks with a theme...** Like everything else at the Egyptian-themed Luxor, the high-energy **Ra** dance club sports gilt everywhere, while videos of the Pyramids flash on giant screens. It easily out-glitzes Caesars Palace's Egyptian offering, **Cleopatra's Barge**, which literally rocks and rolls in 5 feet of water. The rest is predictable—ponderous stone Sphinxes, pharaoh statues, black chariot seats; no mummies, though some guests look embalmed. **Gilley's Saloon, Dance Hall & Bar-B-Que** conveys the rustic barn feel of the original Gilley's in Pasadena, Texas, adding cowboy kitsch (and neon): swinging saloon doors, hay bales, wooden posts, barrels, buckets of peanuts (with shells strewn over the floor), and a dance area resembling a corral. Harrah's **Carnaval Court/La Playa** is as gaudy as they come: Carnaval Court, the Strip's only outdoor lounge, screams with primary colors, Mardi Gras graffiti, and street performers, while inside La Playa goes for a beach theme, with Day-Glo™-hued palms and crocs in Hawaiian shirts. Appropriate live music is provided by Latin, surf pop, and Brazilian performers. The Mirage's upscale **Lagoon Saloon** is a more exotic beach, with designer tropical fabrics, rattan chairs, parquet floors, Indonesian thatching, actual sand and shells incorporated into the bar top, and froufrou frozen drinks. Off the Strip near the convention center, **The Beach** diligently re-creates a SoCal barn: grass thatching, surfboards, posters of bikinied gals, plastic sharks, even real cars dangling from the ceilings. On Maryland Parkway, **Hookah Lounge**, an adjunct of the popular Mediterranean Café, is as plush as a pasha's digs: deep red walls, low tables, banquettes, embroidered cloth walls and ceilings, and of course, exquisitely ornamented water pipes smoked by exotically attired hipsters. Out in Summerlin, the J.W. Marriott's **J.C. Wooloughan** is an authentic Irish pub, built and dismantled in Dublin. Etched-glass panels, intricately carved wood bar, and pub scene murals get the look right; the ambience is helped along by excellent shepherd's pie, bangers and mash, and fish 'n' chips to accompany the excellent selection of beer (Wooly's, Murphy's, Guinness on tap) and Irish whiskey (from Tullamore Dew to Knappogue Castle Single Malt 36-Year).

**Class lounge acts...** The Bellagio offers a number of cosmopolitan nooks: Choose between the super-sophisticated **Fontana Bar**, whose entertainers range from immaculate pop stylists to high-energy swing bands, and the tranquil **Allegro Lounge**, with its smart decor, fine jazz combos, and a vast selection of cognacs, grappas, eaux de vie, single malts, and single batch bourbons. At Paris, **Napoleon's** Empire trappings—burgundy leather chairs, gold-tasseled red curtains, carpet-strewn marble floors—strike the right note for silky jazz and brandies. At the J.W. Marriott, **Gustav Mauler's Lounge** wittily parodies a men's club: marble tables, forest green upholstery, copper accents, and barrel-vaulted ceilings of stained glass and cedar. It's a prime spot for Summerlin's less stuffy young professionals to decompress over a single malt and cigar.

**Tit-illations...** Only in Vegas will you find strip clubs containing an honest-to-God library or a gourmet restaurant. **Club Paradise** strives for class, with opaque glass, cushy sofas and armchairs with remarkably unstained upholstery, and murals of copulating couples and orgies termed "erotic art." Seating is by maître d', name cigars are available, and, if the action doesn't heat up sufficiently, you can go for such flambé dishes as Steak Diane and Cherries Jubilee. The tab can run high, but the girls are equally high-rent, several of them "actual centerfolds" from *Penthouse* and *Playboy*. **Olympic Gardens** likewise cultivates airs: marble exteriors, arched windows, bronze Rodin lookalikes, and a lingerie shop that, however naughty, emphasizes lace over leather. It even offers equal-opportunity ogling, with a ladies' section where buff long-haired men thrust their pelvises. With more than 300 clean-cut dancers per evening, however, it's a bit mass-produced. *Showgirls* was researched and filmed at **Cheetahs**; don't hold that against it. The place isn't overly campy; many dancers have performed *on* the Strip, and management prides itself on the friendly vibe. Most of the gals do gymnastic routines on the poles, tossing their long manes around like whips, playing the G-string like virtuosi. **Girls of Glitter Gulch** is a venerable Downtown tourist trap (souvenir baseball caps, mugs, and T-shirts) where assertive gals strip from sequined gowns down to spangly G-strings. The immense **Palomino Club** ain't what it used to be, but it *is* the only 100 percent nude joint in town that serves alcohol. Palomino offers unique old-fashioned burlesque shows (a bride peels off her wedding dress and veil to Mendelsohn's "Wedding March"; a cheerleader in red-white-and-blue spangles bumps and grinds to "I'm a Yankee Doodle Dandy"). Uniformly pretty, if slightly hard-bitten, the Palomino girls are also quite persistent; this is one of the more mercenary clubs. The similarly nude **Little Darlings** promotes itself as the "Pornocopia of Sex," providing everything from adult boutique (naughty nighties, fluorescent condoms, even dildo candles) to private booths (dancers must remain, as one says, at least "Kinsey average length away"). The girls, who look unnervingly young, are drop-dead gorgeous; many sport tattoos and unusual piercings. But the selling point is the Fantasy Rooms, in which ladies cavort singly or in numbers, stroking, mounting, and punishing various toys.

**Where the Rat Pack might hang out...** Everything about **Bix's**, the only true supper club around, suggests retro-chic: all dinner jackets, classic martinis, swing bands, and lipstick-smeared cigarettes, like you're strolling into a black and white 1940s flick about cafe society. The MGM Grand's **Brown Derby** would be a natural for the boys, a vast clubby space (lounge plus restaurant) with mahogany paneling, recessed lighting, display cases of crystal, caricatures of the famous (many original), and photos of everyone from George Burns to John Wayne. The lounge menu includes the original restaurant's signature crab cakes, Cobb salad, and grapefruit cake.

**See-and-be-scenes...** House of Blues's separate, multi-chambered Foundation nightly hosts a glamorous international moneyed stampede to Mandalay Bay. Typical sightings include residents (Andre Agassi, Wolfgang Puck) and transients (Oscar de la Hoya, Alanis Morissette, Bruno Kirby, Naomi Campbell, Bruce Willis). At Venetian's **V Bar**, a 50-foot-long, opaque glass exterior with strategic translucent gaps tantalizes passersby with peeking glimpses of such regulars as Pamela Anderson, Sheryl Crow, Dennis Hopper, Halle Berry, Lauren Hutton, and Jeremy Irons, who monopolize this urban-chic nightspot's coveted power seats: pearlized silver leather "beds" containing hollowed-out centers for cocktails. **Studio 54**, which hosted The Hef's 75th birthday bash, favors jocks and rockers with their entourages (Charles Barkley, Oscar de la Hoya, Prince); Hard Rock's always-packed **Circle Bar/Viva Las Vegas Lounge** lets stargazers brush against high-wattage carousers like Matt Damon, Ben Affleck, Christina Aguilera, Charlie Sheen, Matthew Perry, and Drew Carey; **Drai's**, the suave Vegas outpost of Angeleno producer/restaurateur Victor Drai (who perpetrated the un-suave *Weekend at Bernie's* and *Woman in Red*), draws its share of air-kissing Hollywood types, from celebrities to agents with statuesque blondes draped like accessories on their arms.

**Vintage Vegas...** Populated by a few old leches and chain-smoking skanks, **Champagnes Café** is straight from an indie flick without knowing it. The joint's so redolent of "old" Vegas (that red decor, the naugahyde banquettes) that if you don't sight Elvis after one drink, there's something wrong with you. **Pogo's Tavern** (named for Walt Kelley's comic-strip possum) sports a classic neon cocktail lounge sign and beer signs that probably haven't changed since owner Jim Holcombe opened in 1968. Despite the slightly dicey northwest neighborhood, it's no dive, with a personable staff, cushy vinyl booths, sports trophies on wood-paneled walls, and musical old-timers who jive live weekends. Riviera's **Le Bistro** is one of the last remaining throwback lounges, from its red neon ribbons, brass accents, and chrome columns (the interior-design version of a '50s lovemobile) to high-energy, black-sequined acts like Lon Bronson's All-Star Band, who've backed everyone from Sinatra to Diana Ross (Drew Carey is an ardent fan). Pink bubble lamps, brass swans, and black lighting make the Downtown topless bar **Girls of Glitter Gulch** true retro Sin City. Just off the Strip, **Carluccio's** was owned and decorated by Liberace—need we say more? It features floor-to-ceiling mirrors, a bar shaped like a grand piano, one of his white grands, and part of a hand-carved turn-of-the-century English pub that he admired, had disassembled, and sent to Vegas. And while the look of **Carnaval Court/La Playa** is more Club Med than Strip Moderne, the ultimate lounge lizard Cook E. Jarr holds court here on weekends, decked out in polyester-and-sequin outfits or shirtless black tuxedos; fervent celeb fans often join him onstage, among them Tom Jones, the Righteous Brothers, and the Beach Boys (Brian Wilson digs his suggestive "I Get Around").

**Love shacks...** Near the convention center, **The Beach** is like a living, breathing beer commercial—only the Bud-weiser lizards are missing. Have a business card ready to exchange at the corporate **Gordon Biersch Brewing Company** down on Paradise Road, where live bands and decent brews draw a yupscale crowd ready to make friends. Nearby **Z'Tejas** is a similar scene with loosened-up 'tude and easier prices. Flamingo-colored **Pink E's Fun Food and Spirits** looks like prom night on peyote, but hog riders (including yuppies) challenge gals in tight spandex at this pool emporium west of Downtown. The astonishing 50-50 male-female ratio (and its chichi ambience, fostered by a strictly enforced dress code) makes Rio's **Club Rio** the best meet market dance club, followed by **Ra**, the Luxor's Egyptian temple of excess, where the combination of hot go-go dancers and sexy promotions virtually thrusts singles into one another's arms. New York-New York's **ESPN ZONE** contains plentiful family-friendly sections, but at the bars, it's "Going, going, gonads": Hormone levels increase expo-nentially as they shoot (the bull) and they score. Much more subdued than its New Orleans namesake, the **Bourbon Street Cabaret** at Orleans draws handsome young singles who obviously think the Big Easy refers to a one-night stand. Well-shod boomers rub against one another in the close confines of **Cleopatra's Barge** (and rub the notably bare-breasted sea nymph figurehead adorning its prow for luck). Go when sultry Singapore soul singer Anita Sarawak slinks through her set. On the Boulder Highway, **Dylan's Dance Hall and Saloon** is the pickup joint for the Chevy pickup crowd; those with fancy footwork and well-filled Wranglers should lasso an admirer or two. The cruisiest place for gay guys and gals alike is on Paradise Road at **Angles/Lace**, with a mixed crowd, primarily clean-cut and youngish. Both sexes boast stylish buzz cuts and more bicep than is absolutely necessary.

**Where to get intimate...** Incongruously set in the back of a Strip coffee shop, the lush **Fireside Lounge** has the air of a swingin' '70s bachelor pad—all that's missing are lava lamps and Teddy Pendergrass crooning on the stereo. Sneak up to the quiet balcony of **The Nightclub** at the Las Vegas Hilton, where many amorous transactions occur amid the streamlined Deco-ish decor. Despite its stripped-soundstage look (nod to legendary studio mogul Jack Warner), **Jack's Velvet Lounge** has a sexy film-noir ambience with lots of intimate, candlelit nooks, oversized sofas smothered in plush pillows, and gauzy curtains. **Seven** offers two choices for serious snuggling: the intensely romantic patio, live jazz wafting in the air, or the Pink Room, with its cushy vermilion sofas and cushioned walls bathed in red light. The exotically tropical **Lagoon Saloon**'s slinky jungle-esque surroundings and sensuous singers (samba, conga, reggae, and jazz) would bring out anyone's inner tiger.

**Rainbow nights...** Ah, the land of pink sequins, Liberace, and lion tamers—you'd think Las Vegas would be a gay mecca. But it's actually a fairly conservative place, despite the Sin City rep, and the gay/lesbian scene is lackluster. **Gipsy** (over on Paradise Road) comes closest to feeling like a classic big-city gay bar, although the decor looks like assorted castoffs from Luxor's and Caesars—etched glass, hanging vines, broken columns, and Greco-Roman statues. Nearby **Angles/Lace** is the classiest, most comfortable bar by far for both sexes (which isn't saying much), with a tiny mermaid fountain on the patio, high-back "thrones" and ottomans, crayon caricatures of regulars, and a fireplace. In the same neighborhood, the leather-and-Levi's set stampedes **The Buffalo**, home to the Satyricons Motorcycle Club and Beary Hairy contests. It's really just a neigborhood hangout with bartenders, pool tables, dirty lino floors, and a trophy case with bowling and pool awards—despite the occasional biker-ish posturing, the guys are softies, talking earnestly of tattoo art. No 'tude at the Western-themed **Backstreet**, beloved by cowguys and gals for its Sunday beer busts. Thursday nights are the most popular, with free line-dancing lessons (best time and place for single dykes to find a partner for dosey-doing).

**Wildest decor...** **Double Down Saloon** is a riot of psychedelic colors, models of skeletons holding cards, murals of skulls with cherry-red lipstick, and graffiti everywhere, even on the hand-painted tables and shredded chairs. Out at Sunset Station, **Gaudi Bar** is patterned (loosely) after the famed Modernista architect's sinuous designs, with nary a straight line. Add mosaics of broken colored glass, cracked ceramics, stalactites, a fountain sprouting improbably, and a bas-relief of Don Quixote—after two martinis, if you stare too hard at the walls, you'd be tilting at windmills, too. At Rio's **Voodoo Lounge**, fluorescent voodoo skulls and snakes adorn the black-lit aubergine ceiling and walls, giving off a romantically macabre Gorey/Addams vibe. **Baby's** calls to mind a '70s sci-fi flick wrap party orchestrated by Fellini: It's a series of tiny rooms decked out in stainless steel, fieldstone, leatherette, and Lucite, with frosted-glass tables illuminated in a spectrum of sherbet colors. Venetian's **Venus** has a Trader-Vic vibe going, with cobalt blue walls, morose hand-carved tikis, hula dancers, space-age murals, and a dazzling diorama of Downtown Vegas. Dig the naked-lady swizzle sticks. Upstairs at **Ghostbar/Rain**, colors shift eerily across the ceiling, while amorphous white plastic chairs, ovoid silver ottomans, and chain-mail curtains give it a spectral, demented aura. At Mandalay Bay, **rumjungle** features a 27-foot wall of fire suspended over a moat and waterwalls lit in ever-changing colors. The lounge section has curved acrylic tables in rainbow colors, tortoiseshell maps, and huge glass orb lamps; faux furs cover S-shaped furniture carved from one enormous fallen oak.

**Rooms with a view...** The big daddy is the glossy **Top of the World**, which commands a 360-degree panoramic view as it slowly rotates atop the Stratosphere, 104 floors above the Strip. Worthy Continental dining, hardwood tables inlaid with polished black granite, and brass lamps complete the "perfect first date" picture. **Ghostbar/Rain**, on the 55th floor of The Palms, features interior floor-to-ceiling picture windows, as well as jaw-dropping Strip views from its deck (where a transparent section vertiginously looks down into the garage and Nine restaurant); the hotel's pulsing pink and purple lights illuminate your face as the moon reflects off Plexiglass surfaces. Patio alcoves at **Jack's Velvet Lounge** overlook the Venetian's outdoor Grand Canal, Treasure Island's Pirate Battle, and the Mirage's lava-belching volcano. Nineteen stories up, **Sky Lounge**'s 270-degree picture windows stare right at New York-New York's Manhattan Express roller coaster, Bellagio's fountains, Aladdin's minarets and domes, and the emerald green MGM Grand. The picture windows of the high-profile **Fontana Bar** overlook Bellagio's faux version of Lake Como, ringed by cypress trees with impossibly romantic sparkling lights, while the fountains' water show provides a spectacle rivaling anything inside.

**True brew...** With its loft-like exposed pipes and track lighting, **Gordon Biersch Brewing Co.** is as much nightclub/yuppieteria as microbrewery, but it ferments some mean lager, pilsner, and Marzen. On the Strip, the **Monte Carlo Brew Pub** also sports the techno-industrial warehouse look, with brick walls and huge copper vats of fermenting brew (six varieties; standouts include Jackpot Ale, High Roller Red, and Winner's Wheat). Twenty somethings enjoy prowling the overhead catwalk and the patio overlooking a grotto-esque pool. **Holy Cow Brewing Company** crafts surprisingly powerful brews, if you can overlook the bovine kitsch decor; try the Amber Gambler and Hefeweizer (shouldn't that have been "Heifer Weizer"???). The younger professional set hangs out Downtown at the handsome **Triple 7 Brewpub** at Main Street Station. The look is 1930s warehouse meets Edwardian railway station; guys will dig relieving themselves on the plastic-wreathed section of the Berlin Wall in the men's room. The draft call at **Crown and Anchor Pub**, near UNLV, is a virtual United Nations of suds, including beers from the Czech Republic, Scotland, Ireland, Germany, Jamaica, Italy, and Mexico. They even do a proper Bondian martini. The British Isles theme is a bit overdone, with nutty nautical touches, darts, Beefeater statues, and heraldic banners. Actual Brit (and Aussie and Kiwi) sightings are more likely at Downtown's **Mad Dogs and Englishmen**—expect to be asked for a fag, mate, and your opinion on whose ruggers and footballers rule. Brass plates and mock-Tudor beams can't disguise the neo-punk aura.

**Martini madness...** **V Bar** dispenses over 10 wildly creative "martinis," such as Pearle Jam (Pearl vodka, Amaretto, Southern Comfort, cranberry and pineapple juices, and grape jam), along with extensive lists of single malts, designer beers, tequilas, and cognacs. Overlooking Caesars' Court of Fountains, the Tuscan-rustic **Terrazza Lounge** (an adjunct of the superlative Italian restaurant) offers a virtual grappa primer, as well as nearly 30 vodka and gin brands combined in creative 'tinis that go down smoothly with the satiny live jazz. **Jack's Velvet Lounge** offers faboo Cosmos, Bloody Marys with just the right pepper kick, and several glacial martinis. It's martini heresy at Sunset Station's **Gaudi Bar**—15 varieties, including chocolate. The decor—a curves-everywhere phantasmagoria—is as outlandish as the designer 'tinis. At least you're on solid ground at **Martini Ranch**, the Texas Station bar where 30 city-slick martinis are served amid longhorns, Texas cowhide, and a fake roaring fireplace.

**Cocktail culture...** The Rio's high-rise **Voodoo Lounge** is famed for flair bartenders, à la Tom Cruise in *Cocktail*, who juggle and throw bottles while mixing more than 40 specialty cocktails in Day-Glo colors. Try the Dambala (Absolut Citron, Midori, Chambord, fruit juices). The exotically lavish **rumjungle** boasts the world's largest rum bar: more than 160 varieties, each bottle underlit by fiber optics, and drinks to match (or set a match to). **Fontana Bar** is the favorite laboratory of Bellagio's master mixologist Tony Abou-Ganim. While purists appreciate the comprehensive single-malt scotches, aged rums, and vintage ports, Tony believes in "treating the bar like a chef's kitchen": Witness his Knob Creek Clermont Smash with mint, bitters, and pineapple. **Z'Tejas** offers dozens of tequilas by the shot, but the margaritas are so memorable you'll forget to have a morning after. Flavored varieties include jalapeño, watermelon, and Chambord; the house special is the Cosmo-Rita (Corazon Blanco tequila, Citronge, fresh lime, and cranberry juice). The oh-so-retro **Fireside Lounge**'s outrageous Scorpion is a flaming bowl—make that football helmet—of 15-plus spirits colored a red that doesn't occur in nature. Bohemian types zone out at **Hookah Lounge** over the aroma-therapeutic fruit- and spice-flavored tobaccos and such knockout signature drinks as the Beirut Bomb (Stoli Vanil, Pearl vodka, Kahlua, and iced espresso). **Venus** specializes in throwback cocktails like the Sidecar, Vesper, Mai Tai, and French 75 alongside current faves like caipirinhas and mojitos). **Shadow**'s backlit bar showcases high-end spirits, and private liquor vaults scream expensively exotic cocktails, poured by show-offy flair bartenders.

**Country roots...** **Gilley's Saloon, Dance Hall & Bar-B-Que** lassos both the real McCoys and folks in Neiman-Marcus Stetsons and Tony Lama boots. You can ride a mechanical bull ($5 for 10 seconds), but you're projected onto big screens so everyone can see what an idiot you look like. **Dylan's Dance Hall and Saloon** boasts the most energetic two-steppers, most eclectic crowd, and most helpful free line-dancing lessons on its 2,000-square-foot dance floor. Genuine ranchers two-step over to the Sam's Town lounge **Roxy's Saloon** for its murals of boomtown dance hall girls, live C&W bands, and exuberant happy hours. Its walls festooned with cowboy boots and banjos, **Armadillo Lounge** lassos name acts, offers two-stepping Thursdays through Saturdays on its barn-sized floor, and hosts karaoke nights where gals admonish each other to "Stand By Your Man" and dudes confess "I'm So Lonesome I Could Cry." **Gold Coast Dance Hall**, in the casino-hotel of the same name, ropes in the older cowpokes, who two-step and swing fluidly around an oval floor nearly as large as a trailer park. Down-home **Backstreet** is where gay and lesbian cowpokes strut their stuff. As one bartender chirped merrily, "You can't keep a gay hoedown."

**Sports bars...** **Barley's Casino & Brew Pub** is a preferred hangout for the after-work crowd to egg on their favorite passers and hurlers while downing pitchers of the cheap cold stuff. **ESPN ZONE** is a two-story paean to sports, with 10,000 square feet of interactive and competitive attractions (climbing wall, virtual reality boxing arena), humongous video walls updating scores, and 165 TV monitors. Couch-jocks love the Screening Room, where they can sprawl in leather recliners to watch a match or surf sports sites. Topless **Cheetahs,** a favorite with athletes, is so eager to please, there are several TVs so you can check up on your favorite sports teams—and many men do, between, um, innings.

**For slackers, goths, and nihilists...** Black is de rigueur for **Club Utopia**, along with militia-style club gear, odd dye jobs, piercings in creative places, and Doc Martens. All wear the requisite alienated look, even when they dance. The local dive **Double Down Saloon** is a Paradise Road haven for nonconformists of all types, from sallow cadaverous punks with vermilion hair to spiffy yup-scale types to tattooed burly bikers and their babes. The quintessential hangout **Mermaid Café** is a vividly colored room (mostly in turquoise) filled with hanging plants, paintings, pottery, and lots of comfy couches and throw pillows. There's always something going on, from poetry and palm readings to tarot readings and massages, along with whatever musical act is up. The sweetly, scruffily neo-Beat **Café Espresso Roma**, across from UNLV, isn't just for caffiends: A revolving cast of stringy-haired skater punks, disaffected philosophy majors, Euro-wannabes, and dreadlocked white poets form study groups, play chess, or skim magazines here.

**Frat parties...** Like a (slightly) more mature version of MTV Spring Break, **The Beach** greets you at the entrance with stainless steel vats filled with brewskis on ice and neon-bikinied gals offering "a cold one." It's an arrested adolescent's wet dream: two vast floors of bars, pool tables, foosball, darts, video games (and poker), pinball, pizza stands, tarot readers, and more than 80 TVs tuned to everything from dirt biking on ESPN to *Jackass* on MTV. **Moose McGillicuddy's** hosts horny young frat boys and sorority babes in an overgrown surfer dude's shack; the astonishing array of shots ensures a shot at your quarry if you wait long enough. The snarky, smart-ass **Tom & Jerry's** feels like *The Real World* goes out on the town. Rated one of the country's top 100 college bars by *Playboy*, it certainly looks the part, with several dingy if intriguingly decorated rooms—glow-in-the-dark alien paintings, a UNLV rainbow student coalition mural—and an excellent juke, from Alanis to B.B. King to the Clash. The Fantasy and Shower Rooms at **Little Darlings** nudie bar draw plenty of local twentysomething bachelors; you could even run into an enthusiastic contingent of gangly college freshmen cheering on the proceedings as if it were a Running Rebels game.

**For twentysomethings...** You feel cool just getting into the Venetian's **V Bar**, mingling with stars, P.R. flaks, Euro-trash, attorneys, and not-so-starving artists parading in Prada. Despite the glam clientele and striking decor—red-lacquered wood scaffolds, black slate bar with cream-colored pony skin stools, and retro double-sided banquettes—there's surprisingly little attitude here. The patrons at **Circle Bar/Viva Las Vegas Lounge** look like finalists on *Making the Band* outfitted by Abercrombie & Fitch to showcase crotches and cleavage. On weekends, this California East meat market gets downright predatory, as singles stalk each other around its elevated concentric circles surrounding the Hard Rock casino floor. There's a much more mellow scene at **Breathe Oxygen Bar**, which purveys wheat-grass smoothies, herbal libations, and enzyme/herb-saturated oxygen mist facials along with hits of 98 percent-pure oxygen through green prongs up your nostrils. Purple drapes, blue lighting, and soothing New Age music—bliss out. There's a similar vibe at **Hookah Lounge,** where corporate poets manqué and goateed goths inhale flavored tobaccos, munch Middle Eastern delicacies, and bob after hours to the acid jazz/trance/techno groove. **Café Espresso Roma**, superficially seems unremarkable: huge hand-painted tiles, indifferent student artworks, and equally indifferent biscotti. But the poetry and live music acts are usually enterprising.

**For thirtysomethings...** The smart set in town hangs out at **Bix's**, enjoying the swing resurgence. This supper club serves admirable nouveau Creole-continental food, but draws more people for its sensational swing evenings (Big

Band Thursdays), and jazzy dance bands that evoke the Lester Lanin days. Romantically minded trust-fund pretties congregate at the Bellagio's **Fontana Bar,** with its brocade booths, plush high-backed shell-patterned chairs, and tiny flickering lamps. **Tommy Rocker's** strives to re-create Margaritaville (it's Parrot Head Central), with tiki thatching, black walls, and surfboards and parrots. Owner/human karaoke machine Tommy Rocker seizes center stage weekends with Jimmy Buffett covers (he also does AC/DC and Queen), and coaxes audience participation on nostalgic rock oldies. Over-indulgence is allowed—nay, expected—at **Caviarteria**, a welcome oasis in the Forum Shops at Caesars where you can order from an international smorgasbord of caviars and salmons, exotic smoked game (wild boar, pheasant, elk, ostrich), and 12 champagnes by the glass. **The Hop/Glo** on Tropicana Avenue is quietly cool, with an intensely danceable R&B mix, occasional Latin and Swing nights, and plenty of plush velvet booths and chairs.

**For fortysomethings...** Bellagio's **Allegro Lounge** is a haven where the performers never seem to play anything composed after 1960 and corporate honchos discourse knowledgeably on the peatiness of Islay single malts. When not dancing, **Shadow**'s concierges "perform" as lounge hostesses in skintight suits behind a sheer scrim screen, like an NC-17 version of Bond flick title credits. This is Caesars' bid to court younger slicksters, but the room is still full of expanding waistlines and receding hairlines. Three miles east of the Strip, congenial candlelit **Pepper's Lounge** features ballroom and swing dancing, with free lessons on Wednesdays; karaoke Sundays and Mondays bring out nostalgiacs of all ages.

**Where locals hang out...** At the **Double Down Saloon**, prominent signs read "You puke, you clean" and "Puke Insurance $20"; psychedelic designs and salacious paintings daub the walls; and customers avail themselves of pool tables, condom machines, live bands, and a sublime jukebox. The house specialty (a jealously guarded secret recipe) is affectionately dubbed "Ass Juice." How could it not be a cherished institution? On the west side of town, **Pink E's Fun Food and Spirits** lures a hip "I don't care if I'm hip" crowd, who like the tongue-in-cheek pink decor, plentiful pool tables (more than 50), and rocking bands with names like Sea Monkeys. **Crown and Anchor Pub** caters to casino industry folk, UNLV students and faculty, and young professionals, who appreciate the vast beer selection, live soccer and rugby telecasts, nightly all-you-can-eat specials, jiving juke, and occasional hot local bands. Locals are greeted *Cheers*-style at **Z'Tejas**, where the subdued lighting, natty surroundings, and nouvelle Southwestern appetizers (half price at happy hour) are ideal for unwinding after work. **Ellis Island Brewery & Casino** is a welcoming casino/lounge just off the Strip: gambling (favorable odds and free bingo), generous cheapo eats and drinks, and a smoky, candlelit, Old Vegas lounge. But folks really come here for nightly karaoke (regulars deck themselves out like their idols, from Tina Turner to Gene Simmons). The **Railhead Saloon** at Boulder Station delivers a sterling selection of almost-has-beens (John Cafferty, Lou Rawls, Jerry Vale, Merle Haggard, Jose Feliciano) might-bes, and celebrity vanity acts (Dogstar with Keanu Reeves) for reasonable prices. Cozy is a charitable word for the size of the room. Heading out toward Henderson, **Barley's Casino & Brew Pub** offers something for everyone: great prices for tall cold draft beers; decent pub grub; a fair selection of cigars; low-key gambling; pool; and plenty of TVs tuned to athletic pursuits.

**Cigars, cigarettes...** At **C2K**'s third-floor Groove Lounge cigar/martini bar, you'll find guys comparing the length and thickness of their stogies, then repairing to the adjacent O2Zone oxygen bar to refresh their lungs. The drinks menu at **Napoleon's** lists several froufrou fruity concoctions, but order an aged armagnac and a cigar from the walk-in humidor: This is one place where neither seems affected. **Gustav Mauler's Lounge** offers Macunudo, Fuentes, Partagas, and premium house blends from the Dominican Republic in a men's-clubby atmosphere. In keeping with its retro-swank rep, **Bix's** offers more than 50 premium brands and a walk-in humidor where you can sniff and twirl to your heart's content. The duplex **Caviarteria** offers the big three Cs: caviar, champagne, and cigars. The upstairs martini bar/cigar lounge has track lighting, faux Cubist artworks, slate-blue chairs and banquettes that look more inviting than they are comfortable, and an excellent selection highlighting Upmanns and Montecristos.

**The piano man...** The suave **Top of the World** at the Stratosphere presents the smooth-as-silk Bobby Dickerson at the keyboard. Michael Anthony Henegan's stylings at **Seven** provide a soothing soundtrack for stylish film folk chattering over dinner. **Gustav Mauler's Lounge's** Teddy Kaye entertains designer martini–sipping execs, while Bobby Barrett performs his uncanny Sinatra shtick at the MGM Grand's posh, retro-Hollywood **Brown Derby** lounge. New York-New York's tourist-packed **Bar at Times Square** offers NYPD (New York Piano Duo), a majestically silly duelling-pianos act that would never fly in the real Times Square.

**Jazzin' it up...** The refined **Terrazza Lounge** at Caesars lures jazz lovers with the classy funk of Ghalib Ghallab's jazz band, running from "Tiny Bubbles" to "Sittin' on the Dock of the Bay"—as done by Herbie Hancock, Al Jarreau, or Stevie Wonder. **Napoleon's** swings to the sinuous sounds of the Ray Cousins Trio; at **Le Bistro**, the Don Menza Big Band hosts wailing Monday jam sessions that often feature visiting musicians from around the jazz world. Fridays at **Pogo's Tavern** are legendary for energetic jazz jams led by Strip veterans, including bass player Chuck Kovacs, trombonist Carl Fontana, and 81-year-old drummer Irv Kluger (who kept the beat for Artie Shaw, Count Basie, and Stan Kenyon). Casual, comfy **Pepper's Lounge** on Thursdays hosts the amazing Carl Lodico Big Band, whose 17 virtuosi backed seemingly all the greats. At Bellagio's smooth **Allegro Lounge**, regulars include Filipino Boy Katindig and his band, the charismatic lounge singer Art Vargas, and the swinging Rocco Barbato and Steven Lee with No Fear (the latter also plays Bellagio's **Fontana Bar** along with Jump Jive and Wail, which really lives up to its name). **Bourbon Street Cabaret** at the Orleans offers the Royal Dixie Jazz Band and other top-notch acts in a setting that feels like one of the quieter, more romantic French Quarter night spots. Along with the inevitable Mardi Gras masks, baby and grand pianos hang from the ceilings.

**Singing a blues streak...** Off the Strip, the **Sand Dollar Blues Lounge** is smokier than *EFX*, but here at least there's fire: blazing blues (and the occasional Dixieland and Zydeco) sessions by the Ruffnecks, the Moanin' Blacksnakes, Al Ek & All-Star Band and Jimmy Mack Blues Attack. The knowledgeable crowd ranges from bikers to corporate types. It's no cover or minimum Thursdays at **Railhead Saloon**'s Boulder Blues Series to hear leading national acts like Coco Montoya and Tab Benoit. The wailing **House of Blues** Live Courtyard series with Willie Jaye Thursdays through Sundays is part revival meeting, part performance.

**Where to hear local bands...** Grubby, bare-bones **Boston Grill & Bar** is hardly *Cheers*, but that's what makes it a prime rock venue. It presents the best mix of acts, from punk to ska to blues; nearly every major local act has paid its dues here. Frat-rat hangout **Tom & Jerry's** brings in one-night and regular stands, like Prince cover band Purple Reign, hard rockers Brass Monkey and Mother Ship, and Acoustic Asylum evenings. Near UNLV, **Café Espresso Roma** remains folk central, with such fine musicians as Steve McCoy and Martin Melancon getting back to their grassroots. Folkies also descend on **J.C. Woologhan's**, especially when stomping Irish bands like Wild Celtic and Mulligan's Edge appear. Surf, punk, and rockabilly bands often storm the **Double Down Saloon**'s tiny corner stage. On Wednesdays, check out wailing Chicago-style Blue Cherry and Friends. Texas Station's **Martini Ranch** books bluesy acts weekends in a space so comfy you can pretend you're home on the range. The **Mermaid Café** roster is heavy on acoustic, blues, and improvisational jazz, but can also run toward sitar and gamelan concerts.

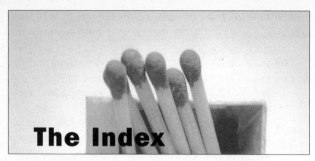

# The Index

**Allegro Lounge.** A supremely relaxed, refined drinking oasis.... *Tel 702/693-7111. Bellagio, 3600 Las Vegas Blvd. S.*
**(see pp. 177, 188, 190)**

**Angles/Lace.** The most "mixed" (gay/lesbian) bar in town, with a younger, slightly uppity crowd.... *Tel 702/791-0100. 4663 Paradise Rd.* **(see pp. 180, 181)**

**Armadillo Lounge.** A laid-back dance club and performance lounge, with C&W karaoke nights.... *Tel 702/631-1000. Texas Station, 2101 Texas Star Lane.* **(see pp. 175, 185)**

**Baby's.** The sexiest, steamiest club in Las Vegas, thanks to the so-hip-it-hurts crowd.... *Tel 702/693-5555. Hard Rock, 4455 Paradise Rd. Closed Sun–Tue.* **(see pp. 173, 175, 182)**

**Backstreet.** Gals who like gals and boys who like boys mosey on down to this amiable Western bar.... *Tel 702/876-1844. 5012 S. Arville St.* **(see pp. 182, 185)**

**Bar at Times Square.** Ebullient nightspot, about as authentically New York as Disneyland's Main Street.... *Tel 702/740-6969. New York-New York, 3790 Las Vegas Blvd. S.*
**(see p. 190)**

**Barley's Casino & Brew Pub.** Huge local hangout for singles action, sports watching, gambling.... *Tel 702/458-2739. 4500 E. Sunset Rd., Henderson.* **(see pp. 185, 190)**

**The Beach.** Like an Annette Funicello/Frankie Avalon movie crossed with Studio 54.... *Tel 702/731-1925. 365 Convention Center Dr.* **(see pp. 176, 180, 186)**

**Bix's.** Sensational supper club throwback.... *Tel 702/889-0800. 9455 S. Buffalo Dr.* **(see pp. 178, 188, 189)**

**Boston Grill and Bar.** Top showcase for local bands.... *Tel 702/368-0750. 3411 S. Jones Blvd.* **(see p. 191)**

**Bourbon Street Cabaret.** Lovingly re-created N'Awlins ambience, with top-notch jazz.... *Tel 702/365-7111. Orleans, 4500 W. Tropicana Ave.* **(see pp. 180, 190)**

**Breathe Oxygen Bar.** Yuppies and ravers fork over for fresh air.... *Tel 702/258-4502. 4750 W. Sahara Ave., Ste. 32* **(see pp. 175, 187)**

**Brown Derby.** Vegas goes '50s Hollywood.... *Tel 702/891-1111. MGM Grand, 3799 Las Vegas Blvd. S.* **(see pp. 178, 190)**

**The Buffalo.** Gay hangout that's not as rough-and-tumble as it looks.... *Tel 702/733-8355. 4640 Paradise Rd.* **(see p. 181)**

**C2K.** High-tech haven for spiffed-up narcissists.... *Tel 702/414-2001 or 702/948-2000. Venetian, 3355 Las Vegas Blvd. S. Closed Mon–Thur.* **(see pp. 173, 189)**

**Café Espresso Roma.** Youthful crowd, not too edgy, with excellent folk acts.... *Tel 702/369-1540. 4440 S. Maryland Pkwy.* **(see pp. 186, 187, 191)**

**Carluccio's.** Gaudy restaurant once owned by Liberace.... *Tel 702/795-3236. Liberace Plaza, 1775 E. Tropicana Ave.* **(see p. 180)**

**Carnaval Court/La Playa Lounge.** Indoor/outdoor versions of beach blanket bingo.... *Tel 702/369-5000. Harrah's, 3475 Las Vegas Blvd. S.* **(see pp. 176, 180)**]

**Caviarteria.** A civilized respite amid the Forum Shops frenzy.... *Tel 702/792-8560. Forum Shops at Caesars, 3500 Las Vegas Blvd. S.* **(see pp. 188, 189)**

**Champagnes Café.** Classic 1970s Vegas where folks drink house liquor and scarf down free buffets.... *Tel 702/737-1699. 3557 S. Maryland Pkwy.* **(see p. 179)**

**Cheetahs.** Genial topless bar.... *Tel 702/384-0074. 2112 Western Ave.* **(see pp. 178, 186)**

**Circle Bar/Viva Las Vegas Lounge.** Jammed, jamming flesh pits....Tel 702/693-5000. Hard Rock, 4455 Paradise Rd.
(see pp. 179, 187)

**Cleopatra's Barge.** Barge replica in 5 feet of water. Great live acts and fun-loving singles.... Tel 702/731-7110. Caesars Palace, 3570 Las Vegas Blvd. S.
(see pp. 176, 180)

**Club Paradise.** "Classy" strip bar.... Tel 702/734-7990. 4416 Paradise Rd.
(see p. 177)

**Club Rio.** A smart set gathers here for its elegant ambience, superb sound system, and theme nights.... Tel 702/252-7777. The Rio, 3700 W. Flamingo Rd. Closed Sun–Tue.
(see pp. 173, 180)

**Club Utopia.** A nonstop rave with eclectic music and oh-so-watchable clientele.... Tel 702/390-4650 or 702/282-1221. 3765 Las Vegas Blvd. S. Closed Sun–Tue.
(see pp. 173, 176, 186)

**Crown and Anchor Pub.** The best variety of on-tap beers, ales, and stouts in town.... Tel 702/739-0281. 1350 E. Tropicana Ave.
(see pp. 183, 189)

**Double Down Saloon.** Hip and trippy, with kickass jukebox and colorful clientele.... Tel 702/791-5775. 4640 Paradise Rd.
(see pp. 182, 186, 188, 191)

**Drai's.** A sybaritic delight, designed for sipping the perfect martini.... Tel 702/737-7111. Barbary Coast, 3595 Las Vegas Blvd. S.
(see pp. 175, 179)

**Dylan's Dance Hall & Saloon**. Honk if you're into honkytonk.... Tel 702/451-4006. 4660 Boulder Hwy. Closed Sun–Tue.
(see pp. 180, 185)

**Ellis Island Brewery & Casino.** A locals' fave for gambling, suds, and karaoke....Tel 702/733-8901. 4178 Koval Lane.
(see p. 189)

**ESPN ZONE.** A nonstop Super Bowl party with games and gadgets galore....Tel 702/933-3776. New York-New York, 3790 Las Vegas Blvd. S.
(see pp. 180, 186)

**Fireside Lounge.** Plush '70s decor makes this makeout joint a trip.... *Tel 702/735-7635. Peppermill Inn, 2985 Las Vegas Blvd. S.* **(see pp. 181, 185)**

**Fontana Bar.** A sophisticated urban-chic cabaret.... *Tel 702/693-7111. Bellagio, 3600 Las Vegas Blvd. S.* **(see pp. 177, 183, 184, 188, 190)**

**Gaudi Bar.** Outrageous decor patterned after the trippy, curvy work of the Modernista architect.... *Tel 702/547-7777. Sunset Station, 1301 W. Sunset Rd.* **(see pp. 182, 184)**

**Ghostbar/Rain.** Mod rooftop lounge and ground-floor state-of-the-art dance club.... *Tel 702/942-7777 or 842-7778. The Palms, 4321 W. Flamingo Rd. Rain closed Mon–Wed.* **(see pp. 174, 182, 183)**

**Gilley's Saloon, Dance Hall & Bar-B-Que.** Raucous Texas import for live country music.... *Tel 702/794-8330. The New Frontier, 3120 Las Vegas Blvd. S. Closed Mon.* **(see pp. 176, 185)**

**Gipsy.** Jungle-ruins decor and snooty gay clientele.... *Tel 702/731-1919. 4605 Paradise Rd.* **(see pp. 175, 176, 181)**

**Girls of Glitter Gulch.** A lot of hustling, but the place and drink prices seem unchanged since the 1970s.... *Tel 702/385-4774. 20 E. Fremont St.* **(see pp. 178, 180)**

**Gold Coast Dance Hall.** Themed music nights, from big band to C&W, lure an older crowd for dancing.... *Tel 702/367-7111. Gold Coast, 4000 W. Flamingo Rd.* **(see p. 185)**

**Gordon Biersch Brewing Co.** Premier yupster pickup joint.... *Tel 702/312-5247. 3987 Paradise Rd.* **(see pp. 175, 180, 183)**

**Gustav Mauler's Lounge.** Where relaxed yuppies chill and smoke.... *Tel 702/869-6700. J.W. Marriott, 221 N. Rampart Blvd.* **(see pp. 177, 189, 190)**

**Holy Cow Brewing Company.** The beer (despite several awards) is secondary to singles mingling.... *Tel 702/732-COWS (2697). 2423 Las Vegas Blvd. S.* **(see p. 183)**

**Hookah Lounge.** Sultry Mediterranean decadence meets hipster music and cocktails.... *Tel 702/731-6030. 4147–53 S. Maryland Pkwy.* **(see pp. 176, 185, 187)**

**The Hop/Glo.** Popular, plush, mid-size club catering to whitebread R&B and swing lovers.... *Tel 702/310-5060. 1650 E. Tropicana Ave.* **(see pp. 174, 188)**

**House of Blues.** Separate club where the well-connected groove after the main show.... *Tel 702/692-7777. Mandalay Bay, 3950 Las Vegas Blvd. S.*
**(see pp. 174, 175, 179, 191)**

**J.C. Wooloughan's.** Authentic reassembled Dublin pub....*Tel 702/869-7725. J.W. Marriott, 221 N. Rampart Blvd.*
**(see pp. 177, 191)**

**Jack's Velvet Lounge.** Cattle call for handsome singles in handsomer space.... *Tel 702/414-1699. Venetian, 3355 Las Vegas Blvd. S.* **(see pp. 181, 183, 184)**

**Lagoon Saloon.** An actual slice of rain forest amid the casino's hubbub, with top acts.... *Tel 702/791-7111. Mirage, 3400 Las Vegas Blvd. S.* **(see pp. 176, 181)**

**Le Bistro.** Brassy old-time lounge, classy swing and soul acts.... *Tel 702/734-5110. Riviera, 2901 Las Vegas Blvd. S.*
**(see p. 179)**

**Little Darlings.** Lissome girls create interpretive dances at this all-nude club.... *Tel 702/366-1633. 1514 Western Ave.*
**(see pp. 178, 187)**

**Mad Dogs and Englishmen.** Gathering spot for yobbo Brits, along with a motley crew of locals.... *Tel 702/382-5075. 515 Las Vegas Blvd. S.* **(see p. 184)**

**Martini Ranch.** Texas Station has several fine bars devoted to specific cocktails (Crazy Mary's for bloodys, Laredo Cantina for margaritas), but this is the best.... *Tel 702/631-1000. Texas Station, 2101 Texas Star Lane.* **(see pp. 184, 191)**

**Mermaid Café.** Wide-ranging crowd, decor, music.... *Tel 702/240-6002. 2910 Lake East Dr.* **(see pp. 186, 191)**

**Monte Carlo Brew Pub.** Good-looking space with youngish crowd, tasty brews and eats, and fine dance music.... *Tel 702/730-7420. Monte Carlo, 3770 Las Vegas Blvd. S.*
**(see pp. 175, 183)**

**Moose McGillicuddy's.** Obnoxious, but wildly popular with the under-25 set.... *Tel 702/798-8337. 4770 S. Maryland Pkwy.* **(see p. 186)**

**Napoleon's.** Luxe cigar/jazz/designer libation spot.... *Tel 702/946-7000. Paris, 3655 Las Vegas Blvd. S.*
**(see pp. 177, 189, 190)**

**The Nightclub.** Urbane little nightspot with superb acts and a nice-looking bunch of traveling business types.... *Tel 702/732-5111. Las Vegas Hilton, 3000 Paradise Rd. Closed Mon.* **(see pp. 174, 181)**

**Olympic Gardens.** The only spot where both men and women get a chance to ogle strippers.... *Tel 702/385-8987. 1531 Las Vegas Blvd. S.* **(see p. 177)**

**Palomino Club.** This once high-class outfit has become seedy, but it still draws its share of clients. Full frontal nudity and alcohol.... *Tel 702/642-2984. 1848 Las Vegas Blvd. N.* **(see p. 178)**

**Pepper's Lounge.** Live Big Band music, big local following.... *Tel 702/731-3234. 2929 E. Desert Inn Rd.* **(see pp. 188, 190)**

**Pink E's Fun Food and Spirits.** Shagadelic pool hall/music venue/eatery, baby.... *Tel 702/252-4666. 4170 S. Valley View Blvd.* **(see pp. 180, 188)**

**Pogo's Tavern.** Beloved hangout for live big band and blues.... *Tel 702/646-9735. 2103 N. Decatur Blvd.***(see pp. 179, 190)**

**Ra.** Phenomenal sound and video systems, savvy DJs, sexy crowd, and awesome gyrating go-go dancers.... *Tel 702/262-4949. Luxor, 3900 Las Vegas Blvd. S. Closed Sun–Tue.* **(see pp. 173, 176, 180)**

**Railhead Saloon.** A great lineup of live music acts, at half the price.... *Tel 702/432-7575. Boulder Station, 4111 Boulder Hwy.* **(see pp. 189, 191)**

**Roxy's Saloon.** The only true C&W lounge in Las Vegas.... *Tel 702/456-7777. Sam's Town, 5111 Boulder Hwy.*

**(see p. 185)**

**rumjungle.** Triplex restaurant/bar/disco with an exotic island theme.... *Tel 702/632-7408. Mandalay Bay, 3950 Las Vegas Blvd. S.* **(see pp. 174, 182, 184)**

**Sand Dollar Blues Lounge.** The name says it all; the bar, many regulars, and the live blues acts have a well-worn integrity that's refreshing in Vegas.... *Tel 702/871-6651. 3355 Spring Mountain Rd.* **(see p. 191)**

**Seven.** Sleek gourmet eatery and dance club.... *Tel 702/739-7744. 3724 Las Vegas Blvd. S.* **(see pp. 174, 181, 190)**

**Shadow.** A refined jiggle-and-juggle scene.... *Tel 702/731-3110. Caesars Palace, 3570 Las Vegas Blvd. S.*

**(see pp. 185, 188)**

**Sky Lounge.** Tranquil lounge with fab jazz and cocktails and late-evening poolside club.... *Tel 702/261-1000. Polo Towers, 3745 Las Vegas Blvd. S.* **(see pp. 174, 183)**

**Studio 54.** Less magic than the Manhattan original.... *Tel 702/891-7254. MGM Grand, 3799 Las Vegas Blvd. S.*

**(see pp. 173, 179)**

**Terrazza Lounge.** Refined, tranquil spot for martinis and music.... *Tel 702/731-7110. Caesars Palace, 3570 Las Vegas Blvd. S.* **(see pp. 184, 190)**

**Tom & Jerry's.** Quintessential college haunt.... *Tel 702/736-8550. 4550 S. Maryland Pkwy.* **(see pp. 187, 191)**

**Tommy Rocker's.** Endearingly tacky tiki hut.... *Tel 702/261-6688. 4275 S. Industrial Blvd.* **(see p. 188)**

**Top of the World.** This rotating lounge/restaurant is the classiest pickup joint in Las Vegas.... *Tel 702/380-7711. Stratosphere, 2000 Las Vegas Blvd. S.*

**(see pp. 182, 190)**

**Triple 7 Brewpub.** Downtown yuppie hangout with admirable brews.... *Tel 702/387-1896. Main Street Station 200 N. Main St.* **(see p. 183)**

**V Bar.** Sleek space and clientele, killer cocktails.... *Tel 702/414- -3200. Venetian, 3355 Las Vegas Blvd. S.*
**(see pp. 175, 179, 184, 187)**

**Venus.** Swanky back-to-the-future tiki bar.... *Tel 702/414-4870. Venetian, 3355 Las Vegas Blvd. S.* **(see pp. 182, 185)**

**Voodoo Lounge.** Sensational views, specialty cocktails, funky decor.... *Tel 702/252-7777. The Rio, 3700 W. Flamingo Rd.* **(see pp. 182, 183, 190)**

**Z'Tejas.** Southwestern-chic watering hole....*Tel 702/732-1660. 3824 Paradise Rd.* **(see pp. 180, 184, 189)**

enterta

nment

High-stepping
gams, jutting
breasts, sequins,
feathers,
rhinestones, and, of
course, incandescent
stars—

for five decades the statuesque showgirl and the headliner strutted arm-in-arm across the Las Vegas stage. Flashy, fleshy production shows still exist, as well as ever more inventive extravaganzas that often out-"Strip" the name acts. But with competition from so many free attractions—animatronic statues, dancing colored fountains, belching volcanoes, pirate battles—Las Vegas productions have become increasingly high-tech (and high-priced). Sure, Elvis or Sinatra might sell out (pending sightings), but with so many options, audiences are fickle and picky.

The scene runs the gamut: headliners, Broadway musical imports (and knockoffs), comedians, magicians, impressionists, trash-talking boxers, and acrobats who paint surreal kinetic pictures. You also have your choice of various professional and collegiate sporting events, from baseball to hockey (both ice and roller varieties), as well as actual performing arts like ballet and theater (including interactive dinner shows such as *Marriage Can Be Murder* at The Egg & I and *Ba-Da-Bing* at Alexis Park). Cutting-edge musicians sell out smaller venues like **The Joint** at the Hard Rock Hotel and **House of Blues** that appeal to the coveted 21-to-39 demographic. The newer stylish casinos strive for more than just a veneer of class by booking the Luciano Pavarottis and Andrea Bocellis. Given the competition, the scene is anything but static, and even star power rarely guarantees long-term solo runs (locals joke a Charlie Daniels impersonator can find work even if Charlie Daniels can't). Many popular entertainers now rent the venues themselves or take low up-front fees in exchange for splitting the proceeds. Even headliners may share the stage with other elements proven to lure gamblers—witness **Clint Holmes** paired with a Sin-emax-themed topless revue, "Skintight," or the sublime comedian **Rita Rudner** joined by Motown oldies groups.

And new venues keep coming on line. In late 2001, the Stratosphere unveiled a 3,606-seat amphitheater as part of its ambitious expansion, hosting championship boxing and such acts as The Beach Boys. Aladdin's new showroom, slated to open spring 2002, will try to have it all, rotating a main revue (*Lumiere*, starring Carmen Electra) with the Hollywood Blondes topless show, then retracting the seating to become the techno-sumptuous Tatou nightclub. Caesars jettisoned its Circus Maximus Showroom and is building a 4,000-seat replica of Rome's Coliseum, where Celine Dion will debut in March 2003. Steve Wynn has commissioned a Cirque du

Soleil fantasia for his re-invented Desert Inn. Several locals'
casinos, following the lead of **Orleans**, present eclectic name
acts (country crooners, older rockers, impressionists, comics,
even boxing matches) at affordable prices; check out Texas Station's Dallas Events Center, the Suncoast Showroom, and
Sam's Town Live!

### Sources

Front desks, hotel room coffee tables, brochure racks, bars, even
taxis practically flaunt free publications, including *Today in Las
Vegas, Showbiz Weekly, Vegas Visitor, Entertainment Today, 411,
Where Las Vegas, Tourguide, Best Read Guide,* and *What's On*.
Peddling every act, from hyped headliner to toe-tapping spectacular to stomach-churning lounge lizard, most list venues,
prices, and show times, while featuring unreliable "reviews" and
gushy celebrity profiles. Many freebie rags include coupons (as
do individual casino fun books and even the local Yellow Pages,
which also shows seating guides for the large arenas) entitling
the bearer to discounts, two-for-one deals, inexpensive dinner
tack-ons, even free admittance with a drink purchase.

Local newspapers, such as *Las Vegas Weekly, City Life,*
and the *Las Vegas Review Journal,* likewise offer complete listings. The first two are the closest to "alt" publications, but
they're simply alternatives to the latter's mainstream Neon section, which is must-reading for its complete coverage. The
**Allied Arts Council** (tel 702/731-5419) is a fine source for
cultural activity off the Strip. You can also contact the **Las
Vegas Convention and Visitors Authority** (tel 702/892-
0711) and request the latest edition of its "Showguide" pam-
phlet before your trip.

Remember that when productions go on the occasional
brief hiatus, the showroom hosts big acts. When magician
Lance Burton vanishes for a week from the Monte Carlo, Paul
Rodriguez appears in his place; Don Rickles subs for Wayne
Newton; Ray Romano fills in for impressionist Danny Gans;
Liza Minnelli, Andrew Dice Clay, or Hall and Oates flesh out
the schedule when **Bally's** flesh-tacular **Jubilee** needs its
sequins buffed; Jay Leno spells **EFX Alive!** at the **MGM
Grand**; and so on.

### Getting Tickets

Order tickets to the hot shows as soon as you know your
dates; weekends and holiday seats are the hardest to obtain.
Many acts sell out months in advance, especially during major

convention and event periods. You're best off buying tickets in person at the casinos and other performing arts/sports venues, eliminating the phone surcharge and enabling you to check seat location. **TicketMaster** (tel 702/474-4000) and **AllState Ticketing** (tel 702/597-5970) also sell seats to many productions in advance.

If you haven't planned ahead, know that several major productions do release seats—usually cancellations—in the morning on the day of performance: perfect timing for most bleary-eyed night crawlers. Or you can brave the lines for seats belonging to no-show ticketholders; these often snake for a city block, moving more slowly than rush-hour traffic on the Strip. For premier shows like "**O**," get there at least three hours prior to the performance.

Showrooms vary in size and layout. The newest are state-of-the-art and comfortable, with fine sight lines and acoustics. Most major showrooms have several tiers, including regular theater-style seating (occasionally raked) and VIP banquettes or tables. For assigned-seating shows, try to finagle center-stage second- or third-level perches. For general admission shows, line up at least half an hour to an hour before the performance to get better seats.

Although reserved ticketing has become the norm, the greased palm remains a cherished institution; $20 is the going rate for an upgrade in top showrooms. There's an art to bribing: Fold the bill into quarters and quickly shake the maître d's hand. He'll palm the "tip" like a card while surreptitiously checking the denomination. Casino chips are equally acceptable (but use just one—the sound of chips clicking against each other is too blatant).

Ticket prices range from $10 to $100, depending on the act; a dozen or so splashy shows exceed the $50 mark, but most are in the $25 to $50 range (which sometimes includes a drink or dinner; always ask what's included). Prices remain the same for all show times (though some fleshier spectacles may go topless only during the later performance). Several decent, low-priced daytime shows cater primarily to families and senior groups.

# The Lowdown

**What money does for the imagination...** Some shows are so sumptuous, you don't mind that their budgets probably exceeded the GNP of an emerging nation.

The aquatic extravaganza called **"O"** occupies a specially designed $70 million theater at the Bellagio (the production itself cost another $20 million). The pool is 25 feet at its deepest, 150 feet at its longest, and 100 feet at its widest, holding 1.5 million gallons, with seven underwater lifts and numerous contraptions to adjust the pool's size. The skeleton of a ship becomes a giant trapeze; walls form tangled mangrove swamps; the pool turns into fire; lunar modules crawl like crustaceans. Imagine an Esther Williams flick crossed with *Blade Runner*. At the MGM Grand, **EFX** offers flying saucers, animatronic aliens, fire-breathing dragons, and rumbling earthquakes (Sensurround Plus!!!). An incredible 3-D movie of time travel enlivens the H.G. Wells sequence: Music notes explode, planes zoom through clouds, and a sea monster devours the room. The lavish sets and costumes recall *The Wizard of Oz, Lord of the Rings,* and *The X-Files* all at the same time. The barrage of mystical, supernatural, and religious elements in **Mystère,** the acrobatic stage spectacle at Treasure Island, creates an effect more sensuous than any flesh show. It starts with a "Big Bang," symbolizing early man embarking on a never-ending journey; "primitives" banging on Japanese Taiko drums coexist with Renaissance archangels, alien masks, and spinning flying saucers. Acrobats balance on cubes, pyramids, and trapezoids, while colors and shapes shift subtly throughout. Besides feathers, rhinestones, and showgirls' breasts, eye-popping **Jubilee,** which fills the stage at Bally's, includes epic set pieces with remarkable special effects: The sinking of the Titanic involves exploding blast furnaces and cascading flumes as the boat strikes the berg, unleashing 5,400 gallons of water. The Sanctum Secorum of dinner extravaganzas, **Caesars Magical Empire** replicates the Roman Forum, adding a realistically starry sky, grottoes, fountains, a bottomless pit, and stalactites and stalagmites. Even the bars contain animatronic skeletons and holographic wizards. The Magical Empire's Secret Pagoda theater features Chinese dragons and delicate Oriental murals, while the Sultan's Palace has arabesques and mosaics and—only in Las Vegas—black-sequined genies as ushers. In a theater transformed into a lush jungle, Mandalay Bay's **Storm** embodies the primeval forces of nature in stunning production numbers featuring fog, strobes, laser lightning, and a genuine thunderstorm. Creative director Jamie King directed tours for Madonna and Britney Spears, so every number goes for music-video overkill. Its wild costumes range from lime-green wigs and leotards to hot pink pants to a blizzard of white sequins and feathers—and that's just for the gogo boys. Other outfits include black-glitter bikinied girls with matador capes, dudes in Jackson Pollock-y overalls, and a singer floating to the ceiling in a gold-and-orange "sunrise" dress. Excalibur's **Tournament of Kings** is surprisingly elaborate for a dinner show, with 3-D sets, an equestrian arena where 48 horses charge about, and ornate, reasonably authentic costumes courtesy of Parisian designer Pierre Fresnay. The swordplay is worthy of Errol Flynn, the pyrotechnics awesome (evil wizard Mordred shoots 20-foot flames from his chest and palm), and there's even hand-to-hand combat with mace and battle axe ("No, not your wife," cracks Merlin to a husband in the audience).

**And the Liberace award goes to...** Those famous animal-act magicians **Siegfried and Roy**, at the Mirage, open with lots of smoke, laser, holograms, and pseudo-mystic incantations. Siegfried and Roy appear out of fog-shrouded pods in space suits with ample codpieces; later a metallic fire-breathing dragon "crushes" the boys, who are straitjacketed and encased in bathysphere-like contraptions before escaping. The poor dancers are outlandishly garbed in leopard outfits with Fabio-like lion wigs, Batsuits with defined pecs and abs, floral headdresses resembling faux-Tiffany lamps, and, natch, lots of pussy tails. **Tournament of Kings** ends up more middlebrow than Middle Ages, as audiences root boisterously for whatever country they're assigned. Knights in shining armor and dragon warriors made up like American Gladiators exhort them to shout medieval encouragements like "Huzzah." At the Imperial Palace, the splashy lookalike show **Legends in Concert** utilizes so much sparkle, glitter, and psychedelic lasering, it resembles a cross between a Merv Griffin talk show set, a college production of *Grease*, and a Midwest disco circa 1972. **Wayne Newton** lands onstage at the Stardust via an unseen UFO and later descends a lit staircase resplendent in a classic tux as American-flag sparklers crackle. He makes frequent smarmy ventures into the audience to kiss swooning women and stops the show cold for photo ops. Well, "Mr. Las Vegas" is entitled, after all. Female impersonator Frank Marino, who's been named to Best Dressed Men *and* Women lists, makes several glamorous costume changes during the Riviera's **An Evening at La Cage**. His gowns range from Gaultier to Givenchy, but the bigger investment is in his 150 elaborate hand-sewn wigs, mostly blonde (he *IS* Joan Rivers). "Put a Viagra pill in my shampoo and look, it even makes my hair big and tall."

**The bare necessities...** Several shows provide a "legit" alternative to nudie bars, and their audience is by no means male-only. A true spectacle of beads, feathers, sequins, rhinestones, and towering headdresses, **Jubilee** is a fitting tribute to its late creator, Donn Arden, nicknamed "the Cecil B. DeMille of the showroom." Its 16-minute, $3 million opening, based on Jerry Herman's "Hundreds of Girls" number, features 74 performers (out of a cast of 100) wearing glittering costumes, while huge mirrors create the illusion that thousands of luscious ladies are descending the staircase. These are the real thing: showgirls who combine Ziegfeld Follies panache with Minsky's pizzazz. At **Crazy Girls,** they go from pink bikinis to biker leather chic. The show is legendary for the ladies' sculptural work—so what if the numbers are obviously lip-synched? It's a cheeky show in the best sense of the word (and word has it that a former lead dancer was actually a remarkably stunning transsexual). Indeed, the Riviera's life-size bronze monument of eight showgirls' backsides (the only ones in town you can fondle) were taken from molds of Crazy Girl cloners. Alas, the showgirls of **Les Folies Bergere,** at the Tropicana, are more erratic than erotic, ranging from apathetic to overly perky. There are a few high points: the opening number, with ladies floating down to the stage in enormous Christmas ornaments; an authentic ballet adagio in artificial snow; and a black-lit burlesque that puts the tease back in striptease. The lissome **Showgirls of Magic** gradually shed their Marie Antoinette ballgowns for the later adults-only performance.

The showgirls in the cut-rate afternoon vaudeville/burlesque **Bottoms Up** would please Russ Meyer: real "knocker"-outs (though as producer/MC, Breck Wall, cracks, "In this show, the men are men and some of the showgirls are, too."). **La Femme,** MGM Grand's import from the venerable Crazy Horse cabaret in Paris, celebrates what founder Alain Bernardin termed "L'Art du nu" (art of the nude). The decor is minimal—suggestive lip-shaped settees, cages, giant hoops, turntables, and conveyor belts-and the costumes basic, from silver wigs and beads to black garters and boots. But the young French girls' supple bodies are stunningly draped and dressed in light, and their precise, almost sculptural posing is remarkably provocative and sensuous. Since Vegas laws prohibit full nudity in alcohol-serving venues, the troupe uses "wigs" of pubic hair (called a *cache-sexe* or merkin), see-through gauzy silk stockings, and very skimpy g-strings. *Mon Dieu!*

**Presto!...** **Siegfried and Roy** are the *Cats* of Las Vegas; they keep going and going like the Energizer bunny. Their white tigers and Timbavati white lions are still miraculous, but the real miracle is how Siegfried and Roy stuff themselves into tight leather and sequin outfits. They're clearly bored with the show and each other, so it's rather amusing when Siegfried saws Roy in half—at crotch level—or they rotate on daggers. Siggy and Roy's taste for the macabre is apparent in the physical production (legions of skeletons brandishing blood red standards, female dancers caught in a spider's web) and tricks (twisting showgirls' heads and torsos 360 degrees, compressing them like accordions in dungeon gadgetry). Ultimately, it's about spectacle, fetishism, and the need for couples therapy. At the Monte Carlo, **Lance Burton**'s sleight-of-hand tricks are captivating (like turning 60 white doves into a shower of confetti); grander illusions include a Houdini-esque stunt where he escapes the hangman's noose and reappears in the middle of the audience, as well as "The Flying Car" (a levitating and vanishing white Corvette). His studly if smirky good looks help, and he's not above changing from black tie and tails into crotch-hugging pants; one escape routine has him in a studded leather straitjacket. Folksy **Steve Wyrick** lacks Burton's panache, but his show at the Sahara (in a theater designed to resemble a rusting aircraft hangar) offers the town's largest illusion, in which he makes a twin-engine Beechcraft with a 40-foot wingspan disappear. In "Blades of Death" he is chained, carved by giant sawblades, vanishes, materializes dangling from a 40-foot helicopter, then strolls through the spinning blades of a 16-foot-diameter 747 turbine engine. Dirk Arthur's accomplished magic act in **Jubilee** might seem incongruous in a show glorifying the American breast obsession. The magical equivalent of a 38D cup, Arthur makes helicopters and sports cars disappear. Arthur trots out his own big cats, too, magically erasing a tiger's stripes. At **Caesars Magical Empire,** during dinner you get simple tricks along the lines of bending spoons and transforming candles into goblets; later on, the intimate Secret Pagoda presents prestidigitation and card tricks, the larger Sultan's Palace hosts bigger-scale illusions like levitations, rope tricks, and turning cockatoos into showgirls. In **Melinda: First Lady of Magic**, bubbly blonde Melinda Saxe bucks the odds in a notoriously chauvinistic field (she's the only woman to win the Society of American Magicians' Magician of the Year Award). Suspicious pyrotechnic flashes accompany the illusions (a Lamborghini vanishing at 200 mph, Melinda astride a disappearing motorcycle in midair) and her most impressive escapes are shown on video, but savvy Saxe spices the production with top-notch specialty acts, sizzling music, revealing costumes, and dirty dancing from a sexy troupe. Like Melinda (whose brother produces both shows), the four gorgeous **Showgirls of Magic** are accomplished dancer/magicians built for display, garbed in everything from black vinyl bikinis to Empire-style gowns. The larger illusions—locked trunk, levitation, sword-skewered cabinet—are garden-variety, but seem more impressive in the reach-out-and-touch cabaret setting. Harrah's **The Mac King Comedy Show** is delightful family afternoon entertainment; with his ingenuous "aw shucks" demeanor, King seems like a teenager trying out tricks on his family. He even flubs a couple of illusions so he can drawl, "That would've been cool, though." In his baggy red plaid suit ("It used to be my grandma's couch") and bowl-shaped haircut, King is old-fashioned goofiness personified; his fun encore tweaks Siegfried and Roy—wrapped in a tarp sketched with their caricatures, he transforms himself into a stuffed white toy tiger.

**The impressionists...** Consummate crowd-pleaser **Danny Gans** effortlessly fits more than 100 voices into his act, including Homer Simpson, Bill Clinton, Sammy Davis Jr., Garth Brooks, and Ella Fitzgerald. While he does some unparalleled straight comic bits (a riotous Hepburn/Fonda scene from *On Golden Pond*), his greatest talent lies in bravura singing renditions. Jimmy Stewart and Kermit the Frog endearingly harmonize on "The Rainbow Connection," and Natalie Cole duets "Unforgettable" with her father. His tour de force is a "12 Days of Christmas" parody starring Paul Lynde, Andy Rooney, Clint Eastwood, Woody Allen, Mia Farrow, et al. **Legends in Concert** rotates its impersonators: You might see versions of Prince,

James Brown, Garth Brooks, Diana Ross, Dolly Parton, Liberace, Marilyn Monroe, Elton John, Rod Stewart, and Elvis (back after an unaccountable hiatus), singing live with backup by a scantily clad dance troupe. Once renowned for the physical similarities (reportedly due to enhancements), now most of the shows' performers seem to have blurry features, like third-generation photo reprints. **An Evening at La Cage** stars Frank Marino as an NC-17 Joan Rivers (Rivers initially sued for $5 million but is now a fan and pal). Out of drag, he looks like an ex–*Teen Beat* cover boy, with pouty lips, a long flowing mane of black hair, and sensuous deep blue eyes. But in drag, honey, he looks born to wear fishnets and stilettos. The other "gals" impersonate divas such as Tina Turner, Patti LaBelle, Roseanne Barr, Cher, and Bette Midler. At the Sahara, **The Rat Pack Is Back** (co-produced by David Cassidy, who's become quite the Vegas performer/impresario) enacts a 46th birthday roast for the Chairman of the Board, with risqué ribbing and razzing from several impersonated celebrities including Dean, Sammy, and Joey, with plenty of vocalizing. The Gold Coast presents small-scale, big-hearted **Honky Tonk Angels,** a star-spangled salute to Patsy Cline, Dolly Parton, and Reba McEntire, along with briefer vocal impressions of Barbara Mandrell, Dottie West, Faith Hill, and The Judds. The three stars vary the song selection frequently, which helps keep the locals coming; in this intimate showroom, they can sass with the snappy five-piece Cool Country Crew and flirt with the guys at the cocktail tables. The wildly popular **The Scintas** at the Rio features singing siblings Frank, Joe, and Chrissi Scinta, a family of unassuming and likeable performers from Buffalo, New York, who warmly draw the audience into each number with personal anecdotes. Chrissi's powerhouse vocals make Whitney Houston's "I Will Always Love You" a moving tribute to their father. The show culminates in a battle of impressions: Neal Diamond, Johnny Mathis, Ray Charles, Louis Armstrong, and a "bulging" Tom Jones, highlighted by Frank's squeezing his crotch to reach the high note on Joe Cocker's "You Are So Beautiful To MEEEEEEE... don't you SEEEEEEE."

**The crooners...** He's baa-aack: "Mr. Las Vegas," **Wayne Newton**, sings, jokes, schmoozes, and even plays more than a dozen musical instruments for enthusiastic sold-out crowds at the Stardust. He energetically works the room, with polished, peppy patter, if perhaps too many self-revealing anecdotes. The act's heart and soul, of course, are still his evergreen renditions of "Danke Schoen" and "Memory." He performs so intensely, he's hoarse by show's end. Harrah's headliner **Clint Holmes** is likewise part of that dying breed, the all-around entertainer: The man can sing, banter, mimic, compose, and dance. The show partly recounts his parents' multiracial marriage (Dad an African-American jazz musician, Mom a white British opera singer) and the prejudice he faced growing up in America. Holmes never appears insincere, offering old-fashioned showmanship without glitz and shtick. And his vocals, ranging comfortably from rock to ballad to jazz to samba to soul to scat, are smooth as a silk negligee.

**Off-Broadway babies...** Musical theater in Las Vegas once consisted solely of tired third-string road tours or gimmicky shows like *Starlight Express*. Then Mandalay Bay wowed with the now-closed *Chicago*, starring seasoned troupers Ben Vereen, Chita Rivera, Hal Linden, and Marilu Henner. The first home-grown product, **EFX**, at the MGM Grand, originally starred Michael Crawford, then David Cassidy, then Tommy Tune, then Rick Springfield (supposedly, Donny Osmond will next tread the boards). The gimmick is that each new "name" incorporates his patented shtick, from Tune ripping off his own choreography to Springfield grabbing an acoustic guitar and serenading audience plants with "Jessie's Girl." But even their megawatt personalities are upstaged by the spectacular $45-million production. Lavish stage effects at least disguise the insipid score and feeble plot (a man hoping to recapture his youthful dreams of being a magician time-travels to the worlds of Merlin, P.T. Barnum, Houdini, and H.G. Wells). **Michael Flatley's Lord of the Dance** is ostensibly a tale of ancient warring clans and epic battles between the forces of light and dark (represented—duh—by the Lord of the Dance and the Dark Lord), but plot and ersatz Stonehenge set take a backseat to the scintillating footwork of the 40 dancers. Off-Broadway's **Blue Man Group** features those mysterious, bald, impish, indigo-hued characters seen in Pentium TV commercials. Trademark bits have been kept in the show—splattering paint across drums to create instant abstract art, banging out music on lengths of PVC pipe, juggling Jello, rolling toilet paper down the aisles—abetted by cool special effects like neon stick figures springing to life and joining the new 16-piece band (in fluorescent demon garb). It's a multisensory guerilla goof, but the Blue Men deftly forge a connection with the audience night after night, clambering through the rows to turn viewers into part of the act. Limited-run shows are especially beloved by risk-averse casino management: The Broadway Series at the **Aladdin Theater for the Performing Arts** brings in top-notch road tours of *Fosse*, *Fame*, *Cats*, and *Les Miz*; **Orleans Showroom** has the Broadway Theater Company, whose shows (*Mame*, *Damn Yankees*, *Dreamgirls*) headline faded stars like Tab Hunter and Anne Jeffreys; and Rio's **Samba Theater** mounts the occasional lavish production, such as the West Coast premiere of *Footloose: The Musical*.

**Headlining showrooms...** Las Vegas showrooms still present a flashbulb-popping lineup of artists. Elvis's former home, the **Las Vegas Hilton**, keeps several class acts like Johnny Mathis under exclusive contract and remains the top venue for touring Broadway shows. It's top-heavy with country performers, one reason why the Academy of Country Music has named it "Casino of the Year." Paris offers the ornate **Le Théâtre des Arts**, which books an eclectic array of acts, tending toward soul and sass: Dennis Miller, Natalie Cole, Sinbad, Whoopi Goldberg, and Earth, Wind & Fire. With 7,000 seats, **Aladdin Theater for the Performing Arts** is almost stadium-size, yet the $25 million renovation so improved sight lines and acoustics that it feels half the size; expect Stevie Nicks to Alice Cooper. Rio's **Samba Theater** is Penn and Teller's favorite residence when in town. The **MGM Grand Hollywood Theater**, which duplicates the decor of the grand old movie palaces, presents has-beens teetering on the edge of self-parody, like Paul Anka, David Copperfield, Tom Jones, and Rodney Dangerfield alongside edgier acts like Carrot Top and George Carlin. Among local casinos, the **Orleans Showroom** books mostly aging faves who know how to put on a show, from Ray Charles to Debbie Reynolds, Air Supply to Anne Murray.

**Music rooms for the hip...** Hip smaller spots for music like **House of Blues** at Mandalay Bay and **The Joint** at the Hard Rock Hotel bring in the spectrum from legends to legends-in-the-making, like Sheryl Crow, kd lang, Tom Petty, Ringo Starr, Billy Joel, Alanis Morissette, Bob

Dylan, and Neil Young. Both sport signature decor (folk art for **House of Blues**, wonderful posters and signed celebrity guitars at The Joint). And both attract the sexiest crowds in town. An offshoot of the legendary Manhattan boîte, **Blue Note Jazz Club** books star performers that run the musical scales from blues to Brazilian to Big Band; recent names include Kenny Rankin, Kool & the Gang, Spyro Gyra, Dizzy Gillespie Alumni All Stars, Pat Metheny, Chick Corea, and Chuck Mangione. The food is excellent too, a Latin/Asian-tinged New American fare. The **Huntridge Performing Arts Center** and its adjacent, smaller Sanctuary venue book cutting-edge acts, as well as indie and alt icons like Beck, Sarah McLachlan, and Courtney Love. Great sound system, stunning Art Deco interior.

**Yukking it up...** Las Vegas has far too many comedy rooms (and even more comedy acts when you factor in lounges, coffeehouses, specialty production acts, and headliners— the ones with TV sitcoms or development deals). Alas, the fabled raunch these days is rarely cutting-edge, merely smirky tit-illating jokes from schlock jocks. The N.Y./L.A. stand-up institution **Catch a Rising Star** distinguishes itself from several other comedy venues with occasional name acts, such as Kevin Pollak and *Hollywood Squares* regular Caroline Rhea. The improv institution **Second City** draws on a cast of veterans from Second City's Chicago, Toronto, and Detroit companies, combining classic sketch comedy (a great recent bit: Leopold and Ray, a pair of Vegas illusionists somewhat defensive about their sexuality), audience interaction, blackouts, and original songs, with a nightly segment of think-on-their-feet improvisation.

Every major production incorporates some comedy routine, from juggling to stand-up. A slapstick, musical Dennis Miller type, Joe Trammel at **Crazy Girls** keeps things tittering with sly pop-culture references and impressions (*Lord of the Dance*, Don Ho, The Village People), enhanced by a dizzying array of hats and props. **Bottoms Up**'s rapid-fire burlesque sketch format, which supposedly inspired the 1960s show *Rowan & Martin's Laugh-In*, always includes the topical with the topless, as well as hysterically funny novelty songs ("I'm Not Myself Anymore" recounts the story of 27 organ transplants). Impressionist **Danny Gans** specializes in gentle lampoons and parodies: Regis Philbin plays *Who Wants to Be a Millionaire* with the Simpsons, and unlikely celeb duets include Michael Bolton and Dr. Ruth on "When a Man Loves a Woman" and Stevie Wonder serenading Shirley MacLaine with "I Just Called to Say I Was You."

**Top-priced tickets...** Is it the lavish production values, the performers' talents, or both? (Or neither?) Whatever the justification, a handful of Vegas shows blithely charge more than $75 a ticket—and the audience pays it. **Mystère,** performed by Montreal's delightfully idiosyncratic Cirque du Soleil, defies description. It's part Pilobolus, part Flying Wallendas, part Olympic gymnastics competition, part Charlie Chaplin—as designed by Hieronymus Bosch and filtered through a Dada sensibility. Haunting images abound: a "baby" floating in a glowing carriage, spaceships and giant snails taking over the stage. Imps frolic and acrobats in whimsical costumes tumble and soar, all to an evocative score influenced by Japanese, African, South American, and classical traditions. As a cast member planted in the audience declares, "There's not a damn thing going on, but it's very Europe and very hip." At the Bellagio, **"O"** is a play on *eau,* the French word for water, and Cirque du Soleil's other show is fluid in every sense. It's literally a three-ring circus, with clowns, dancers, and gymnasts in the air, in the water, and on solid ground. Typically, the images are transcendent. Expect hunchbacks, whip-cracking ringmasters, horse-riding skeletons, snowmen roasting on a spit, and acrobats contorting themselves into crabs. The long-running **Siegfried and Roy** showcases stunning animals, over-the-top production values, and two men who become animated only when talking about their beloved white tigers. Singer-impressionist-comedian-actor **Danny Gans** has become the darling of Las Vegas, his show so popular that it sells out a month in advance in the handsome, $12 million theater built for him at the Mirage. Gans actually lowered prices from his stint at Rio, but they're still high. At **Caesars Magical Empire,** statuesque golden-clad hostesses offer to take your photo in a chariot, while magicians, seers, sorcerers, and wizards in flowing imperial robes brandish gilded staffs.

**Best values...** At half the price of Siegfried and Roy, **Lance Burton** bewitches with his down-home demeanor and upscale tricks, in a tasteful magic show free of superfluous smoke, lasers, and melodramatic cape-twirling.

(Not be outdone, **Steve Wyrick**, he of the disappearing airplane at the Sahara, undercuts Lance by another $20.) **Crazy Girls** delivers more bang, so to speak, for the buck than other flesh shows. It isn't just the Playboy pets come to life; it's the occasional kinkiness: voyeuristic mirrors and leather-booted, spanking dominatrices. **Showgirls of Magic** delivers the whole package for $25.95 (including two drinks, with dinner deals available): magic, comedy, dancing, singing, traditional showgirl costumes, and buff bods (topless in the later performance) in a showroom smaller than many stars' dressing rooms. Look also for reasonably priced acts at the **Orleans Showroom** (Crystal Gayle, Neil Sedaka, the Smothers Brothers), or the wholesome hoedown **Honky Tony Angels** at the Gold Coast. Major afternoon acts, including the **Mac King Comedy Magic Show** and the inventively bare-all (almost) **Bottoms Up**, are bargains at their advertised prices ($11.50 to $14.95); promotional vouchers go even further, slashing prices in half or providing free admission with drink purchase.

**Family outings...** In **Tournament of Kings**, King Arthur invites his fellow monarchs to participate in a competition—the usual Ye Olde Renaissance Faire stuff, but given the million-dollar treatment. It's full of physical, chest-thumping action—and besides, kids love eating without utensils. **Blue Man Group** bangs on pipes, lobs marshmallows, expels Twinkies, squirts toothpaste, rolls toilet paper down the aisles—how could kids not eat it up? **The Mac King Comedy Magic Show** is right on a child's wacky level: Who could resist being coaxed onstage for a "fishing lesson" that culminates with King's spitting a live goldfish from his mouth? **EFX Alive!** features the best animatronics on the Strip, including dragons, aliens, elves, imps, sprites, fairies, goblins, and gremlins of both sexes; throw in flying camels, showgirls, and trapeze and tumbling acts rivaling Cirque du Soleil's. (Younger children will probably not even notice the mild raunch.) Away from the Strip, the remarkably innovative **Rainbow Company Children's Theater** presents occasionally warped variations on classic fairy tales with a tinge of Roald Dahl-ness that keeps parents on the edge of their seats.

**Best movers and shakers...** Jubilee's classically trained showgirls are poetry in motion, though with so many costume changes one showgirl confides, "It's like running a marathon in stilettos." The finale defies the laws of anatomy and physics, with elaborate Bob Mackie–designed headdresses that would topple lesser topless acts. **Mystère's** international acrobats and aerialists possess bodies as elastic as cords. Acrobats twirl precisely on Chinese poles, bungee aerialists seem weightless, and the troupe uses the theater's sides for "rock climbing." The show's aerial fairy ballet is magnificent, at once ethereal and muscular. That's nothing compared to the same troupe's water show **"O,"** at the Bellagio, whose 75 performers were trained for underwater work. Some of the 16 "nageurs," or synchronized swimmers, won Olympic gold for Canada in 1992, but they had to learn more flowing strokes to swim gracefully through colored lights and bubbles. **Michael Flatley's Lord of the Dance** takes traditional Irish step dancing up a notch, incorporating upper-body movement, as well as improbable flamenco, ballet, and disco elements. The 40 dancers define nimble. The stylishly slutty **Crazy Girls** are more soft-core porn cheerleaders than dancers, but the witty choreography displays their assets (performing and otherwise) to the best advantage. **Storm**, produced by Ricky Martin's management (hence the mostly Latin score), has the Strip's best-looking cast (male and female)—even the band is hunky and flexible. Silver-clad skateboarders flip off ramps; aerialists dangle in silk straps; all 50 cast members scale walls, tap-dance up a thunderstorm, and work up a sexy sheen. **La Femme's** Gallic girls, all ballet-trained, exhibit poise and gymnastic flexibility, spinning in hoops, posing in tableaux vivants, straddling chairs, and executing the Crazy Horse trademark move, the *cambré du corps*, with provocatively arched backs and outthrust hips. The bodacious dancers (male and female) in **Melinda: First Lady of Magic** enact steamy bump-and-grind routines in costumes showing the bare minimum.

**Stadium seating...** The outdoor **Sam Boyd Stadium** sees everything from the UNLV football team to huge music acts. Its arena counterpart, the **Thomas & Mack Center**, is an acoustic vacuum, with poor sight lines and a murky sound system that a smart teenage band could duplicate in a garage. Its new mini-arena, Cox Pavilion, handles the

spillover, from Vince Gill to *Barney's Musical Kingdom*.
The **MGM Grand Garden** is where Barbra Streisand
returned to the stage in 1993 after a 25-year absence and
Madonna swam in for her 2001 Drowned World tour.
The Rolling Stones, Bette Midler, Elton John, Champions
on Ice, and Rod Stewart are other high-octane acts booked
here. The **Mandalay Bay Events Center** hits some of the
highest notes with primo performers like Pavarotti and
James Taylor and championship boxing bouts (Lennox
Lewis, Prince Hamed Nareem). Hipper acts like the Goo
Goo Dolls draw the twentysomething set here. The state-
of-the-art **Las Vegas Motor Speedway** (with 117,000
grandstand seats plus luxury boxes) is not only a regular
pit stop on the NASCAR circuit, but hosts such down-
home events as the George Strait Chevy Truck Country
Music Festival.

**Classical moments...** Las Vegas remains more plucked-
brow than highbrow. Still, several worthy music and
dance companies play at numerous venues throughout
town. The premier venue, the **UNLV Performing Arts
Center**, has three stages: the 1,870-seat proscenium
Artemus W. Ham Concert Hall (superlative acoustics),
the 550-seat Judy Bayley Theatre (modified thrust
layout), and the Alta Ham Fine Arts Blackbox Theatre
(flexible seating for up to 175). PAC's regular season
includes touring classical musicians, Best of the New
York Stage, and the World Stage Series (Montreal's Les
Ballet Jazz, Ladysmith Black Mambazo). The 95-piece
**Las Vegas Philharmonic** runs the scale from a Pops
series where guest John Williams conducted his "Theme
from Star Wars" to a monumental mounting of Mahler's
Resurrection Symphony, featuring two vocal soloists and
a 165-voice chorus. **The Nevada Ballet Theater** specializes in classics like *Coppelia*, but is notable for inventive
adaptations like *Bram Stoker's Dracula*. The **University
Dance Theater**, UNLV's burgeoning student troupe,
performs both classical and modern pieces with remarkable energy; the season includes internationally renowned
guest artists. **Las Vegas Civic Ballet** usually performs at
the **Reed Whipple Cultural Center**; many performances
double as unofficial auditions for the Strip shows, so
dancers and choreographers alike strut their stuff for
agents and casting directors with cell phones bulging in

**ENTERTAINMENT | THE LOWDOWN**

their pockets. The cream is annually skimmed from the company, making the quality unpredictable. The Las Vegas-Clark County Library District is also a major player on the music, dance, and theater scenes; its leading lights are the **Summerlin Library & Performing Arts Center Theater** and **Clark County Library Theater**. Along with the **Reed Whipple Cultural Center** and the **Charleston Heights Arts Center**, they present invariably excellent chamber music groups, young artists recitals, string quartets, folkloric performances, and even ballroom dancing.

**The theatah...** Fringe theaters are popping up all over town, occasionally mounting productions in some unlikely venues; even senior citizens' centers are fertile meeting spots. The same culture culprits listed above (see Classical moments) stage the more provocative, enterprising troupes' work. **Actors Repertory Theater** is the lone Equity venue in town, presenting fare that tends toward the crowd-pleasing: lavishly mounted musicals (*Oliver*) in the small **Summerlin Library & Performing Arts Center Theater,** farces (*Run for Your Wife*), and the occasional prestige play (*Angels in America*). **Rainbow Company Children's Theater,** ensconced at the **Reed Whipple Cultural Center,** produces delectably twisted kiddie material that doesn't condescend to audiences. Productions are imaginative and nonconformist, as such titles as *No One Will Marry a Princess With a Tree Growing Out of Her Head* attest. **Signature Productions** presents family-friendly musicals like *The Secret Garden* and *Guys and Dolls*; quality is that of a top-notch community players ensemble, with surprisingly high production values. The **Huntridge Performing Arts Theater** ropes in unusual, challenging productions: anything loosely defined as performance art. Don't miss Jim Rose, icon and protector of the bizarre, who holds actual freak shows (mostly transvestite wrestlers and folks desperate to break into the *Guinness Book of World Records* by eating live chickens or broken glass) in his *Side Show Circus*.

**A sporting chance...** The wide range of spectator sports includes golf championships at the IPC course, a pro rodeo, and PBA tournaments at Castaways. The UNLV sports program, tarnished by NCAA probations, is coming back. **Sam Boyd Stadium** hosts football; the university's ugly fieldhouse, the **Thomas & Mack Center**, presents UNLV Runnin' Rebels basketball as well as the even more highly ranked Lady Rebels. The Dodgers' AAA farm team, the **Las Vegas 51s**, is baseball like it oughta be, right atop the action, even from the $5 general admission seats (field seats are just $8; be prepared for foul balls and flying bats). Enjoy the *Bull Durham* touches, like high-fiving mascot Cosmo the Alien and the crashed spaceship in the Cashman Field bleachers, while you can: Management has announced plans to erect a new Downtown stadium in the next three years. The 1,500-acre, $200-million **Las Vegas Motor Speedway** revs up regular NASCAR Winston Cup events, Craftsmen Truck competitions, drag races (the public can enroll in the Friday night slate), demolition derbies, and Moto-X series on over a dozen tracks, including a 1.5-mile super-speedway, Tri-Oval. The biggest boxing bouts are held at Caesars Palace (see Casinos), **MGM Grand Garden Arena**, and the **Mandalay Bay Events Center**. Ringside seats (when you can get them) run $1,500 and up to watch celebrities like Leonardo DiCaprio, Michelle Pfeiffer, Shaquille O'Neal, Drew Carey, and Madonna chew the fat about whether Mike Tyson will chew his latest opponent's ears. So non-high-rollers shouldn't overlook the cozier confines of the **Orleans Showroom**, where Friday night matches might include the IBF Featherweight Championship: $75 and up for ringside seats.

**Overrated...** Sure, **Siegfried and Roy** can make elephants disappear, but the overwrought production lumbers along, somehow combining the insipid innocence of *Born Free* with undertones of S&M. And the stars are astonishingly inept at patter—their heavy Bavarian accents sound like the Dana Carvey/Kevin Nealon "Ahnald" parody on *SNL*. **Storm**'s music is all-too-familiar ("Hot Hot Hot" *again*, with tired twirling torches, no less). Add the portentous, inane voice-over narration and video clips about Mother Nature and you've got a storm that lacks thunder. **Danny Gans**, though undeniably brilliant, overdoes the cloying schmaltz, corn, and religion. And please, Danny, a moratorium on dated material: parodies (*Rocky, Scent of a Woman*), impressions of dead celebs like George

Burns, and anything Clinton. **Lance Burton**, in his supposedly family-oriented show, does bring kids onstage, but his snarky humor, Jack Nicholson intonations, and cast of buxom gals in naughty outfits make the act anything but PG. The topless beauties in **Folies Bergere** merely go through the motions, and the show, running since 1961, uses recorded elevator music that makes Zamfir sound like Smash Mouth. Despite the presence of pop star Rick Springfield, **EFX Alive!** doesn't rock. Club wear and lots of air guitar can't overcome the over-amped coffee-jingle music and asinine lyrics ("Dreams can be magic when you believe/...stars in your jacket, rainbows up your sleeve").

# The Index

**Actors Repertory Theater.** Professional live theater company, playing at different venues off the Strip.... *Tel 702/647-7469.* **(see p. 218)**

**Aladdin Theater for the Performing Arts.** Horseshoe-shaped venue with fabulous acoustics, accommodating touring rockers and Broadway shows....*Tel 702/785-5000 or 702/474-4000. Aladdin, 3667 Las Vegas Blvd. S. Show times and prices vary.* **(see p. 212)**

**An Evening at La Cage.** The impressions aren't always sharp, but the humor is: You wouldn't want to cross these cross-dressers, especially Mistress of Ceremonies Frank Marino as Joan Rivers.... *Tel 702/796-9433. Mardi Gras Plaza, Riviera, 2901 Las Vegas Blvd. S. Shows 7:30 & 9:30pm. Closed Tue.* **(see pp. 207, 210)**

**Blue Man Group.** Hip deconstruction of modern culture, more fun than a food fight....*Tel 702/262-4400. Luxor Theater,*

*3900 Las Vegas Blvd. S. Shows 7pm nightly (also 10pm Fri–Sat).* **(see pp. 211, 215)**

**Blue Note Jazz Club.** Jazz, R&B, Latin, and blues greats in an elegant supper setting. *Tel 702/862-8307. Desert Passage, 3663 Las Vegas Blvd. S. Show times and prices vary.*
**(see p. 213)**

**Bottoms Up.** Gleefully sexist vaudeville/burlesque at equally old-fashioned prices....*Tel 702/733-3333. Flamingo Show-room, 3555 Las Vegas Blvd. S. Shows 2 & 4pm. Closed Sun.* **(see pp. 207, 213, 215)**

**Caesars Magical Empire.** Awful "gourmet" food, but even the hokey comic magicians can't detract from resplendent set-tings.... *Tel 702/731-7333. Caesars Magical Empire, Cae-sars Palace, 3570 Las Vegas Blvd. S. Dinner/show every 45 minutes 4:30–11:30pm. Audience must be 12 years old and over.* **(see pp. 205, 208, 214)**

**Catch a Rising Star.** Spiky acts waiting to get lionized on Leno.... *Tel 702/587-7600. Excalibur, Medieval Village Showroom, 3850 Las Vegas Blvd. S. Shows 7:30 & 10:30pm.* **(see p. 213)**

**Charleston Heights Arts Center.** A snug auditorium that hosts everything from theater to dance, with a penchant for edgy works.... *Tel 702/229-6383. 800 S. Brush St.*
**(see p. 218)**

**Clark County Library Theater.** This 500-seat thrust the-ater, the crown jewel of the library system, presents some of the more stimulating cultural fare in town.... *Tel 702/733-7810. 1401 E. Flamingo Rd.* **(see p. 218)**

**Clint Holmes.** Triple-threat performer—warm, winning, and electric.... *Tel 702/369-5111. Harrah's, 3475 Las Vegas Blvd. S. Shows 7:30pm. Closed Sun.* **(see p. 211)**

**Crazy Girls.** The supreme giggle, wiggle, and jiggle show, with no pretensions to being anything but.... *Tel 702/796-9433. Mardi Gras Plaza, Riviera, 2901 Las Vegas Blvd. S. Shows 8:30 & 10:30pm (also midnight Sat). Closed Mon.*
**(see pp. 207, 213, 215, 216)**

ENTERTAINMENT | THE INDEX

**Danny Gans.** Clean-cut and instantly likeable, this red-hot impersonator is the newly anointed King of Vegas.... *Tel 702/791-7111. The Mirage, 3400 Las Vegas Blvd. S. Shows 8pm. Closed Mon, Fri.* **(see pp. 209, 213, 214, 219)**

**EFX Alive!.** It's blinding and deafening; the book and score are insipid; but the production values boggle the mind.... *Tel 702/891-7777. MGM Grand, 3799 Las Vegas Blvd. S. Shows 7:30pm (10:30pm shows Tue, Fri–Sat). Closed Sun & Mon.* **(see pp. 205, 211, 215)**

**Honky Tonk Angels.** Impersonations of country greats at hillbilly prices....*Tel 702/251-3574. Gold Coast, 4000 W. Flamingo Rd. Shows 8pm. Closed Mon–Tue.*
**(see pp. 210, 215)**

**House of Blues.** This glam venue attracts trendoid twenty- and thirtysomethings with eclectic acts like Ruben Blades, Dwight Yoakam, Etta James, and Dennis Miller.... *Tel 702/632-7580. Mandalay Bay, 3950 Las Vegas Blvd. S. Show times and prices vary.* **(see pp. 212, 213)**

**Huntridge Performing Arts Theater.** Huge following among college students and ravers; acts here are the height of indie cool.... *Tel 702/562-8307 and 386-4168. 1208 E. Charleston Blvd. (The Sanctuary is behind the Huntridge, at 1125 S. Maryland Pkwy. Tel 702/471-6700.)*
**(see pp. 213, 218)**

**The Joint.** Intimate, yet prestigious enough to attract everyone from Billy Joel to B.B. King to Blondie. Drawbacks include stratospheric prices and near-fire-hazard crowding (avoid the balcony, which has the worst sight lines).... *Tel 702/693-5066. Hard Rock Hotel, 4455 Paradise Rd. Show times and prices vary.* **(see p. 212)**

**Jubilee.** Ziegfeld himself would have been proud of this show's lavish production, incredible set pieces, and top-notch specialty acts, all "glorifying the American girl" from top to bottom.... *Tel 702/739-4567. Jubilee Theatre, Bally's, 3645 Las Vegas Blvd. S. Shows 7:30 & 10:30pm. Closed Fri. Audience must be 18 and older.*
**(see pp. 205, 207, 208, 215)**

**La Femme.** Parisian Crazy Horse import, *très authentique*.... *Tel*

702/891-7777. *MGM Grand, 3799 Las Vegas Blvd. S. Shows 8 & 10:30pm. Closed Tue. Over 21 only.* **(see pp. 207, 216)**

**Lance Burton: Master Magician.** The new breed of magician, with matinee-idol looks, hypnotic sleight-of-hand routines, and elegant staging.... *Tel 702/730-7160. Monte Carlo, 3770 Las Vegas Blvd. S. Shows 7 & 10pm (no late show Sun). Closed Mon.* **(see pp. 208, 214)**

**Las Vegas Civic Ballet.** Uneven range of modern dance, and the occasional classic, at the Reed Whipple Cultural Center.... *Tel 702/229-6211. 821 Las Vegas Blvd. N.* **(see p. 217)**

**Las Vegas Hilton.** Chic, simple black theater seats 1,700, with excellent sight lines (the farthest seats are just 81 feet from the stage). Styx, LeAnn Rimes, Damon Wayans, and Pat Benatar are typical headliners.... *Tel 702/732-5111. Hilton Theater, 3000 Paradise Rd. Show times and prices vary.* **(see p. 212)**

**Las Vegas Motor Speedway.** State-of-the-art facility for NASCAR, motocross, demolition derbies, and tractor pulls....*Tel 702/644-4443. 7000 Las Vegas Blvd. N. Times and prices vary.* **(see pp. 217, 219)**

**Las Vegas Philharmonic.** Classical orchestra usually performs at the Artemus Ham hall on the UNLV campus.... *Tel 702/386-7100. 4505 S. Maryland Pkwy.* **(see p. 212)**

**Las Vegas 51s.** AAA baseball, played at Cashman Field.... *Tel 702/386-7200 and 702/798-7825. 850 Las Vegas Blvd. N. April–Sept.* **(see pp. 217, 219)**

**Le Théâtre des Arts.** Sumptuous venue booking edgy comedy (Steven Wright), soul survivors (Patti LaBelle, Al Jarreau), and aging crooner-hunks (Julio Iglesias, Clint Black)....*Tel 702/946-4507. Paris, 3655 Las Vegas Blvd. S. Show times and prices vary.* **(see p. 212)**

**Legends in Concert.** Running since 1983, it's the splashiest of the impersonation shows.... *Tel 702/794-3261. Imperial Theatre, Imperial Palace, 3535 Las Vegas Blvd. S. Shows 7:30 & 10:30pm. Closed Sun.* **(see pp. 206, 209)**

**Les Folies Bergere.** The longest-running production show in the history of Las Vegas entertainment (more than 25,000 performances). Given the tepid production and dinner, all one can ask is *pourquoi?*.... *Tel 702/739-2411. Tiffany Theatre, Tropicana, 3801 Las Vegas Blvd. S. Shows 7:30 (covered) & 10pm. Closed Thur.* **(see p. 207)**

**The Mac King Comedy Magic Show.** Klutzy-magician persona, Pee Wee Herman-ish nuttiness, and crowd-pleasing magic tricks.... *Tel 702/369-5111. Harrah's, 3475 Las Vegas Blvd. S. Shows 1 & 3pm. Closed Sun–Mon.*
**(see pp. 209, 215)**

**Mandalay Bay Events Center.** Where to view stars like Luciano Pavarotti, Ricky Martin, Alanis Morissette, Tori Amos, and Oscar de La Hoya.... *Tel 702/632-7580. Mandalay Bay, 3950 Las Vegas Blvd. S. Show times and prices vary.* **(see pp. 217, 219)**

**Melinda: First Lady of Magic.** Energetic, fast-paced show combining magical illusions with ample flesh....*Tel 702/948-3007. Venetian, 3355 Las Vegas Blvd. S. Shows 6:30pm Thur–Tue (also 8:30pm Tue, Thur) Closed Wed.*
**(see pp. 209, 216)**

**MGM Grand Garden.** This 15,122-seat arena patterned after Madison Square Garden hosts it all: major sporting events, ice shows, ballroom and Latin dance championships, and megawatt musical acts like the Backstreet Boys and Britney Spears.... *Tel 702/891-7777. MGM Grand, 3799 Las Vegas Blvd. S. Show times and prices vary.*
**(see pp. 217, 219)**

**MGM Grand Hollywood Theater.** This intimate space (630 seats) lets audiences feel close to the headliner act(ion); you might be eye level with Tom Jones's thrusting pelvis.... *Tel 702/891-7777. MGM Grand, 3799 Las Vegas Blvd. S. Show times and prices vary.* **(see p. 212)**

**Michael Flatley's Lord of the Dance.** Extraordinary hoofers render the Gaelic folk whimsy bearable.... *Tel 702/740-6815. Broadway Theater, New York-New York, 3790 Las Vegas Blvd. S. Shows Tue–Wed 7 & 9pm, Thur–Fri 9pm, Sat 3 & 8pm, Sun 7pm. Closed Mon.* **(see pp. 211, 216)**

**Mystère.** Mystifying, even maddening, yet hypnotic, Cirque du

Soleil's acrobatic tour de force.... *Tel 702/894-7722. Treasure Island, 3300 Las Vegas Blvd. S. Shows Wed–Sun 7:30 & 10:30pm. Closed Mon & Tue.* **(see pp. 205, 214, 216)**

**The Nevada Ballet Theater.** Classical ballet troupe performs mostly at UNLV PAC... *Tel 702/243-2623. 1651 Inner Circle.* **(see p. 217)**

**"O."** The peerless Cirque du Soleil's version of an aquacade, with synchronized swimmers, acrobats, gymnasts, and clowns.... *Tel 702/693-7722. Bellagio Theater, 3650 Las Vegas Blvd. S. Shows 7:30 & 10:30pm. Closed Wed–Thur.* **(see pp. 205, 214, 216)**

**Orleans Showroom.** Smaller showroom, bigger acts: a high-quality, low-price venue booking old reliables like Willie Nelson and the Everly Brothers.... *Tel 702/365-7075. Orleans, 4500 W. Tropicana Ave. Show times and prices vary.* **(see pp. 212, 215)**

**Rainbow Company Children's Theater.** Superb children's theater with a sophisticated edge.... *Tel 702/229-6211. Reed Whipple Cultural Center, 821 Las Vegas Blvd. N. Showtimes and prices vary.* **(see pp. 215, 218)**

**The Rat Pack Is Back.** Salute to Sinatra & Co.... *Tel 702/737-2515. Sahara, 2535 Las Vegas Blvd. S. Shows 8pm Tue, Fri–Sun, 6:30 & 9pm Mon & Wed. Closed Thur.* **(see p. 210)**

**Reed Whipple Cultural Center.** Home to the Las Vegas Civic Ballet, the Rainbow Company Children's Theater, and touring acts in all media.... *Tel 702/229-6211. 821 Las Vegas Blvd. N.* **(see pp. 217, 218)**

**Sam Boyd Stadium.** The UNLV football stadium hosts sports events and mammoth outdoor acts like U2, Paul McCartney, and the Dave Matthews Band.... *Tel 702/895-3900. UNLV campus, 7000 E. Russell Rd.* **(see pp. 216, 219)**

**Samba Theater.** Gorgeous concert space with museum-quality artwork....*Tel 702/252-7776. Rio, 3700 W. Flamingo Rd. Show times and prices vary.* **(see p. 212)**

**The Scintas.** Performing family act with warm anecdotes,

razor-sharp parodies, and cuddly ballads....*Tel 702/252-7776. Rio, 3700 W. Flamingo Rd. Shows 8pm Fri–Tue (additional show Tue 10:30pm). Closed Wed–Thur.* **(see p. 210)**

**Second City.** Fabled Chicago troupe in inspired improvisations and skits....*Tel 702/733-3333. Flamingo, 3555 Las Vegas Blvd. S. Shows 8pm Tue–Sun (also 10:30pm Tue, Sat) Closed Mon.* **(see p. 213)**

**Showgirls of Magic.** Top-flight specialty acts, low prices, lower-cut costumes....*Tel 702/597-6028. Parisian Cabaret, San Remo, 115 E. Tropicana Ave. Shows 8 (covered) & 10:30pm (over 18 only). Closed Mon.*
**(see pp. 207, 209, 215)**

**Siegfried and Roy.** Yes, the lions, tigers, and elephants are magnificent. Several tricks remain magical, but the leather-clad duo exude contempt for the audience.... *Tel 702/792-7777. Mirage, 3400 Las Vegas Blvd. S. Shows 7:30pm (also 10:30pm Tue, Fri–Sat). Closed Wed–Thur.*
**(see pp. 208, 214, 219)**

**Signature Productions.** Local theater company performs at numerous library theaters and cultural centers.... *Tel 702/878-7529. 3255 Mustang St.* **(see p. 218)**

**Steve Wyrick, World Class Magician.** Laid-back, lightweight Texas charm, with heavy-duty tricks.... *Tel 702/737-2515. Sahara, 2535 Las Vegas Blvd. S. Shows 7 & 10pm (no late show Sun–Mon). Closed Tue.* **(see pp. 208, 215)**

**Storm.** Sexy music-video-like production, themed to the natural elements....*Tel 702/632-7580. Mandalay Bay, 3950 Las Vegas Blvd. S. Shows 7:30pm (also 10:30pm Wed, Fri, Sat). Closed Tue.* **(see pp. 205, 216, 219)**

**Summerlin Library & Performing Arts Center Theater.** A charming, state-of-the-art 299-seat proscenium theater staging varied events.... *Tel 702/256-5111. 1771 Inner Circle.* **(see p. 218)**

**Thomas & Mack Center.** Generic barn for the Runnin' Rebels basketball teams, the new hockey team (the WCHL's Wranglers), and enormous music acts. An adjacent arena hosts smaller events.... *Tel 702/895-3900. UNLV campus, 4500 Maryland Pkwy.* **(see pp. 216, 219)**

**Tournament of Kings.** Good, evil, jousting, dragons, swashbuckling, fireballing wizards, and Cornish game hen eaten with fingers: Camelot ham-a-lot.... *Tel 702/597-7600. Excalibur, 3850 Las Vegas Blvd. S. Shows 6 & 8:30pm.*
**(see pp. 206, 215)**

**University Dance Theater.** Worthy student dance troupe at UNLV performs modern and classical works at various venues and also lures top guest artists.... *Tel 702/895-3827.*
**(see p. 217)**

**UNLV Performing Arts Center.** More than 600 annual performances fill this major venue: artists like Yo Yo Ma, Dance Theater of Harlem, Stars of the Bolshoi, Kenny G., and the London Symphony Orchestra.... *Tel 702/895-2787. 4505 S. Maryland Pkwy. Show times and prices vary.*
**(see p. 217)**

**Wayne Newton.** Mr. Las Vegas knows how to put on a show.... *Tel 702/732-6325. Stardust, 3000 Las Vegas Blvd. S. Shows 9pm. Closed Fri.* **(see pp. 206, 210)**

# hotlines & other basics

**Airports...** **McCarran International Airport** (tel 702/261-5743, 5757 Wayne Newton Blvd.) is conveniently situated, 5 minutes from the nearest Strip mega-resorts. (It has well over 1,000 slot machines if your fingers are itching; the airport keeps 75 percent of the revenues for maintenance, land acquisition, and construction.) Flying in at night you can see the Strip from the runways. It's served by virtually every major domestic airline and several international carriers, from Japan Airlines to Virgin Atlantic. And if you find yourself with time to kill at the airport, there are options beyond one-armed banditos and airport food. In the baggage claim area, the **Senator Howard W. Cannon Aviation Museum** displays some of Howard Hughes's personal items and a replica of Alamo Airways' "crash wagon"—a cherry-red 1956 Thunderbird with the legend "For Flying Tourists" painted on the doors. In the gorgeous Deco-ish D Gate terminal, you'll find a huge kids' play area, 24-hour fitness club, and handsome 25-foot murals; C Gate has a large changing exhibition space, with shows of abstract sculpture cobbled together from desert *objets trouvés* or vintage atomic-blast photos. Terminals A and B display mannequins garbed in 1960s pilot, ground crew, and stewardess gear of the now-defunct Bonanza Air Lines and Hughes AirWest. There are great Strip views from Gates A and B, or check your bags and head for Sunset Road off Escondido Street, a superb runway observation area that doubles as "Lookout Point" for randy teens.

**Airport transportation to the city...** Private shuttle buses prowl the arrivals terminal 24 hours daily; flag any of them down. **Bell Trans** (tel 702/739-7990) is the most reliable, with 20-passenger minibuses that patrol all the Strip and Downtown hotels. Rates range from $3.50 to $5. Leaving Las Vegas, call at least 2 hours in advance for departure from your hotel. Several hotels also offer limousine service; check when you make reservations. If you choose to go by taxi, know that there is a $1.20 surcharge for airport drop-off and pickups; taxi fare from the airport to Strip hotels runs $9 to $12, to Downtown about $15. There is no bus from the airport to Strip hotels.

**All-night pharmacies...** The vast **Sav-on** (Tel 702/731-5373, 1360 E. Flamingo Rd. at Maryland Pkwy.) carries all your health-care and hygienic items.

**Buses...** **Citizens Area Transit** (tel 702/CAT-RIDE) operates modern, handicapped-accessible buses over a comprehensive route system between 5:30am and 1:30am. The one-way fare is $1.25 for adults, 60¢ for children. Route 301 buses, catering primarily to tourists, run up and down the Strip around the clock, starting at the Downtown Transportation Center (Stewart and 4th streets) and ending at the intersection of Sunset and Las Vegas Boulevard (adult fare $2). A bus stop can be found on nearly every block. The 302 offers evening Strip express service at fewer stops. The hunter-green, oak-paneled **Las Vegas Strip Trolley** (tel 702/382-1404, fare $1.50 in exact change) cars run every 15 minutes daily 9:30am to 1:30am from Hacienda Avenue north to the Sahara, with a loop to the Las Vegas Hilton.

**Car rentals...** The usual culprits service the Las Vegas area; most offer inventories including 4WDs, SUVs, Jeeps, minivans, convertibles, and sports cars. **Allstate Car Rental** (tel 702/736-6147/8 or 800/634-6186), Nevada's largest independently owned agency, offers the greatest number of special packages. National brand names include: **Avis** (tel 702/261-5595 or 800/367-2847), **Budget** (tel 702/736-1212 or 800/922-2899), **Dollar** (tel 702/739-8408 or 800/842-2054), **Enterprise** (tel 702/795-8842 or 800/325-8007), **Hertz** (tel

702/736-4900 or 800/654-3131), **National** (tel 702/261-5391 or 800/227-7368), and **Thrifty** (tel 702/896-7600 or 800/367-2277). If you want to tool around in exotic style, **Rent-A-Vette** (tel 702/736-2592) offers a wide array of convertibles, sports cars, and Harley Davidsons.

**Child care...** Most major Strip properties have baby-sitters either on staff or on call; locals' casinos often have superb on-site childcare or play centers. **Nannies of Las Vegas** (tel 702/395-4009, 2960 W. Sahara Ave., Suite 200) utilizes savvy, mostly longtime residents practiced in taking care of casino employees' kids and high rollers with strollers. For extended stays, they offer thoroughly vetted live-in and au pair services, with and without accent. **Around the Clock Child Care** (tel 702/365-1040 or 800/798-6768) screens its sitters not only with references but by running checks with the sheriff, health department, and FBI. **Four Seasons Babysitting Service** (tel 702/384-5848) also provides bonded caregivers. Sitters are on call 24/7, but advance notice may be required. There is usually a minimum charge (four hours at $25 to $40 for one or two children), with subsequent hourly rates and surcharges on holidays and for additional children.

**Climate...** No matter how many times they tell you it's a "dry heat," even at 22% average humidity, 110 in the shade will still fry an egg. National Weather Service records for the Las Vegas Valley show average daily highs in the 100s for June, July, and August, which cools off to the low 70s at night. Highs in the 80s are more typical for October and May, with 50s and 60s the normal highs November through March, when lows sometimes drop into the 30s.

**Convention center...** Las Vegas Convention Center (tel 702/892-0711, 3150 Paradise Rd.) has 1.9 million square feet of meeting space (the world's largest, and soon to be expanded by another 1.3 million square feet), with nearly 100 meeting rooms, full banquet facilities, and high-tech audiovisuals. Its rival, Sands Convention Center (tel 702/733-5556, 210 Sands Ave.), near the Venetian, has 1.2 million square feet and comparable facilities.

**Coupons...** They're everywhere. Check the freebie magazines, available everywhere, such as *Today in Las Vegas*, *Tour Guide*, *Showbiz Weekly*, *Vegas Visitor*, *Entertainment Today*, *Las Vegas Today*, and *What's On*—they may offer coupons worth a few bucks off a show or tour and two-for-one deals on entertainment, even meals. The Yellow Pages has a section devoted to cut-out cut-rate coupons. And ask if your casino provides a "fun book" of discounted hotel activities and facilities.

**Dentists...** If you must grin and bear it while on vacation, ask your concierge or check out local dentists' credentials by contacting the **Southern Nevada Dental Society** (tel 702/733-8700).

**Doctors...** The **Clark County Medical Society** (tel 702/739-9989, 2590 Russell Rd., 9am–5pm Mon–Fri) makes referrals, with more than 600 recommended physicians, including specialists, in its database. For minor injuries and illnesses as well as referrals, **Family Medical Group** (tel 702/735-3600, 4550 E. Charleston Blvd.) is open daily 8am till 10pm; it offers free shuttle service from your hotel to a medical facility, a pharmacy if necessary, and then back to your hotel.

**Driving around...** Cars are virtually a necessity of life in Las Vegas. The main highways into town are I-15 and I-515. Visitors can hardly avoid traffic-clogged Las Vegas Boulevard South, better known as the Strip, which runs more or less north-south parallel to I-15; the main east-west arteries crossing it are Charleston Blvd., Sahara Ave., Flamingo Rd., Tropicana Ave., and Desert Inn Rd. Seat belts are mandatory (traffic cops are vigilant).

**Emergencies...** Dial **911** for police, fire, and ambulance services. Many locals feel the best emergency room in town is **University Medical Center** (emergency room tel 702/383-2661, 1800 W. Charleston Blvd. at Shadow Lane, open 24 hours). Another good 24-hour bet is **Sunrise Hospital and Medical Center** (tel 702/731-8080, 3186 Maryland Pkwy. between Desert Inn and Sahara roads).

**Events hotline...** Culture vultures should call the **Las Vegas Cultural Affairs Arts Line** (tel 702/229-5430) for bimonthly updates on non-Strip performances, including poetry readings, music and dance recitals, and theater, as well as gallery exhibits. Also check the websites listed below under Visitor information for updated listings.

**Festivals and special events...** The worst times to visit this eternal Mardi Gras are during the major conventions, which occupy not only the convention center but also several major hotels.

January: Mid-January brings the vast (130,000-plus conventioneers) Consumer Electronics Show, showcasing the latest in—guess what.

March: Castaways (tel 800/826-2800), with the world's largest bowling alley, hosts the annual PBA Classic, as well as the PBA International. Hoops fans may want to check out the men's and women's WAC Basketball Tournament at the Thomas & Mack Center (see Entertainment).

April: April brings out the beady-eyed sharks and celebrities alike for the 21-day World Series of Poker (Binion's Horseshoe, tel 702/382-1600). April's big convention headache is the National Association of Broadcasters (95,000 attendees), always good for stargazing. The TPC at the Summerlin hosts the TruGreen Chem-Lawn Las Vegas Senior PGA Classic in late April.

October: The PGA Invensys Classic at Las Vegas (tel 702/242-3000) is played at three area courses.

November: Comdex (nicknamed Comsex by locals for the private shows for horny techno-geeks). With more than 200,000 attendees, it's hard to book a room anywhere.

December: It's a hoot and a hootenanny with the world's top male and female rodeo stars competing in National Finals Rodeo (tel 702/895-3900), held at the Thomas & Mack. This World Series of ropin', wrestlin', and ridin' every kind of fiesty animal corrals nearly 200,000 rowdy attendees. Pigskin fans can check out Las Vegas Bowl (tel 702/895-3900) at Thomas & Mack Center, where the Big West and Mid-American Conference champions butt heads.

**Gay and lesbian resources...** The gay/lesbian scene is quiet and the community virtually invisible despite rhinestones and showboys. There are several free publications with resource information, including the biggie, *The Bugle*. The **Gay and Lesbian Center** (tel 702/733-9800, 812 E. Sahara Ave.) sponsors various discussion groups, programs, and the occasional mixer.

**Limos...** Casinos, wedding chapels, strip joints, and the brothels of nearby Nye County own and operate complimentary limousines. Plus there are fleets of limos for rent by the hour or day. If you want to cruise the Strip in a limo with moon roof, wet bar, hot tub, and a buxom driver, **Bell Trans** (tel 702/739-7990) and **Las Vegas Limo** (tel 702/739-8414) both have sleek fleets. The average price for a town car is $30, a basic limo runs about $35 to $57, and a super stretch averages about $80 per hour.

**Newspapers and magazines...** The *Las Vegas Sun* is a bit more maverick and locally oriented than the conservative *Las Vegas Journal* (or RJ), which is best for its Friday Neon section (must-reading for its complete arts coverage; look also for John Smith's columns on Las Vegas wackiness). The weeklies (*City Life* and *Las Vegas Weekly*) are far hipper. *Las Vegas Life* and *Las Vegas Magazine* are the usual glossy city monthlies with insider information, potshots at local bigwigs, the occasional muckraking piece, intriguing columns on local life, and fairly reliable dining, cultural, and shopping listings.

**Parking...** Most hotel/casinos and malls offer free parking, either as valet parking service (see You Probably Didn't Know) or in huge multilevel self-park garages. Generally, valet parking is the way to go. There's always a free space somewhere—but it may be a hike.

**Post offices...** Stamps are usually available at hotel front desks or sundry shops. The **Main Post Office** (1001 E. Sunset Rd.) is open till 10pm on weeknights. The **Downtown Station** (301 Stewart Ave.) is a few blocks' walk from the big hotels in that area. **Strip Station** (3100 S. Industrial Blvd.) is one block west of the Strip at Stardust Way.

**Radio and TV stations...** The major network affiliates are KVBC Channel 3 (NBC), KVVU Channel 5 (FOX), KLAS Channel 8 (CBS), and KTNV Channel 13 (ABC). Public broadcasting is KLVX Channel 10. UPN (Channel 33) and WB (Channel 21) are usually available. The radio stations follow pretty much the same format as any major American city with a small local music scene— they're often most notable for priceless commercials hyping buffets and "fantabulous" shows. Vital traffic reports are delivered every quarter hour or so during the morning and evening rush hours. C & W dominates the airwaves, with KWNR FM 95.5 the leader. Top-40 stations are KMZQ FM 100.5, KFMS FM 101.9, and KLUC FM 98.5; the first is a "lite" station that's heavy on female balladeers, the latter two play a few more dance tracks. The only classic-rock station is KKLZ FM 96.3 (supposedly the LZ stands for Led Zep). KXTE FM 107.5 and KCEP FM 88.1 are the sources for alt sounds. KJUL FM 104.3 and KSFN AM 1140 showcase the golden-oldie headliners: Sinatra, Mathis, Streisand. KNPR FM 89.5, the local NPR affiliate, offers the best classical play list. Listen for Nate Tannebaum's "Guess Who's Playing the Classics," where local headliners and politicos share their favorite classical pieces. UNLV's station, KUNV FM 91.5, plays mostly jazz sounds. And there's plenty of talk radio, including such faves as Dr. Laura and Rush Limbaugh (KXNT AM 840) and Howard Stern (KXTE FM 107.5), as well as the expected psychobabble drones and chatty entertainment gossips. KXTE FM 107.5 is also home to Howard's primary local shock jock competition: Carlota, host of "X-Treme Radio," a breath of fresh airwaves amid all the buffet commercials and traffic reports. Expect descriptions of "my infamous cavity searches with both hands tied behind my back" and the like. Go, girl.

**Restrooms...** Every hotel casino and lobby has facilities, some quite ornate. Favorites: **Via Bellagio** (the hotel's shopping arcade), with gold-plated fixtures; **New York-New York**'s Rockefeller Restroom (Murano glass chandeliers and wall sconces, gilded mirrors, silk flowers, custom tile work, and portraits of Mae West over marble and painted fireplaces); and the beaded, translucent glass bathrooms with TV screens outside **Mandalay Bay**'s China Grill.

**Taxis...** Several taxicab companies serve the Las Vegas Valley. Fares are fairly stratospheric (meters drop at $2.20 to $2.40, generally 35 cents for every 1/5 mile thereafter or minutes of waiting time). Try **Desert Cab Company** (tel 702/386-2687); **Yellow/Checker Cab/Star Company** (tel 702/873-2000); and **Whittlesea Taxi** (tel 702/384-6111).

**Ticketing...** Remember that for top shows, weekend tickets are tighter than a showgirl's spandex. **TicketMaster** (tel 702/474-4000) and **AllState Ticketing** (tel 702/597-5970) sell seats to many productions in advance. (See Entertainment for specific tips.)

**Tours...** **Gray Line** (tel 702/384-1234) is the gray lady of day tours, with air and bus tours to Hoover Dam, Laughlin, Lake Mead, the Grand Canyon, and Red Rock Canyon. **Las Vegas Tour and Travel** (tel 702/739-8975) also offers a complete set of options, including various helicopter tours and a Grand Canyon excursion. There are numerous other companies, specialty and otherwise, in the freebie rags and phone book. Prices are comparable.

**Travelers with disabilities...** Las Vegas is admirably attentive to the needs of the physically challenged. The bus system is fully outfitted; nearly every hotel has handicapped rooms; pools, spas, casinos, and public restrooms are wheelchair-accessible. Malls have ramps and push-button or electronic entrances. Some hotels even offer special games for hearing- or visually impaired players. (This isn't playing good Samaritan—casino resorts must do so to keep their licenses.) But the distance between casino/hotels on the Strip is forbidding, and the casinos themselves are often difficult to negotiate via wheelchairs due to crowds. The **Nevada Association for the Handicapped** (tel 702/870-7050, 6200 W. Oakey Blvd.) is an invaluable resource, providing advice on hotels and restaurants that meet your needs as well as transportation, equipment rental, and help with finding personal attendants. The **Las Vegas Convention and Visitors Authority** also has a helpful ADA coordinator (tel 702/892-7525).

**Visitor information...** The best sources for comprehensive information are the **Las Vegas Convention and Visitors Authority** (tel 702/892-0711 or 800/332-5333, 3150 Paradise Rd., open 8am–6pm Mon–Fri, till 5pm Sat, Sun) and the **Las Vegas Chamber of Commerce** (tel 702/735-1616, 711 E. Desert Inn Rd., open 8am–5pm Mon–Fri). Both offer free guides, maps, and brochures, most notably the Chamber's jam-packed Visitors Guide. The LCVA's websites, *www.lasvegas24hours.com* and *www.vegasfreedom.com* have the most information on every aspect of Las Vegas, including playful videocam highlights of hotels imploding and plentiful related links for discount hotels, show bookings, et al. The *Las Vegas Review Journal* website, *www.lvrj.com* is another good info source. Two comprehensive sites partnered with major city publications are *www.vegas.com* (marginally less pandering in its coverage) and *www.lasvegas.com*. More adventuresome travelers can surf *www.indievegas.com,* which provides details on everything alt from raves to body art. And there are dozens of other sites dealing with entertainment, gambling, hotels, sightseeing, topless clubs, flying Elvis impersonators, and Area 51. **Clark County Parks and Recreation** (general information tel 702/455-8200, 2601 E. Sunset Rd.) is an invaluable source for recreation (including free tennis) and special events (pop concerts, art classes) that lure locals.

Actor's Repertory Theater, 218, 220
Adventuredome, 106, 115, 126
Airport transportation to the city, 230
Airports, 229
AJ Hackett Bungy, 107, 126
AJ's, 62, 87
Aladdin Resort & Casino, 22, 28, 46
Aladdin Theater for the Performing Arts, 212, 220
Aladdin, 136, 142, 143, 146, 147
Albion Book Company, 160, 161, 164
Alexis Park Resort and Spa, 35, 44, 46
Allegro Lounge, 177, 188, 190, 192
All-night pharmacies, 230
Alternate Reality, 160, 164
Amen Wary Home, 163, 164
AmeriSuites, 45, 46
An Evening at La Cage, 207, 210, 220
André's French Restaurant, 62, 74, 83, 87
Angles/Lace, 181, 192
Aqua, 60, 71, 74, 77, 87
Armadillo Lounge, 175, 185, 192
Armani, 162, 164
Arts Factory, The, 120, 127
Attic, The, 161, 163, 164
Aureole, 61, 71, 74, 77, 87

Baby's, 173, 175, 182, 192
Backstreet, 182, 185, 192
Bali Trading Company, 163, 164
Bally's Las Vegas, 32, 33, 37, 39, 46, 203
Bally's Steakhouse, 67, 78, 87
Bally's, 140, 146, 147
Bar at Times Square, 190, 192
Barbary Coast Hotel, 35, 47
Barbary Coast, 141, 143, 148
Bare Essentials, 163, 164
Barley's Casino & Brew Pub, 185, 190, 192
Beach, The, 176, 180, 186, 192
Bellagio Buffet, 65, 67, 87
Bellagio Conservatory, 108, 127
Bellagio Gallery of Fine Arts, 119, 127
Bellagio, 136, 144, 146, 148
Bellagio, 16, 17, 18, 23, 25, 28, 33, 37, 38, 43, 44, 47, 57
Bernini, 162, 164
Best Western Mardi Gras Inn, 31, 47
Big B's, 161, 164
Big Kitchen Buffet, 66, 88
Billy Bob's Steakhouse, 79, 81, 88
Binion's Horseshoe, 143, 145, 148
Bix's, 178, 188, 189, 192
Blue Man Group, 221, 215, 220
Blue Note Jazz Club, 213, 221

Bonanza Gifts Shop, 158, 164
Bootlegger Ristorante, 65, 70, 88
Boston Grill and Bar, 191, 193
Bottoms Up, 207, 213, 215, 221
Bourbon Street Cabaret, 180, 190, 193
Breathe Oxygen Bar, 175, 187, 193
Brown Derby, 178, 190, 193
Buffalo Exchange, 162, 165
Buffalo, The, 181, 193
Build-A-Bear Workshop, 158, 165
Burgundy Room, 62, 65, 88
Buses, 230

C2K, 173, 189, 193
Caesars Magical Empire, 205, 208, 214, 221
Caesars Palace, 136, 142, 143, 145, 147, 148
Caesars Palace, 17, 19, 21, 28, 32, 34, 38, 39, 41, 47, 57
Café Espresso Roma, 186, 187, 191, 193
Café Lago, 63, 66, 68, 88
Car rentals, 230
Carluccio's, 180, 193
Carnival Court/La Playa Lounge, 176, 180, 193
Carnival World Buffet, 65, 88
Casino Legends Hall of Fame, 117, 118, 127
Casino Legends Hall of Fame, 160, 165
Catch a Rising Star, 213, 221
Caviarteria, 188, 189, 193
Celebrity Deli, 69, 88
Centaur Galleries, 163, 165
Champagnes Café, 179, 193
Charleston Heights Arts Center, 218, 221
Charlie Palmer's Steakhouse, 73, 79, 88
Cheetahs, 178, 186, 193
Child care, 231
China Grill, 74, 82, 88
Chinois Las Vegas, 72, 75, 88
Circle Bar/Viva Las Vegas Lounge, 179, 187, 194
Circus Circus Buffet, 66, 81, 88
Circus Circus Midway, 105, 115, 127
Circus Circus, 136, 141, 143, 148
Circus Circus, 15, 29, 35, 47
Clark County Library Theater, 218, 221
Cleo's, 160, 165
Cleopatra's Barge, 176, 180, 194
Climate, 231
Clint Holmes, 202, 211, 221
Club Paradise, 177, 194
Club Rio, 173, 180, 194
Club Utopia, 173, 176, 186, 194
Commander's Palace, 64, 67, 73, 85, 89

Convention center, 231
Coupons, 231
Coyote Café and Grill Room, 61, 85, 89
Crazy Girls, 207, 213, 215, 216, 221
Crown and Anchor Pub, 183, 189, 194

Danny Gans, 209, 213, 214, 219, 222
Dead Poet Books, 161, 165
Delmonico Steakhouse, 59, 79, 89
Dentists, 232
Desert Paradise Resort, 45, 47
Doctors, 232
Double Down Saloon, 182, 186, 188, 191, 194
Dragon's Lair, 160, 165
Drai's, 175, 179, 194
Driving around, 232
Dylan's Dance Hall & Saloon, 180, 185, 194

EFX Alive!, 203, 205, 211, 215, 222
Eiffel Tower Experience, 121, 127
Eiffel Tower, 59, 71, 73, 83, 89
808, 60, 72, 75, 89
El Cortez Hotel & Casino, 27, 34, 47
El Sombrero, 68, 84, 89
Elements/Tremezzo, 70, 77, 89
Ellis Island Brewery & Casino, 189, 194
Elvis-a-Rama Museum, 116, 117, 118, 127
Emergencies, 232
Emeril's New Orleans Fish House, 60, 77, 89
Empress Court, 71, 76, 89
ESPN ZONE, 180, 186, 194
Ether M's Chocolate Factory, 106, 109, 127
Events hotline, 232
Excalibur Medieval Village/Fantasy Faire, 105, 106, 127
Excalibur, 141, 143, 148
Excalibur, 15, 17, 22, 26, 29, 36, 41, 48

FAO Schwarz, 158, 165
Ferraro's, 65, 71, 90
Festival Buffet, 66, 90
Festivals and special events, 232
Fiesta, The, 136, 140, 148
Fireside Lounge, 181, 185, 195
Fitzgerald's, 144, 147, 148
Flamingo Hilton, 38, 48
Flyaway Indoor Skydiving, 107, 128
Fontana Bar, 177, 183, 184, 188, 190, 195

Fortune's, 76, 90
Fountains of Bellagio, 105, 112, 128
Four Seasons Las Vegas, 17, 21, 30, 33, 35, 43, 48
Francesco's, 69, 78, 90
Fred K. Leighton, 161, 165
Fremont Street Experience, 105, 108, 114, 128

Galerie Lassen, 159, 165
Galleria di Sorrento, 159, 165
Gallery of Legends, 160, 165
Gambler's Book Shop, 161, 166
Gambler's General Store 159, 166
Gameworks, 111, 115, 125, 128
Garden Court Buffet, 66, 90
Garduno's Cantina, 67, 85, 90
Gaudi Bar, 182, 184, 195
Gay and lesbian resources, 233
Get Booked, 161, 166
Ghostbar/Rain, 171, 174, 182, 183, 195
Gilley's Saloon, Dan Hall & Bar-B-Que, 176, 185, 195
Gipsy, 175, 176, 181, 195
Girls of Glitter Gulch, 178, 180, 195
Glass Pool Inn, 28, 38, 48
Gold Coast Dance Hall, 185, 195
Gold Coast, 136, 140, 147, 148
Gold Spike, 141, 149
Gold Spike, 27, 48
Golden Nugget Buffet, 66, 67, 90
Golden Nugget, 142, 145, 149
Golden Nugget, 20, 33, 48
Gordon Biersch Brewing Co, 175, 180, 183, 195
Guggenheim Las Vegas, 119, 128
Guggenheim/Hermitage Museum, 119, 128
Gustav Mauler's Lounge, 177, 189, 190, 195

Hamada of Japan, 77, 90
Hard Rock Hotel & Casino, 18, 19, 28, 37, 39, 41, 48
Hard Rock, 140, 141, 144, 146, 149
Harrah's, 140, 147, 149
Holy Cow Brewing Company, 183, 195
Honky Tonk Angels, 210, 215, 222
Hookah Lounge, 176, 185, 187, 196
Hop/Glo, The, 174, 188, 196
Hotel San Remo, 31, 48
Houdini's Magic Shop, 158, 159, 166
House of Blues, 174, 175, 179, 191, 196
House of Blues, 202, 212, 213, 222
House of Blues, 67, 72, 86, 90

Hugo's Cellar, 62, 71, 90
Huntridge Drugstore
  Restaurant/Tavern, 65, 68, 76, 90
Huntridge Performing Arts Theater,
  213, 218, 222
Hyatt Regency Lake Las Vegas
  Resort, 25, 30, 36, 49

Ice, 162, 166
Imperial Palace Auto Collections,
  117, 128
In Celebration of Golf, 160, 166
Isis, 80, 90

J.C. Woolloughan's, 177, 191, 196
Jack's Velvet Lounge, 181, 183, 184,
  196
Jackie Gaughan's Plaza Hotel &
  Casino, 27, 49
Jazzed Café and Vinoteca, 59, 69,
  73, 91
Jeanne Lottie, 162, 166
Joint, The, 202, 212, 222
Josef's Brasserie, 77,79, 83, 91
Jubilee, 203, 205, 207, 208, 215,
  222
Judith Leiber, 162, 166
La Barca Seafood Restaurant, 78,
  84, 91
La Concha Motel, 31, 49
La Femme, 207, 216, 222
Lady Luck, 141, 149
Lagoon Saloon, 176, 181, 196
Lake Mead/Hoover Dam, 102, 103,
  122, 128
Lance Burton: Master Magician,
  208, 214, 223
Las Vegas 51s, 217, 219, 223
Las Vegas Art Museum, 120, 129
Las Vegas Civic Ballet, 217, 223
Las Vegas Cyber Speedway, 111,
  120, 129
Las Vegas Hilton, 142, 143, 146,
  149
Las Vegas Hilton, 17, 31, 49, 57
Las Vegas Hilton, 212, 223
Las Vegas Motor Speedway, 107,
  121
Las Vegas Motor Speedway, 217,
  219, 223
Las Vegas Museum of Natural His-
  tory, 109, 114, 129
Las Vegas Philharmonic, 212, 223
Lawry's The Prime Rib, 65, 80, 91
Le Bistro, 179, 196
Le Cirque, 56, 58, 71, 72, 74, 83,
  91
Le Théâtre des Arts, 212, 223
Le Village Buffet, 66, 81, 91
Legends in Concert, 206, 209, 223
Les Folies Bergere, 207, 223
Liberace Museum, 102, 116, 118,
  129

Lied Children's Museum, 114, 129
Limos, 233
Lindo Michoacan, 84, 91
Little Darlings, 178, 187, 196
Lost City of Atlantis, 105, 108,
  110, 129
Lotus of Siam, 76, 91
Lutèce, 59, 78, 91
Luxor Hotel & Casino, 17, 21, 29,
  35, 42, 44, 49
Luxor, 143, 149
Luxor's King Tut's Tomb and
  Museum, 104, 118, 129

M&M's World, 106, 118, 130
Mac King Comedy Magic Show,
  The, 209, 215, 224
Mad Dogs and Englishmen, 184,
  196
Madame Tussaud's Celebrity
  Encounter, 112, 116, 130
Main Street Station, 145, 147, 149
Main Street Station, 26, 43, 49
Mandalay Bay Events Center, 217,
  219, 224
Mandalay Bay Resort & Casino, 16,
  17, 19, 25, 28, 37, 39, 41, 42, 49
Mandalay Bay, 141, 149
Manhattan Express, 104, 106, 130
Manhattan of Las Vegas, 62, 70, 92
Marjorie Barrack Museum, 109,
  118, 120, 130
Martini Ranch, 184, 191, 196
Masquerade Show in the Sky, 105,
  112, 130
Mayflower Cuisinier, 75, 92
McCormick and Schmick's, 75, 92
Mediterranean Café and Market,
  68, 89, 92
Melinda: First Lady of Magic, 209,
  216, 224
Mermaid Café, 186, 191, 196
MGM Grand Garden, 217, 219,
  224
MGM Grand Hollywood Theater,
  212, 224
MGM Grand Hotel & Casino, 14,
  15, 17, 18, 29, 32, 33, 36, 40, 42,
  49, 203
MGM Grand Lion Habitat, 109,
  115, 130
MGM Grand, 136, 145, 149
Michael Flatley's Lord of the
  Dance, 211, 216, 224
Michael's, 59, 65, 92
Mirage Volcano, 105, 108, 130
Mirage, 136, 142, 146
Mirage, 14, 17, 20, 29, 40, 41, 50
Mizuno's, 77, 92
Mon Ami Gabi, 63, 79, 83, 92
Monte Carlo Brew Pub, 175, 183, 197
Monte Carlo Resort & Casino, 24,
  43, 50

Monte Carlo, 141, 144, 147, 150
Moose McGillicuddy's, 186, 197
Mount Charleston, 104, 121, 131
Mr. Lucky's, 59, 68, 81, 92
Mystère, 205, 214, 216, 224

N'Awlins Store, 160, 166
Napa, 58, 60, 73, 92
Napoleon's, 177, 189, 190, 197
Neon Museum, 114, 131
Nevada Ballet Theater, The, 217, 225
New York-New York Hotel & Casino, 17, 24, 41, 50
New York-New York, 140, 142, 150
Newspapers and magazines, 234
Neyla, 61, 62, 92
Nightclub, The, 174, 181, 197
NikeTown, 158, 166
Nob Hill, 61, 85, 92
Nobu, 75, 78, 93

"O.", 204, 205, 214, 216, 225
Olio, 70, 72, 82, 93
Olive's, 74, 82, 93
Olympic Gardens, 177, 197
Orleans Hotel & Casino, The, 15, 24, 30, 50
Orleans Showroom, 212, 215, 225
Orleans, 136, 140, 145, 150, 203
Osteria del Circo, 69, 81, 93
Oxo/Spiedini, 70, 72, 86

P. F. Chang's China Bistro, 59, 75, 82, 93
Palace Station, 136, 140, 141, 150
Palm, The, 64, 79, 93
Palomino Club, 178, 197
Pamplemousse, 62, 83, 93
Paradise Electro Stimulations, 163, 166
Paris, 142, 150
Paris, 23, 32, 37, 39, 44, 50
Parking, 234
Pepper's Lounge, 188, 190, 197
Pharaoh's Pheast, 66, 81, 93
Picasso, 58, 60, 74, 93
Piero's, 70, 93
Pink E's Food and Spirits, 180, 188, 197
Pink Pony Café, 68, 94
Pink Taco, 72, 82, 84, 94
Pinot Brasserie, 73, 77, 83, 94
Pogo's Tavern, 179, 190, 197
Post offices, 234
Postrio, 61, 74, 94
Prime, 58, 63, 74, 79, 94
Pullman Grille, 79, 80, 94

Ra, 173, 176, 180, 197
Race for Atlantis, 108, 115, 131
Radio and TV stations, 234
Raffles Café, 68, 81, 94

Railhead Saloon, 189, 191, 197
Rainbow Company Children's Theater, 215, 218, 225
Rainforest Café, 74, 81, 94
Range, The, 62, 79, 94
Rat Pack Is Back, The, 210, 225
Ré Society Gallery, 160, 166
Red Rock Canyon National Conservation Area, 102, 104, 109, 121, 125, 131
Red Rooster Antique Mall, 163, 167
Red Square, 80, 82, 86, 94
Reed Whipple Cultural Center, 217, 218, 225
Regent Las Vegas, 20, 36, 38, 42, 50
Regent, 142, 150
Renoir, 58, 71, 94
Reserve, The, 136, 141, 145, 147, 150
Restrooms, 235
Retro Vintage Clothing, 161, 167
Rio All-Suite Casino Resort, 140, 144, 146, 150
Rio All-Suite Casino Resort, 17, 28, 42, 43, 50, 57
Riviera Hotel & Casino, 32, 34, 37, 51
Ron Lee's World of Clowns, 158, 167
Rosemary's, 61, 74, 85, 95
Rosewood Grille, 60, 65, 78, 95
Roxy's Saloon, 185, 198
Royal Star, 64, 76, 95
rumjungle, 174, 182, 184, 198

Sahara Hotel & Casino, 26, 35, 51
Sam Boyd Stadium, 216, 219, 225
Sam Woo BBQ, 68, 76, 95
Sam's Town, 136, 140, 150
Sam's Town, 24, 30, 51
Samba Brazilian Steakhouse, 72, 79, 84, 95
Samba Theater, 212, 225
Sand Dollar Blues Lounge, 191, 198
Scintas, The, 210, 225
Second City, 213, 226
Second Street Grill, 61, 75, 95
Secret Garden and Dolphin Habitat, 108, 109, 110, 115, 131
Serge's Showgirl Wigs, 159, 167
Seven, 174, 181, 190, 198
Shadow, 185, 188, 198
Shark Reef, 110, 115, 131
Shauna Stein, 162, 167
Showcase Slots and Antiquities, 163, 167
Showgirls of Magic, 207, 209, 215, 226
Siegfried and Roy, 208, 214, 219, 226

Signature Productions, 218, 226
Sir Galahad, 74, 81, 95
Sky Lounge, 174, 183, 198
Slightly Sinful, 159, 163, 167
Slots of Fun, 141, 147, 150
Smith & Wollensky, 74, 80, 95
Soco, 162, 167
Spago, 60, 64, 95
Speed: The Ride, 107, 111, 131
Stage Deli, 56, 69, 95
Star Canyon, 80, 84, 95
Star Trek: The Experience, 108, 111, 114, 117, 118, 131
Stardust Resort & Casino, 33, 35, 51
Stardust, 143, 150
Stash, 162, 167
Steak House, The, 67, 78, 96
Steve Wyrick, World Class Magician, 208, 215, 226
Storm, 205, 216, 219, 226
Stratosphere Casino Hotel & Tower, 22, 26, 30, 43, 51
Stratosphere Tower/Strat-O-Fair/Thrill Rides, 106, 107, 111, 121, 132
Stratosphere, 146, 150
Studio 54, 173, 179, 198
Summerlin Library & Performing Arts Center Theater, 218, 226
Sundance Helicopters, 121, 132
Sunset Station Hotel & Casino, 24, 30, 51
Sunset Station, 136, 145, 151

Taxis, 235
Terrazza Lounge, 184, 190, 198
Texas Station, 136, 140, 141, 142, 151
Thomas & Mack Center, 216, 219, 226
Ticketing, 235
Tiger Habitat, 108, 109, 132
Tillerman, The, 64, 77, 96
Tom & Jerry's, 187, 191, 198
Tommy Rocker's, 188, 198
Top of the World, 182, 190, 198
Tournament of Kings, 206, 215, 227
Tours, 235
Trattoria del Lupo, 64, 69, 96
Travelers with disabilities, 235
Treasure Island Pirate Battle, 104, 105, 132
Treasure Island, 22, 26, 29, 51
Triple 7 Brewpub, 183, 198
Tropicana Resort & Casino, 34, 37, 38, 52
Tropicana, 144, 151
Tsunami, 61, 75, 82, 96

Unika, 163, 167
University Dance Theater, 217, 227

UNLV Performing Arts Center, 217, 227

V Bar, 170, 175, 179, 184, 187, 199
Valentino, 63, 70, 73, 96
Valentino's 161, 167
Valley of Fire State Park, 122, 132
Venetian Gondolas, 104, 107, 132
Venetian Resort-Hotel-Casino, 15, 17, 19, 23, 32 40, 41, 42, 44, 52, 57
Venetian, 136, 142, 146, 151
Venetian, 68, 71, 96
Venus, 182, 185, 199
Visitor information, 236
Viva Mercado, 84, 96
Voodoo Lounge, 182, 183, 190, 199

Wayne Newton, 206, 210, 227
Wet 'n' Wild, 107, 110, 132
Wild Sage, 67, 85

Z'Tejas, 180, 184, 189, 199

Bellagio Galleries of
Fine Art
(1 ⟹ Chihuly Ceiling

Venetian - 2 Guggenheim
branches

---

Paris: only Patisserie
by famous Parisian
(44); all
French restaurants —

Luxor - Sega Virtual Land

Circus Circus ? Arcade

Mirage - Secret Garden
        Dolfin Habitat
        White Tiger
            Habitat

MGM Grand - Lion
            Habitat

    3-12 y.o.
        Activity Center
    + video arcade

Stratosphere - ~~Midway~~
Thrill rides, games.
        Strat - o - Fair
                midway

Orleans -
    70 lane bowling alley
    18 - screen multiplex
    Time Out Arcade